# PICTORIAL GUIDE TO
# SHRUBS
# & CLIMBING PLANTS

## Marshall Cavendish

# INTRODUCTION

**Editors:** Margaret Daykin, Anne Wiltsher
**Designers:** Trevor Vertigan, Andrea Ryan

© Marshall Cavendish Limited 1986

Printed and bound in Italy by L.E.G.O. S.p.A.

Published by
Marshall Cavendish Books Limited
58 Old Compton Street London W1V 5PA

ISBN 0 86307 607 6

Shrubs and climbing plants are the basis for any garden and browsing through this beautifully illustrated pictorial guide, presented in alphabetical order, will allow you to choose at leisure the varieties you wish to grow.

One of the attractions of growing shrubs is that they are relatively easy to cultivate; some climbing plants are less so, but their effect can be stunning so it is worth persevering. Full instructions for soil preparation, planting and cultivation are given in the general introductions to each section. There are also easy-reference tables to tell you what to plant where, as well as a useful section on pruning at the back of the book.

Even the most reluctant, armchair gardener will be inspired to grow the fragrant climbers and beautiful flowering shrubs featured here, and to create a garden well worth sitting in.

# CONTENTS

Pictorial Guide to Shrubs                                    8

Pictorial Guide to Climbing Plants                         102

Pruning Shrubs and Climbing Plants                         131

Index                                                      138

# PICTORIAL GUIDE TO
# SHRUBS

A SHRUB may be defined as a perennial woody plant, branching naturally from its base without a defined leader (a single main shoot), and not normally exceeding 30 feet high. Shrubs may be deciduous or evergreen and range from plants no more than an inch or two high, such as some heaths and creeping willows, to huge rhododendrons. Some woody plants may grow either as large shrubs or trees according to position, soil type and pruning. When the lower part of the plant is woody and the upper shoots are soft, it is referred to as a sub-shrub.

## Shrub gardening

There can be no other form of gardening that has enjoyed a more rapid growth in popularity since the Second World War than the cultivation of shrubs. This is understandable, since the great majority are easy to grow, tolerant of a wide range of soil conditions—apart from the calcifuges, or lime-haters, such as rhododendrons, camellias and other similar groups of shrubs. Most shrubs are also relatively undemanding as far as maintenance operations are concerned.

In Britain gardeners are fortunate as the climate makes it possible to grow plants from almost every country in the world. Shrubs are no exception and plant hunters such as Robert Fortune, George Forrest and Frank Kingdon-Ward have explored five continents to provide an astonishing wealth of material for gardens. Camellias and rhododendrons from the Himalaya and other parts of Asia can be grown with the striking Chilean firebush, *Embothrium coccineum*. Brooms from Spain, Portugal, Morocco and Madeira grow happily alongside miniature shrubs from the Alps and the Canadian Rockies. South African shrubs grow next to whin and gorse from the Scottish moors.

**Ways of using shrubs** There are many different ways of making use of shrubs in the garden. Although the 'shrubbery' of Victorian gardens, which was generally an uninteresting collection of dingy laurels and privets, still lingers on in some of our parks and open spaces, it has all but disappeared from private gardens.

Today shrubs are used individually, at focal points of interest, as lawn specimens, in borders devoted entirely to them, or in conjunction with herbaceous perennials and bulbous plants in a mixed border (a type of planting that is becoming increasingly popular).

**Preparation of the site** Just because shrubs *are* so easy to grow, it is a mistake to imagine that you can just stick them into a hole in the ground and then leave them to their own devices. Proper and careful planting is one of the most important operations contributing to their successful cultivation.

The initial preparation of the site should be done, whenever possible, a few months before planting is due to be carried out, in order to give the soil ample opportunity to settle. This may not always be possible, in which case a certain amount of raking and treading may be necessary on light sandy soils, while on heavier clays extra precautions will have to be taken to avoid leaving air pockets round the roots.

Deep and thorough cultivation, either by trenching or double digging, to break up the subsoil, as well as the top spit, is the ideal to be aimed at.

Although the roots of the shrubs will eventually travel far in search of nourishment and moisture, this preliminary cultivation will ensure that they get away to a good start in their first season.

Before the shrubs are put in, the surface soil should be broken down to a reasonably good tilth. Getting it into this condition will provide an opportunity of raking in a slow-acting organic fertiliser, such as steamed bone flour, meat and bonemeal or fish manure. Any of these, applied at the rate of 3–4 ounces per square yard should provide adequate reserves for the first growing season.

With a new garden, on former pasture or woodland, the chances are that the

A border of mixed shrubs selected for either their flower or foliage colour makes a decorative feature.

soil will already contain sufficient humus. First, the turf should be sliced off and placed at the bottom of the second spit or, as far as woodland sites are concerned, all fallen leaves, leafmould, etc., should be collected up and incorporated in the soil as digging progresses.

Where existing beds and borders are being given over to shrubs, it may be necessary to provide humus-forming materials in the form of sedge peat, leafmould, garden compost, spent hops, or rotted down straw, when the site is prepared.

**Planting** Whether a single specimen shrub is being planted, or hundreds of shrubs are set for a hedge, the actual planting process must be carefully carried out if the plants are to give of their best. Planting holes must be large enough and deep enough to accommodate the roots without bunching or overcrowding, and it is a good idea to leave a slight mound at the base of the hole on which the plant can rest while the roots are spread out and soil is worked among them. On light sandy soils this latter procedure will be simple, but with sticky clays, particularly if planting coincides with a wet spell, it may be necessary to fill in the holes with compost or dry sifted soil. Most shrubs will benefit by being planted in a mixture consisting of equal parts of sifted soil, peat or leafmould and bonfire ash.

Many evergreen shrubs, including rhododendrons, will arrive from the nursery with their roots 'balled' in sacking. When these are planted, the root ball should remain intact. It is not even necessary to remove the sacking, as it will soon rot away, but if it is left in position it is advisable to cut the ties that secure it round the plant.

The shrub should be gently jiggled up and down to ensure that all the roots are in contact with the soil and to prevent air pockets. Planting is usually a job for two—one holding the shrub in position and giving it an occasional shake, the other working the soil round the roots and firming it with the boot, or where small shrubs are concerned, with the hands.

Depth of planting is important. The soil mark on the stem made at the nursery can be used as a guide and shrubs should be planted with the soil slightly above this to allow for the slight sinking that is likely to take place.

Normally, staking will not be necessary, although in positions exposed to

1 Many shrubs are included in the garden for the brilliant colour of their foliage in autumn. Fothergilla monticola is one of these.
2 Rhododendrons are among the most popular of spring-flowering shrubs.

1 The Camellia is one of the most superb flowering shrubs when grown under suitable conditions. Camellia × williamsii 'Donation' at Wisley.
2 Choisya ternata, the Mexican Orange, will tolerate some shade.

1 The Camellia is one of the most superb flowering shrubs when grown under suitable conditions. Camellia × williamsii 'Donation' at Wisley.
2 Choisya ternata, the Mexican Orange, will tolerate some shade.

strong winds it may be advisable to provide a temporary support for the first season to guard against root damage from wind rock. In any case, it is always advisable to go round newly planted shrubs after a spell of rough weather or prolonged frost to refirm the soil round the base.

The best time to do this is after the soil has had a chance to dry out. Although they like firm planting no shrubs like their roots encased in soil that has been consolidated into a concrete-like consistency, which is what will happen if an attempt is made to firm heavy clay soils when they are still waterlogged.

There are two schools of thought where the initial planting of a new shrub border is concerned. Some garden writers advocate planting at distances sufficient to allow each shrub to develop to its fullest capacity without over-crowding. Others advise planting well in excess of the final requirements and later ruthlessly sacrificing any that are not required.

There are drawbacks to each of these methods. In the latter instance, although it is easy to see when shrubs are begin-ning to exceed their allotted space above ground, it is difficult to say when overcrowding of the roots starts to take place. Waiting till the branches are jostling one another may cause con-siderable damage to the roots of those that remain when the unwanted surplus is removed.

On the other hand, in a shrub border with every plant at a distance from the others sufficient to allow room for the ultimate spread of its roots there will be plenty of wide open spaces for several years to come. These can be filled during spring and summer by bulbs and perennials.

The best solution is to provide temporary stopgaps in the form of relatively short-lived shrubs, or common ones of vigorous habit that will not be greatly missed when the time comes to get rid of them to make room for the more permanent occupants of the border.

Brooms are ideal for this purpose. No matter how carefully they are pruned they invariably become leggy and untidy in the course of four or five years. But in their prime they make a colourful display. The many lovely hybrid forms of the native broom, Cytisus scoparius, range from white through every shade of cream and yellow to rich mahogany reds and purples. A good representative selection would include 'Cornish Cream', 'Dorothy Walpole', a rich

crimson, 'Lady Moore', a bicolor with rich red wings and keel, the lovely apricot and buff 'C. E. Pearson' and the dainty carmine and rose-red 'Johnson's Crimson'. For the edge of the border or the rock garden there are the early-flowering C. praecox and the prostrate C. × kewensis both of which bear masses of cream coloured blossom.

Other 'expendables' include the flower-ing currants, some of the more rampant mock oranges, such as Philadelphus coronarius, as well as the taller forsythias and such coarse-growing shrubs as Buddleia davidii.

**Winter flowering shrubs** By judicious planning and selection it should be possible to have shrubs in flower throughout the year. Winter-flowering

shrubs make an invaluable contribution to our gardens, bringing colour and, in many instances, penetrating fragrance during the darkest days of the season.

By mid-November, when the early heavy frosts have stripped the deciduous shrubs and trees of most of their leaves, the first pinkish-white flower clusters of Viburnum fragrans will be starting to open. This is one of the loveliest and most useful of winter shrubs; it con-tinues to produce relays of richly fragrant blossoms right up to the end of February. There is a white variety, candidissima, with flowers lacking the pinkish tinge of the type, but which contrast even more effectively with the bare, cinnamon-brown twigs.

The witch hazels start to flower

1

2

3

towards the end of December and in most years it is possible to fill a vase with their curious spidery, cowslip-scented blossoms at Christmas. *Hamamelis mollis*, the Chinese species, with showy golden-yellow flowers—showy by winter standards, at any rate, is the one most widely grown. The form *brevipetala* has shorter petals of orange, while those of *pallida* are a pale sulphur-yellow.

*H. japonica* comes into flower a little later; the blooms of this species are more striking, their golden-yellow strap-like petals being set off by a purple calyx. They lack, however, much of the scent of the *mollis* varieties.

More fragrant still—half a dozen small sprigs will scent a room—is the

1 The Azara species are good shrubs for chaiky soil. Azara lanceolata has bright yellow double flowers along the arching stems.
2 The Firethorn, Pyracantha rogersiana, has red berries.
3 Garrya elliptica, excellent in shade.

winter sweet, *Chimonanthus praecox*, with waxy, pale yellow flowers, the centres blotched with purple. In the variety *grandiflorus* they are of a pure clear yellow. The plant type starts to bloom in December, the flowers of the latter open a few weeks later and sacrifice some of their scent for showiness.

February will see the bare branches

of the mezereon, *Daphne mezereum*, covered in purple, hyacinth-scented blossom. This is a short-lived shrub and might well qualify to fill gaps in the border if it did not make such a valuable winter contribution to the garden. Fortunately, fresh supplies come easily from seed, and provided the scarlet fruits—which incidentally are extremely poisonous—are protected from the birds, which are very partial to them, the task of providing replacements is a simple one as the seed will germinate freely in any good garden soil.

From spring to summer the main display starts with shrubs such as the viburnums, brooms and lilacs and reaches its zenith at midsummer.

With the many plants to choose from,

## Shrubs for specific purposes

### For partly shaded situations
*Acer japonicum* (Japanese maple)
*Aucuba japonica* (spotted laurel)
Berberis (various) (barberry)
*Buxus sempervirens* (box)
Camellia
*Choisya ternata* (Mexican orange)
*Cotoneaster simonsii*
*Daphne mezereum* (mezereon)
*Garrya elliptica* (silk tassel bush)
Genista (various) (brcom)
Hedera (various) (ivy)
Hypericum (St John's wort)
Ilex (holly)
*Kerria japonica* (Jew's mallow)
*Viburnum tinus* (laurustinus)
*Mahonia aquifolium* (Oregon grape)
Pernettya
Pyracantha (firethorn)
*Ruscus aculeatus* (butcher's broom)
*Sambucus nigra aurea* (golden elder)
*Vinca major and Vinca minor* (periwinkle)

### Foliage effects
*Artemisia abrotanum* (southernwood, lad's love)
Arundinaria and Phyllostachys (bamboo)
†*Cornus alba sibirica* and *C. alba variegata* (dogwood)
*\*Cotinus coggygria* (smoke bush)
†*Elaeagnus pungens variegata* (wood olive)
*\*Euonymus alata*
Hebe (shrubby veronica)

*\*Hypericum patulum* (St John's wort)
*Laurus nobilis* (sweet bay)
*Pachysandra terminalis*
*Phlomis fruticosa* (Jerusalem sage)
*\*Ribes americanum* (American black currant)
*Romneya coulteri* (Californian tree poppy)
*Rosmarinus officinalis* (rosemary)
*Ruta graveolens* (rue)
*Santolina chamaecyparissus* (cotton lavender)
*Senecio maritima*
*Sorbaria arborea*
*Spiraea arguta* (bridal wreath)
*Viburnum davidii*
*\*Vitis coignetiae*
†*Weigela florida variegata*
*\*Good autumn leaf colour
†Variegated foliage

### Berried shrubs
*Arbutus unedo* (strawberry tree)
*Aronia arbutifolia* (red chokeberry)
*Aucuba japonica* (spotted laurel)
Berberis (various, barberry)
*\*\*Celastrus orbiculata* (climbing bittersweet)
*Clerodendrum trichotomum*
*Gaultheria procumbens* (partridge berry)
*Hippophaë rhamnoides* (sea buckthorn)
Ilex (various, holly)
Pernettya
*\*\*Pyracantha* (firethorn)
*Skimmia japonica*
*Symphoricarpos albus laevigatus* (snowberry)
*Vaccinium myrsinites* (evergreen blueberry)

Viburnum (various)
*\*\*Wall shrubs

### Shrubs for chalk
*Aesculus parviflora* (bottlebrush buckeye)
*Azara microphylla*
Berberis (all) (barberry)
*Buddleia davidii* (butterfly bush)
*Choisya ternata* (Mexican orange)
Cistus (rock rose)
Cotinus
Cotoneaster (all)
Deutzia
*Erica carnea, E. × darleyensis* (heaths)
Escallonia (Chilean gum box)
Forsythia (golden bells)
*Hibiscus syriacus* (tree hollyhock)
Syringa (all) (lilac)
Philadelphus (mock orange)
Potentilla (shrubby cinquefoil)
Rhus (all)
Spiraea (all)
Symphoricarpos (all) (snowberry)
Viburnum (all)

### Waterside planting shrubs
Arundinaria, Phyllostachys (bamboo)
*Cornus alba, C. stolonifera* (dogwood)
Cortaderia (pampas grass)
Philadelphus (mock orange)
Sambucus (elder)
*Viburnum opulus sterile* (snowball tree)
Weigela

planning and planting for continuity of display should be easy. To obtain a lavish display of blossom for as long as possible it will be necessary to include in the planting plan shrubs such as *Caryopteris clandonensis,* and the tree hollyhock, *Hibiscus syriacus,* the flowering season of which covers the months of late summer and autumn.

Lilacs rank among the favourite shrubs of late spring and the most decorative are the hybrids of *Syringa vulgaris.* Among both singles and doubles, old favourites still reign supreme, with 'Souvenir de Louis Spath' as the best purple and 'Maud Notcutt' most popular as the most outstanding single white. Lesser-known single forms include 'Esther Staley', an unusual shade of pale lilac verging on pink, and 'Maurice Barnes', the best examples of the true 'lilac' colour.

Many prefer the doubles with their chunky tightly-packed conical flower trusses, although they lack some of the elegant form of the singles. 'Katherine Havemeyer' (soft mauve), 'Madame Lemoine' (white) are all established favourites. All of them, both single and double have the typical enchanting perfume of lilacs and are vigorous shrubs, reaching a height of 15–20 feet.

In the smaller garden there will not be much room for these giants, but some of the lilac species are much more compact and would prove useful where space is restricted. Their flowers may be smaller and less showy than those of the larger hybrids but they yield nothing to these where fragrance is concerned. *Syringa macrophylla,* for example, makes a dainty shrub, only 4–6 feet in height, with elegant purple flower spikes that are extremely fragrant and have an attractive habit of continuing to bloom at intervals throughout the summer. *S. persica alba,* a white-flowered form of the incorrectly-named 'Persian' lilac is a delightful Chinese shrub with narrow leaves and handsome panicles of white flowers.

In late spring the shrub border is redolent with fine perfumes. The mid-season viburnums, with their distinctive clove scent will be in bloom then; also *V.* x *burkwoodii,* a vigorous cross between *V. carlesii* and *V. utile,* with its large globes of white, *V.* x *carlcephalum,* another *carlesii* hybrid, with in this instance, *V. macrocephalum* as the other parent, whose large fragrant flowers measure 4–5 inches across and *V. carlesii* itself, still ranking as one of the most popular garden shrubs.

**Midsummer beauty** Philadelphus, or

1 Daphne mezereum, one of the shrubs that produces its flowers early in the year. The blooms come on the bare wood and are fragrant.
2 Euonymus fortunei gracilis.
3 Aucuba japonica has fine foliage.

mock orange, often wrongly called syringa, will be among the next batch of favourites to come into flower. Its fragrance can be cloying and is too heavy for some tastes. In many of the newer varieties, however, the somewhat funereal smell of *P. coronarius,* is more subdued, and the superb decorative value of their white flowers could never be in dispute. For the smaller gardens of today, there are a number of compact hybrids, much less coarse in habit than the once popular *P. coronarius.* 'Enchantment' is one of the loveliest of these, with elegant, arching branches thickly festooned with double white flowers in June and July. 'Manteau d'Hermine', only 4 feet tall at maturity, also produces its double white blossoms freely. 'Sybille', another delightful shrub of modest dimensions, bears an abundance of dainty white, purple-scented blooms. *P. microphyllus* can be particularly recommended for the small garden. Its leaves are very small and the unusual four-petalled flowers have a distinctive fruity perfume.

Weigelas, still listed sometimes as Diervilla, are useful midsummer shrubs of medium height and girth. Their flowers, borne along the entire length of the previous years' shoots are long and tubular, rather like miniature foxgloves. *W. florida,* a native of Korea and northern China, was discovered by Robert Fortune in the garden of a Chinese mandarin in the last century; it is the hybrids of this attractive species that have produced our popular garden forms.

'Feerie', *W. vanhouttei* and *W. styriaca* are all good, with flowers of varying shades of pink. 'Eva Rathke' and 'Bristol Ruby' have flowers of a stronger colour. 'Eva Rathke' has the longest flowering season. Its deep crimson flowers appear from mid-May until August.

Deutzias, shrubs that deserve wider recognition, will also be in flower at this period. Their habit of growth, narrow at the base but arching elegantly outwards when they attain a height of 4-5 feet, makes them invaluable where ground space is at a premium. The flowers, which are like small tassels, are profusely borne, while in winter the bare cinnamon branches are of great decorative value. *D. elegantissima* is the form most commonly encountered. The pinkish-purple blossoms are profusely borne on arching sprays, while in the variety *pulchra* they are a pearly pink. 'Codsall Pink' is a strong grower and can reach a height of 10–15 feet. This form flowers later than most, starting at the end of June and continuing into July.

No shrub garden would be complete without the summer-flowering viburnums. The snowball bush, *V. opulus sterile,* is the most popular of these. Its globular flowers, green at first, but turning pure white later, make an established specimen of this lovely summer shrub an unforgettable sight when the branches are smothered in white snowballs. It is, however, rather a vigorous grower for small gardens and for these *V. tomentosum plicatum* would be a more appropriate choice. This seldom exceeds 6 or 7 feet in height and the 'snowballs' are in the form of half-globes which are borne in symmetrical pairs along the branches, giving the effect of a stylised Chinese scroll painting. The variety *grandiflorum,* with larger leaves and flowers than those of the type is the best form to grow.

**Continuity of display** In the rather barren weeks that follow the peak flowering period, hydrangeas are a first-class standby. Apart from the large-leaved species, which require partial shade, they will thrive either in full sun or semi-shade. In the former posi-

15

colour so brilliantly, the barberries and cotoneasters play a prominent part. *Berberis thunbergii* has small leaves of a clear green that produce brilliant flame in autumn. The leaves of the variety *atropurpurea*, which are deep purple throughout the summer, assume even more dazzling colours before they fall. *B. verruculosa* is an evergreen species, but many of its dark green leaves turn scarlet, while some of the foliage of the closely related *Mahonia aquifolium*, another evergreen, turns coppery-red in autumn and winter.

Although, botanically, the cut-leaved Japanese maples are not shrubs, but small trees, they have so many of the characteristics of the former that they are usually included in this category.

The Japanese maples are very slow growers and the purple-leaved *Acer palmatum dissectum atropurpureum* and its green-leaved counterpart, *palmatifidum*, both with leaves like the finest lace, never exceed 8–10 feet in height. The leaves of the former turn a vivid deep scarlet, while those of the latter colour to a lighter but no less distinctive hue.

Anyone who gardens on the moist peaty soils in which rhododendrons and azaleas thrive ought to find room for *Enkianthus campanulatus*, which enjoys similar conditions and puts on a spectacular autumn display in orange and red. The Ghent azaleas, too, can be very colourful in autumn, as also can the

tion, however, copious watering or regular mulching will be required during the first few seasons after planting. *H. macrophylla* is the well-known and deservedly popular pot hydrangea of the florists' shops. It will also do well out of doors in most parts of the British Isles, although in exposed positions and inland districts the blossom buds, which begin to swell very early in the year, may suffer frost damage. This can often be prevented by leaving the previous year's flower-heads on the plants as protection, but in really cold areas it would be safer to plant one of the completely hardy species such as *H. paniculata*, *H. villosa*, *H. serrata* or the oak-leaved hydrangea, *H. quercifolia*.

Another genus of late-flowering shrubs, useful for bridging the gap between the summer and the beauties of autumn leaf colour is represented by the hypericums, or St John's worts, of which, the best-known member is the prolific, weed-smothering *H. calycinum*, the rose of Sharon. For the shrub border, however, the taller species and hybrids are a good deal more useful and decorative. Their flowers, like giant buttercups with a central boss of contrasting stamens, make them among the finest shrubs for a late summer display. 'Hidcote' and 'Gold Cup' are both outstanding forms of *H. patulum*,

**The various forms of Hibiscus produce flowers in August, a month in which few shrubs flower.**

with large cup-shaped flowers 2–2½ inches across. *H. elatum* 'Elstead' is another attractive form, with oval leaves of a fresh vernal green, and masses of small yellow flowers in July and August that are followed by scarlet fruits.

But the outstanding member of the group is undoubtedly the hybrid, 'Rowallane'. Unfortunately, it is not completely hardy in all parts of Britain and needs a sheltered position in many areas. Its magnificent golden chalices are 2½ inches in diameter and well-developed specimens reach a height of 8 feet in milder districts.

To wind up the floral display for the season there is the so-called shrub hollyhock, *Hibiscus syriacus*, together with the blue-flowered *Caryopteris* x *clandonensis*, which is best treated as a herbaceous perennial and cut back almost to ground level each spring.

**Shrubs for autumn leaf colour** The beauty of the shrub border is not restricted to its floral display. From September until final leaf fall comes a brilliant cavalcade of coloured foliage, followed by, and sometimes simultaneous with, beauty of winter berry and bark.

Among the shrubs the leaves of which

common yellow *Azalea pontica (Rhododendron ponticum)*, when its sage-green leaves burst into tints of flame and coral.

One of the most unusual and striking shrubs for autumn colour, is a member of the euonymus genus, of which the spindle tree is probably the most representative. *E. alata* has leaves that turn a bright glowing pink. After they fall, continuing winter interest is provided by the curious corky wing-like excrescences on the stems.

All the cotinus and rhus, related genera, are noted for their brilliant autumn colour. The stag's horn sumach, *R. typhina laciniata,* is particularly spectacular, but this small tree colours rather early for the main autumn display and the display itself is somewhat short-lived. Much more satisfying are the brilliant orange and scarlets of *Cotinus americanus (Rhus cotinoides),* or the bright yellow of the smoke bush, *Cotinus coggygria (Rhus cotinus).*

Among wall shrubs and climbers many of the vines and creepers colour magnificently, particularly the giant-leaved *Vitis coignetiae, Vitis inconstans* (syns. *Parthenocissus tricuspidata veitchii, Ampelopsis veitchii*), and the true Virginian Creeper, *Parthenocissus quinquefolia.* Where space is restricted, the smaller-leaved and less rampant *Parthenocissus henryana* is useful for providing a wall tapestry of brilliant colour.

On the ground, too, creeping and prostrate shrubs such as *Cotoneaster* **1**

1 Viburnum plicatum tomentosum 'Lanarth' has its horizontal branches covered in creamy-white flowers in June.
2 The shrub planting at Mount Usher, Eire, includes Azaleas and Malus. Conifers provide the background.

3 The broad green leaves of Sibiraea laevigata, a deciduous flowering shrub for summer effect.

**2**

**3**

horizontalis, Gaultheria procumbens and others will be putting down a red carpet, while the hypericums, that have only just finished their flowering season, will be adding to the autumn colours. Hypericum patulum forrestii has the most brilliant foliage of any of these.

**Beauty of berry and bark** Just as decorative, but with a longer-lasting effect are the berries of many shrubs. These will continue the display from leaf fall until the New Year—sometimes even later in districts where birds are not numerous.

Once again, the barberries and cotoneasters are well in evidence, with species and varieties bearing fruits of many colours, ranging from the vivid coral red of *Berberis* 'Bountiful' to the grape-purple of *B. darwinii*. Among the striking forms are *B.* 'Buccaneer' and *B. thunbergii*, both with bright red berries and both, incidentally, also providing attractive leaf colour. 'Cherry Ripe' has fruits that are salmon-red and pear-shaped; the compact, free-flowering Formosan species, *B. morrisonsienis*, bears larger red fruits than most.

More than a dozen kinds of cotoneaster share this same valuable quality. The better known varieties include *C. horizontalis*, whose herring-bone set branches are packed with scarlet button berries and *C. simonsii*, a popular shrub for hedging and cover planting, with no less brilliant berries the size of peas. Taller forms and species include *C. cornubia* with large berries borne profusely, *C. frigidus* with clustered crimson fruits and *C. salicifolius*, the willow-leaved cotoneaster, that bears heavy crops of bright red fruits. Among the prostrate forms suitable for the rock garden, or for use as ground cover, *C. dammeri* decks its trailing shoots with berries like blobs of sealing wax, while *C. adpressus* has both autumn fruits and bright scarlet foliage.

The pernettyas are a group of attractive small-leaved evergreen shrubs with showy marble-sized berries of an unusual beauty. Not many of them, however, are self-fertile so that a specimen of the type plant, *P. mucronata*, will have to be included to cross-fertilise the more decoratively-berried forms. These last-named include 'Donard Pink' and 'Donard White' (the names are descriptive of the colour of their berries), *lilacina*, with lilac-pink fruits and 'Bell's Seedling' with extra-large, dark-red berries.

The vacciniums, like the pernettyas, are ericaceous plants, and they include the edible North American swamp blueberry, *V. corymbosum*, and others such as *V. macrocarpum*, the American cranberry, a prostrate evergreen, the large scarlet berries of which are used for cranberry sauce traditionally associated with the Christmas turkey. *V. myrsinites*, the evergreen blueberry, is a graceful compact shrub that bears

1 Cotinus coggygria is good for autumn foliage colour. The colour heightens late in the season.
2 Vitis coignetiae has attractive autumn leaf colour.

its blue-black berries in May and June when they are of doubtful value for garden decoration.

It is not always realised that certain shrubs are dioecious, for example, the male and female flowers are borne on separate plants, so that a specimen of each sex will need to be planted if berries are to result. Japanese laurels or aucubas all share this specialised sex characteristic, which makes it difficult for the owner of a small garden, with limited space at his or her disposal, to include many of them in the planting plan. But for those with room to spare all of these are well worth growing, not only for the beauty of their berries but also for the year-long decorative qualities

**Pruning** It is impossible, in the space available, to lay down principles of pruning in any but the most general terms. As a general rule, however, spring-flowering shrubs can be pruned after they have finished blooming. Those that flower in summer and autumn, on the current year's wood, can have their season's growths cut right back in March of each year.

Shrubs should normally be allowed to develop their natural form and dimensions, but any particularly vigorous growths that appear in the second and third seasons after planting should be tipped when they are between 6 and 9 inches long to induce the formation of laterals to build up a solid framework.

Most shrubs, once established, will need little or no attention as far as pruning is concerned, apart from cutting out weak, straggling, diseased or dead shoots. In any case, drastic pruning is an operation that should always be undertaken with caution and should normally be resorted to only when shrubs have been neglected or when, like buddleias, forsythias, flowering currants and the larger philadelphuses, they grow too rampantly and exceed their allotted quarters, or trespass on paths and lawns.

Avoid, at all costs, indiscriminate clipping with the garden shears. Such treatment will not only reduce all your shrubs to a monotonous uniformity of shape but will also result in weak, straggling growth. See also Pruning ornamentals.

**Propagation** This, too, is a vast subject. Many shrubs can be grown easily from seed, although not all of them ripen their seed in this country and it may be necessary to obtain it from specialist seedsmen. Brooms, for example, will germinate as easily and as freely as sweet peas; other shrub seeds, berries in particular, need to be stratified, that is, over-wintered in moist sand, to rot the fleshy seed covering, before they can be sown with any hope of success.

Propagation from hard-wood cuttings is another simple method by which many shrubs may be increased. These cuttings should consist of ripened side shoots that have not flowered, pulled off the parent stem with a heel of bark attached, and inserted in a moist shady bed in July and August. They are left until the end of the following season, when sufficient root and top growth should have developed to enable them to be grown on in a nursery bed.

Shrubs that may be propagated easily by this method include cornus, weigela, deutzia, philadelphus, rhus, cotinus, hydrangea and many other well-known kinds. Hedging shrubs such as privet or *Lonicera nitida* are easier still. Trimmings stuck into the soil almost anywhere will usually root very quickly.

of their handsome, evergreen foliage.

Finally, to act as a foil to the winter-flowering shrubs, there are other plants whose main attraction lies in their strikingly-coloured bark or interesting branch formation.

The dogwoods, both the scarlet and yellow-stemmed species, love moisture. They will respond to waterside planting and nothing looks more striking in January sunshine than a group of the scarlet-stemmed Westonbirt dogwoods

1 The feathery foliage of Rhus typhina laciniata colours well in autumn.
2 One of the plants grown for its bold red berries is Skimmia japonica.
3 Red berries of Viburnum hupehense.

*(Cornus alba sibirica)* at the edge of a pond or stream, while the curiously twisted stems and branches of *Corylus avellana contorta,* popularly known as Harry Lauder's walking stick, make an unusual and interesting tracery against

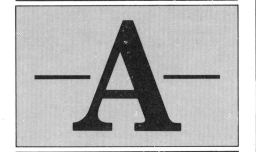

# A

**Abelia** (a-beel-e-a)
Commemorating Dr Clarke Abel
(1780-1826), a physician attached to Lord
Amherst's mission to China in 1816-17
(*Caprifoliaceae*). A genus of slightly tender evergreen and deciduous flowering
shrubs, moderate in size, daintily flowered and graceful in habit, although not
spectacular. They will grow well by the
seaside and do not object to chalky soils.
**Species cultivated** *A. chinensis* (D), 4 feet,
fragrant flowers, white, flushed pink,
summer to autumn. *A. floribunda* (E),
3–5 feet, rosy-red flowers, summer. *A.
grandiflora* (SE), 4–6 feet, pink and
white flowers, summer to autumn. *A.
schumanii* (D), 5 feet, rosy-lilac flowers,
summer to autumn. *A. serrata* (D),
3–4 feet, small white or blush-pink
flowers, late spring to summer. *A.
triflora* (D), 12–15 feet, fragrant white
flowers flushed with pink, early summer.
**Cultivation** Any ordinary well-drained
soil and a sunny position will suit
abelias. Except in milder counties, they
do best against a warm, sheltered wall.
Plant in October or April.

Any pruning should be done after
flowering by cutting out some of the
older shoots and shortening the more
straggly growths, although pruning is
seldom necessary. Propagation is by cuttings rooted in July in a cold frame or in
a propagating case with bottom-heat.
Long shoots may be layered in spring.

**Abeliophyllum** (a-beel-e-off-illum)
The name means with leaves like those of
*Abelia* (*Oleaceae*). There is but one
species in this genus, the Korean *A.
distichum* (D), a shrub about 2–3 feet
tall, which has clusters of fragrant
white flowers with orange centres from
January or February to April.
**Cultivation** Ordinary, well-drained soil is
suitable. A sheltered, sunny site should
be provided. Like the forsythias, to
which this plant is related, any pruning
should be done after flowering is over as
the blooms are produced on shoots made
during the previous year. Propagation
is by cuttings in late summer or autumn.

**1 Abelia grandiflora bears slightly
fragrant flowers from June until October.
2 The fragrant white flowers of Abeliophyllum distichum.**

## Abutilon (a-bu-til-on)

Arabic name for a species of mallow (*Malvaceae*). Greenhouse and half-hardy shrubs, some with handsome mottled foliage. The chalice-shaped flowers are borne in summer and autumn.

**Species cultivated** *A. globosum* (SE), 6–8 feet, a shrub for a tub; should be over-wintered under glass. Varieties flowering June–November: 'Ashford Red', salmon-red; 'Orange Glow', clusters of orange bells. *A megapotamicum* (E), 4–8 feet, may be grown in the open against a warm wall in sheltered gardens. Flowers yellow and scarlet with a conspicuous cluster of brown anthers, summer and autumn. *A.* x *milleri* (SE), 4–8 feet, bell-shaped orange flowers with crimson stamens, leaves dark green mottled with yellow. *A. ochsenii* (SE), (also known as A. 'Margherita Mann'), 6–8 feet, purplish blue flowers with darker centre, June–July. For a sheltered sunny wall. *A. striatum thompsonii* (SE), 6–10 feet, often used for summer bedding, bears orange flowers from June to September and has leaves variegated with yellow. *A. vitifolium* (SE), 10–25 feet, under glass, blue flowers shading to white. May be grown in the open in sheltered districts, but sometimes short lived; var. *album*, a pure white form.

**Cultivation** All enjoy sun and well-drained soil. Plant under glass in October and April, or in the open in May. Pot in March in John Innes compost. Overgrown plants may be cut back in March but regular pruning is not necessary. Under glass the minimum winter temperature should not fall below 45°F (7°C), and 65°F (18°C) is an adequate summer temperature. Propagation is by seed sown in March in a cold-frame or cool house. Cover the seed lightly only and use a well-drained, sandy compost. Cuttings taken in spring or early summer will root in a sandy compost in a close frame, or with mist propagation in a temperature of about 65°F (18°C).

**1 Abutilon 'Master Hugh' 2 Abutilon viti-folium album 3 The showy yellow and scarlet flowers of Abutilon megapotamicum, a South American species**

# -B-

1

**Berberis** (ber-ber-is)
From berberys, the Arabic name (Berberidaceae). The barberries are hardy evergreen or deciduous shrubs furnished with needle-like spines. There are nearly 500 species, some notable for blossom and some for beauty of fruit or leaf. Some species provide particularly good autumn foliage colour. Unfortunately our only native barberry, B. vulgaris, is known to be a host plant of the wheat rust, and its cultivation is frowned upon in farming districts, where it is rooted out of hedgerows. B. vulgaris has a form with bronze coloured leaves which look particularly good when seen with the golden yellow flowers and later with the fruit, which is edible.

Of all barberries the South American B. darwinii is probably the best known and still the loveliest when seen in full bloom in April and May. This barberry makes a good impenetrable hedge. At one time the plants now called mahonia were lumped with the barberries; they are distinguished from these close relations by their large pinnate leaves, and provide some excellent garden plants (see Mahonia).

**Species cultivated** (Note, all have either yellow or orange flowers and blue-black fruits unless otherwise noted). *B. actinacantha* (E), 4–5 feet, leaves stiff and hard, flowers chrome-yellow. *B. aggregata* (D), 4–5 feet, coral-red berries,

1 **Berberis gagnepainii makes a dense flowering hedge 2 One of the most popular of all Barberries is Berberis darwinii with holly-like leaves and rich orange-yellow flowers 3 Berberis Barbarossa', a hybrid with scarlet fruits**

**2**

good autumn leaf colour. *B. amoena* (SE), 1–2 feet, fruits coral-red. *B. angulosa* (D), 3 feet, large yellow flowers. *B. aristata* (D or SE), 8–10 feet, yellow flowers with reddish tinge, fruits red. *B. asiatica* (E), 6 feet, leaves white below, leathery. *B. bergmanniae* (E), 7–8 feet, compact plant. *B. buxifolia* (E), 5–6 feet, leaves grey below; var. *nana*, 1½ feet, slow-growing. *B. calliantha* (E), leaves white beneath. *B. candidula* (E), 2 feet, dome-shaped shrub. *B. chitria* (D), 10–12 feet, dark red berries in long trails. *B. chillanensis* (D), 6 feet, flowers yellow and orange; var. *hirsutipes*, which differs only botanically, is the form grown. *B. chrysophaera* (E), 5–6 feet, large flowers. *B. coxii* (E), 8–10 feet, leaves whitish below. *B. darwinii* (E), 5–6 feet, early flowering, the most popular barberry; var. *prostrata*, dwarfer variety. *B. diaphana* (D), 3–6 feet, fruits red, good autumn colour. *B. dictiophylla* var. *albicaulis* (D), 5–6 feet, leaves white below, fruits covered with white powdery bloom. *B. dumicola* (E), 4 feet, flowers tinged red. *B. francisci-fernandii* (D), 8–12 feet, vigorous, berries sealing-wax red. *B. gagnepainii* (E), 4–5 feet, dense growth, suitable for hedging. *B. georgei* (D), 3–4 feet, fruits crimson, good autumn colour. *B. gilgiana* (D), 3–4 feet, fruits dark red. *B. hakeoides* (E), 8–10 feet, golden flowers freely produced. *B. henryana* (D), 6–8 feet, red berries. *B. hispanica* (D), 6 feet, flowers orange-yellow. *B. hookeri* (E), 4–5 feet, leaves white below; var. *viridis*, leaves green below. *B. hypokerina* (E), 4 feet, large, holly-like leaves, white below. *B. insignis* (E), 6 feet, large leaves and flowers, slightly tender. *B. jamesiana* (D), 6–8

**1** Berberis thunbergii atropurpurea, which grows to about 5 feet, and has reddish-purple leaves, makes an excellent deciduous hedge **2** The coral-red berries of the hybrid Berberis x rubrostilla are among the largest of all barberry fruits

feet, coral berries. *B. julianae* (E), 8–10 feet, fruits covered with white bloom. *B. kawakamii* (E), 4–6 feet, young leaves coppery; var. *formosana*, fruits with mauve bloom. *B. koreana* (D), 3–4 feet, stoloniferous habit, large leaves, good autumn colour, fruits red. *B. lempergiana* (E), 7–9 feet, fruits covered with white bloom. *B. linearifolia* (E), 3–4 feet, one of the most beautiful species, with orange-red flowers. *B. lycium* (SE), 8–9 feet, fruits with white bloom. *B. manipurana* (E), 8–10 feet, fruits with grey bloom. *B. mitifolia* (D), 3–4 feet, fruits crimson. *B. montana* (D), 6 feet, flowers large, 1 inch across, yellow. *B. morrisoniensis* (D), 3 feet, red berries, good autumn leaf colour. *B. orthobotrys* (D), 4–6 feet, bright red fruits, good autumn leaf colour. *B. panlanensis* (E), 3–4 feet. *B. prattii* (D), 6–7 feet, fruits bright pink, freely produced. *B. pruinosa* (E), 6 feet, leaves white below, fruits with white bloom. *B. replicata* (E), 5 feet, leaves white below. *B. sargentiana* (D), 6 feet, leaves yellowish below. *B. sherriffii* (D), 6 feet, leaves grey below, fruits with grey bloom. *B. taliensis* (E), 2–3 feet, slow-growing. *B. telomaica* (D), 6 feet, young shoots and leaves blue-white, fruits red. *B. thunbergii* (D), 4 feet, scarlet fruits, fine autumn leaf colour; vars. *atropurpurea*, 5 feet, leaves good reddish-purple, fine foliage shrub, good for hedging; *erecta*, dwarf fastigiate variety; *minor*, 18 inches,

dense growth. *B. umbellata* (D or SE), 6 feet, young shoots bright red, fruits red. *B. valdiviana* (E), 5–6 feet, large leaves, dense growth. *B. valdisepala* (D), 5–6 feet, similar to *B. yunnanensis*, with smaller flowers and fruits. *B. veitchii* (E), 6 feet, young shoots red, leaves large, spiny, flowers bronze. *B. vernae* (D), 6–10 feet, fruits orange red. *B. verruculosa* (E), 4–5 feet, leaves white beneath, slow-growing, compact. *B. virescens* (D), 6–7 feet, fruits red, good autumn leaf colour. *B. vulgaris* (D), 8 feet, the native barberry, of which many vars. are recorded including *purpurifolia* with wine-purple leaves. *B. wilsonae* (E), 2–3 feet, coral berries, fine autumn leaf colour; several vars. including *globosa*, dwarf form and *stapfiana*, taller. *B. yunnanensis* (D), 5–6 feet, fruits bright red, good autumn leaf colour. *B. zabeliana* (D), 5–6 feet, fruits dark red, leaves colour well in autumn. **Hybrids and cultivars** *B.* × *antoniana* (E), 5 feet, orange flowers on long stalks. 'Barbarossa' (D), 5–6 feet, fruits red, freely borne. 'Bountiful' (SE), 3 feet, free fruiting, coral-red berries. *B.* × *chenaultii* (D), 3–4 feet, large yellow flowers, arching habit. 'Buccaneer' (D), 5 feet, large red fruits. 'Cherry Ripe' (D), 5–6 feet, bright red fruits, one of the finest hybrid berberis. *B.* × *irwinii* (E), 3 feet, dwarf, compact; vars. *coccinea*, *corallina*, *corallina compacta*, *gracilis nana*, *picturata*, all more dwarf. *B.* × *lologensis* (E), 6 feet, apricot flowers. *B.* × *macrantha* (D), 10–12 feet, fruits dark red with purple bloom. *B.* × *rubrostilla* (D), 4 feet, very large coral-red fruits. *B.* × *stenophylla* (D), 6–8 feet, gracefully arching habit, free-flowering, useful for hedging.

## Buddleia (bud-lee-a)

Named after the Rev. Adam Buddle, English botanist *(Loganiaceae)*. Deciduous and evergreen free-flowering hardy and half-hardy shrubs. They are easily grown in any light soil, including chalky loam, in full sun, and frequently seed themselves. The colourful, fragrant flowers are a great attraction to a wide variety of butterflies. Making such rapid growth they have not always a particularly long life, but are easily propagated. In recent years a number of attractive named varieties have been produced.

**Species cultivated** *B. alternifolia* (D), 12 feet, hardy, of weeping habit, flowers, lavender, fragrant, on one-year-old wood, May, China; var. *argentea*, leaves silvery with downy hairs, can be trained against a sunny wall or grown as a specimen standard on a lawn. *B. asiatica* (SE), shrub or small tree, fragrant white flowers, winter, East Indies, conservatory or cool greenhouse. *B. auriculata* (E), 7–10 feet, half-hardy, small, sweetly fragrant creamy-white flowers in winter, may be grown against a warm, sheltered wall in the south, otherwise needs the

1 The tangerine coloured flowers of Buddleia globosa, familiarly known as the Orange-ball Tree. 2 Buddleia davidi is the most popular kind, known as the Butterfly Bush because its deep purple spikes of fragrant bloom in late summer attract these insects.

protection of a greenhouse or conservatory. *B. candida* (D), 6–8 feet, grey, flannel-like leaves, violet flowers in short spikes, half-hardy, as above. *B. caryopteridifolia* (D), 7–10 feet, lilac flowers in spring, hardy only in the south and west. *B. colvilei* (D), 20 feet, half-hardy, flowers rose-coloured, in drooping panicles, June, Himalaya, requires the protection of a warm wall. *B. crispa* (D), 6–10 feet, leaves and stems woolly-white, flowers fragrant, lilac, orange-throated, July, N. India, sunny sheltered site; var. *farreri*, flowers rosy-lilac, April. *B. davidii* (syn. *B. variabilis*) (D), 10–15 feet, dark lavender, July to October, China. *B. fallowiana* (D) 8 feet, powder-blue, silver-grey leaves, June, China; var. *alba,* white 'Lochinch' is a rich blue cultivar. *B. forrestii* (D) 6–10 feet, leaves brown below, flowers maroon

to pale mauve, fragrant, August, September, China. *B. globosa* (SE), orange ball tree, 10–15 feet, fragrant tangerine-orange flowers, June, Chile, and Peru. *B. lindleyana* (D), 6–10 feet, purplish-violet flowers in slender spikes, July–August, China, somewhat tender. *B. officinalis* (D or SE), 6–10 feet, grey-woolly leaves, fragrant mauve flowers, winter, China, needs protection of cool greenhouse. *B. pterocaulis* (D), 6–8 feet, mauve flowers in stout spikes, Yunnan, Burma, rather tender. *B. salvifolia* (SE), 6–8 feet, flowers fragrant, pale lilac or white with orange eye, July, South Africa, hardy only in milder counties. *B. sikkimensis* (D), 6–8 feet, shoots and leaves woolly white, flowers lilac, summer, Sikkim, rather tender. *B. sterniana* (D), 6–9 feet, leaves large, woolly white, flowers pale lavender with orange eye, spring, China, rather tender. *B.* ×*pikei* (D), 8–10 feet, rosy-mauve, fragrant, June. *B.* ×*weyeriana* (D), 10–15 feet, a hybrid between *B. davidii* and *B. globosa,* it has spikes of ball-shaped yellow and pink inflorescences in summer. 'Golden Glow' is the form usually offered; in this variety the flowers are tangerine, pink and mauve in colour.

**Cultivars** of *B. davidii* include 'Black Knight', deepest purple, July and August, 'Charming', lavender-pink, July and August, 'Dubonnet', deep purple, 'Empire Blue', violet-blue with orange eye, 'Fascination', lilac-pink, 'Fromow's Purple', deep purple-violet, July and August, *nanhoensis*, dwarf variety, slender mauve spikes, summer, 'Pink Pearl', lilac-pink with yellow eye, 'Royal Red', long spikes of purple red, July and August, 'White Bouquet', white with yellow centre, 'White Cloud', pure white, 'White Profusion', July and August.

**Cultivation** Plant in autumn or in April in an ordinary light soil. Prune *B. davidii*, its named varieties and *B. fallowiana* by cutting hard back in March or April. *B. alternifolia* is thinned out after flowering, cutting out some of the old wood when necessary. *B. globosa* and *B.* × *weyeriana* should be thinned and cut back after flowering. Pruning of others depends on whether they flower on wood produced in the same season, when they should be pruned in late winter, or whether they bloom on shoots produced during the previous season, when they should be pruned immediately they have finished flowering. Propagate *B. davidii* and its varieties by hardwood cuttings in the autumn in a cold frame in sandy soil. Propagate *B. alternifolia*, *B. globosa* and other species by taking cuttings of half-ripened wood in June and July and planting in sandy soil under a hand light or bell glass.

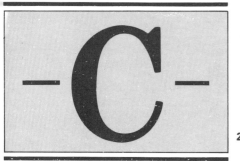

**1** Callicarpa giraldiana in flower, one of the best species for autumn colour. **2** C. rubella a deciduous shrub reaching 10 feet needing cool greenhouse culture

**Callicarpa** (kal-ee-karp-a)
From the Greek *kallos*, beauty, *karpos*, fruit *(Verbenaceae)*. A genus of erect hardy and half-hardy deciduous shrubs from 6 to 8 feet tall, neat in habit and attractive for the clusters of violet-blue or lilac berries in autumn, which remain all the winter; interesting, but not outstanding shrubs. The tiny flowers are borne in small clusters in late summer.

**Species cultivated: Greenhouse** *C. americana*, 4 feet, mauve-blue berries, southeast USA. This needs cool greenhouse conditions with a minimum winter temperature of 45°F (7°C). Prune before repotting in March. It may be grown out of doors in sheltered gardens in the milder counties.

**Hardy** *C. giraldiana* (syn. *C. bodinieri giraldii*), 6 feet, one of the best garden species with good autumn tints to its foliage and blue-mauve berries freely produced, China. *C. dichotoma*, 5 feet, coarser growth, purplish leaves, pink flowers, deep lilac fruits, China, Korea. *C. japonica*, 4 feet, compact growth, violet-blue berries, Japan; var. *angustata*, long narrow leaves, China.

**Cultivation** Plant these shrubs in November in sheltered sites, prune in February, cutting back fairly hard, as flowers and fruits are produced on the current season's wood. Propagation is by cuttings 4 inches long, rooted during June and July in a shaded cold frame.

## Calluna (kal-oo-na)

From the Greek *kalluno*, to clean, or brush, as the twigs were used for making brooms *(Ericaceae)*. A low evergreen flowering shrub of 6–18 inches high, calluna is the Scottish heather, but known in the south as ling; the chief plant of moorlands, it gives large areas of purple colour in late summer. There is but one species, *C. vulgaris,* but many varieties and cultivars of it. Some may be used as cut-flowers and many wild forms are worth propagating. Natural variations occur in the colour, form, and grouping of the flowers, and some plants have leaves covered with soft down which gives a grey colour and different texture. There are also taller varieties. An open site is most suitable; a lime-free soil is essential.

**Cultivars** include *aurea*, 4 inches, yellow-tipped foliage, white flowers, September and October; *plena*, 18 inches, double-flowered white, August and September; *alportii*, 2 feet, very upright, bright carmine flowers, August and September; 'Blazeaway', 1½ feet, spectacular reddish foliage, autumn and winter; 'David Eason', 1½ feet, purple-red flowers, September to November; *foxii nana*, 4 inches tall cushion plants, flowers pink; *hammondii aurea*, 2½ feet, golden foliage, white flowers, August and September; 'H. E. Beale', attractive double pink

flowers; *serlei*, 3 feet, white flowers, September; *serlei aurea*, 2 feet, golden foliage, white flowers, August and September. Others are listed by nurserymen.
**Cultivation** Plant in spring or autumn and if the soil is neutral, topdress with peat each spring. If plants become leggy cut them back in March or April. Propagate by cuttings 1 inch long of non-flowering shoots in July or August, rooted in a sand and peat mixture under a handlight, or in a frame.

## Camellia (kam-el-e-a)

Commemorating George Joseph Kamel (or Camellus), a Jesuit who travelled widely in the East *(Theaceae)*. Plants were brought to this country in one of the East India Company's ships in 1792. The leaves of *C. sinensis* produce the tea we drink. In their natural habitat camellias are undershrubs, which dislike a lime soil, and revel in moist conditions of leafmould. The value of the camellia as an outdoor evergreen flowering shrub, is not always fully appreciated; for long treated as tender, it is now taking its place with rhododendrons and azaleas among hardy shrubs. The leaves are dark glossy green, the flowers white, pink, or red, sometimes attractively striped, mostly borne in March and April (earlier under glass). Height varies according to conditions and can be 15 feet or more. Plants have the advantage of flowering when very young, at only 1½ feet. These shrubs require a position sheltered from cold winds and early morning sun; it is the latter, causing a quick thaw which damages the blooms on frosty mornings. Light woodland or north-facing borders should be chosen. There are several species, but not all are grown.

**Species cultivated** *C. cuspidata*, small white, single, cup-shaped flowers and purple-tinted leaves, pleasing but not outstanding. *C. granthamiana*, bronze-red young leaves, large white flowers. *C. hongkongensis*, young leaves bluish-brown, flowers crimson, 2 inches across. *C. japonica*, the common camellia and the most widely known. This species has over 10,000 varieties and cultivars with single, semi-double and double rosette-like flowers (see list of cultivars); it is reasonably hardy. *C. reticulata*, large rose flowers, not quite as hardy, and more suitable for the milder counties, but freer flowering and more spectacular. *C. saluenensis* is also free flowering, and is used in hybridising, 3 inch wide flowers, rose, carmine or white. *C. sasanqua* produces white to rose single or double fragrant flowers from October to April. *C. taliensis*, flowers white or cream, 2 inches across, September–December. *C. tsai*, young leaves coppery, numerous small white flowers, tender. *C. × vernalis*, white, sometimes flushed pink, 3 inches or so across, January to April The race of hybrids known as *C. × williamsii (japonica × saluenensis)* was raised at Caerhays Castle, Cornwall, and these deserve a place in every garden, as they have the hardiness of *C. japonica* with the freedom of flowering of *C. saluenensis*. Some of them also have the attractive habit of dropping their dead flowers, whereas with many camellias these remain on the bushes, brown and somewhat unsightly. In recent years many new cultivars of *C. japonica* have been raised in the USA and more of these will gradually find their way into British gardens.

**Cultivars** (a selection only of the many in cultivation) 'Cornish Snow', numerous 2½ inch wide white flowers. *C. japonica:* 'Adolphe Audusson', large dark red flowers; 'Donckelarii', semi-double, crimson marbled white; 'Lady de Saumerez', carmine, free flowering; *magnoliaeflora*, petals point forward, shell pink; *mathotiana*, double, in red *(rubra)*, white *(alba)* and pink *(rosea)*. The newer race of japonicas from USA includes 'Drama Girl', semi-double, very large flowers, rose-pink; 'Kramer's Supreme', paeony flowered, bright red;

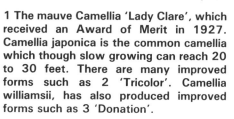

1 The mauve Camellia 'Lady Clare', which received an Award of Merit in 1927. Camellia japonica is the common camellia which though slow growing can reach 20 to 30 feet. There are many improved forms such as 2 'Tricolor'. Camellia williamsii, has also produced improved forms such as 3 'Donation'.

'Snowman', paeony flowered, very large white; 'Virginia Robinson', semi-double, pink. *C. reticulata:* 'Butterfly Wings', rose-pink, semi-double; 'Chang's Temple', paeony-flowered, flowers pink with white blotches, up to 8 inches wide; 'Crimson Robe', semi-double, carmine, up to 6 inches across; 'Mary Williams', large, clear pink; 'Purple Gown', paeony-flowered, purplish-red, up to 8 inches across. *C. sasanqua:* 'Mine-no-Yuki', semi-double, white; 'Papaver', soft pink; *rosea plena*, double, pink, good foliage; *versicolor*, single, white, tipped pink. *C. × williamsii* hybrids: 'Coppelia', flowers open flat, pale pink; 'Donation', semi-double, peach pink, an

outstanding variety; 'November Pink', winter-flowering in mild areas; 'St. Ewe', madder pink, single to semi-double.

**Cultivation: Outdoors** Camellias should be given well-drained soil, free of lime, with leafmould or peat added and a light dressing of bonemeal. Plant in April or October; no pruning is required except to remove dead wood. Propagation is by layers in autumn, by stem cuttings with a heel in summer, or by leaf-bud cuttings rooted in March in bottom heat. They are good plants for tubs, using John Innes compost, or a mixture of lime-free loam, peat, leafmould and sand.

**Greenhouse** This treatment is necessary for the more tender species, including *C. sasanqua* and its varieties, in colder areas. Pot in May using John Innes compost; keep the plants syringed and well-watered. In winter they should have sufficient heat to keep out frost, a minimum of about 45°F (7°C). Bud-dropping may be due to either water-logging or dryness at the roots. Propagation is the same as for outdoors.

## Ceanothus (see-an-o-thus)

Derived from *keanothus,* the ancient Greek name for another plant *(Rhamnaceae).* Evergreen and deciduous flowering shrubs from North America, known as Californian lilacs. The majority have blue flowers and they are an asset to any garden. They are fairly hardy in this country (evergreen species the least so) if they are given a sheltered position, but liable to be cut back by frosts otherwise. They are easily trained and are very suitable for a warm wall. The hybrids are most satisfactory for decorative garden use. The evergreen species flower in early summer and the deciduous species in the autumn.

1 Ceanothus thyrsiflorus will stand all but the most severe winters. Evergreen the flowers are produced in May. An Award of Merit was given in 1935. 2 C. 'Trewithen'. 3 C. dentatus flowers in May and is usually grown on a wall

**Species cultivated** *C. americanus* (D), 3–4 feet, flowers white, summer. *C. arboreus* (E), 6 feet, deep blue, spring. *C. austromontanus* (E), 10–12 feet, rich blue, May–December in warm localities. *C. cyaneus* (E), 8 feet, cornflower-blue flowers, June and July. One of the hardiest. *C. dentatus* (E), 6–10 feet, deep blue, May; vars. *floribundus,* 6–8 feet, powder-blue, April and May; *Impressus,* low or prostrate form. *C. divergens* (E), 1½–2 feet, prostrate in habit, powder-blue, July–September. *C. fendleri* (D), up to 4 feet or semi-prostrate, white or pale mauve, June and July. *C. foliosus* (E), dwarf, spreading, deep blue, May. *C. gloriosus* (syn. *rigidus grandifolius*) (E), 10–12 feet, lavender blue, fragrant, April and May. *C. griseus* (syn. *C. thyrsiflorus griseus*) (E), 10–15 feet, lilac, May. *C. incanus* (E), 5–8 feet, creamy white, April and May. *C. papillosus* (E), 10–12 feet, deep blue, May and June; var. *roweanus,* 6 feet, narrower leaves. *C. prostratus* (E), prostrate, 6–10 feet across, blue, spring. *C. pumilus* (E), dwarf, creeping habit, pale blue, spring. *C. rigidus* (E), 5–6 feet, purple-blue, spring; var. *pallens,* larger leaves, paler flowers. *C. thyrsiflorus* (E), 10–15 feet, bright-blue early summer; var. *repens,* semi-prostrate, Cambridge-blue.

**Cultivars** 'A. T. Johnson' (E), 10–15 feet, rich blue, spring and autumn; 'Autumnal Blue' (E), 10–15 feet, blue, late summer and autumn; *C.* × *burkwoodii* (E), 6–10 feet, bright blue, summer to autumn; 'Cascade' (E), 10–15 feet, powder-blue, May and June; 'Ceres' (D), 6–10 feet, lilac-pink, summer; 'Delight' (E), 10–15 feet, deep blue, May and June; 'Dignity' (E), 10–15 feet, deep blue, May and June, sometimes again in autumn; 'Gloire de Plantieres' (D), 5–8 feet, deep blue, summer; 'Gloire de Versailles' (D), 6–10 feet, sky-blue, fragrant, summer and autumn; 'Henri Defosse' (D), 6–10 feet, violet blue, summer; 'Indigo' (D), 6–10 feet, summer; *C.* × *lobbianus* (E), 10–15 feet, bright blue, May and June; 'Marie Simon' (D), 6–10 feet, pink, summer; 'Perle Rose' (D), 6–10 feet, rosy-carmine, summer; 'Pinquet Guindon' (D), 6–10 feet, lavender: 'Topaz' (D), 6–10 feet, bright blue, summer and autumn; *C.* × *veitchianus* (E), 10–15 feet, deep bright blue, May and June, a good hardy hybrid.

**Cultivation** Ceanothus prefer a light soil and a sheltered position and are shrubs mainly for the South of England. Plant in March or April; if planted in autumn they must have protection from frosts during the first winter. Evergreen species should be pruned after flowering; if growing against a wall they may need fairly hard cutting, whereas a bush in the open needs only sufficient pruning to keep it shapely. Deciduous kinds are pruned in April. Propagation of evergreen kinds is by cuttings 2–4 inches long made from firm sideshoots with a heel, rooted in a cold frame in October. Deciduous kinds are propagated in the same manner but cuttings should be 3–5 inches long. The seed of some species is occasionally available; it should be sown in spring and germinated at 59–65°F (15–18°C).

## Chaenomeles (ki-nom-el-eez)

From the Greek, *chaino*, to gape or split, *meles*, apple, a reference to the fruits *(Rosaceae)*. Japanese quince, but better known as 'japonica'. The common quince which is grown for its fruit is now in a separate genus, *Cydonia*. Natives of northern Asia, the chaenomeles are among the most colourful of spring flowering hardy deciduous shrubs. They will thrive in any ordinary soil, including those containing chalk. Planted in any aspect, they do equally well in flower borders, against walls or fences or even grown as a hedge. The fruit is used only in small quantities in preserves.

**Species cultivated** *C. japonica*, 3 feet, spreading, compact growth, orange-red, fruits used in jelly, April. *C. cathayensis*, 10 feet, white suffused pink, large fruits,

April. *C. lagenaria*, 6–10 feet, scarlet blood red, against a sheltered wall, will often start to flower from January and continue until June. *C. × superba (C. japonica × C. lagenaria)*, 3–5 feet, blood red. Cultivars include *atrococcinea*, blood red; *cardinalis*, salmon-pink; 'Knap Hill Scarlet', orange scarlet; *moerloesii* Apple Blossom', pink and white; *nivalis*, white; *rosea flore pleno*, rose-pink, double; 'Rowallane Seedling', rosy crimson, large flowers; *rubra grandiflora*, low-growing, large crimson flowers; *simonii*, dwarf, semi-double, blood red; 'Vermilion'. 'January Pink' is an attractive hybrid between *C. cathayensis* and *C. lagenaria*, which has rosy pink flowers from January onwards but fruits later.

**Cultivation** Any ordinary soil is adequate. Plants will grow in any aspect but prefer sun. They resent root disturbance and young plants are usually grown in pots. Plant from November to March. Wall or trained specimens should have the young breast wood shortened back by 4–5 inches in the summer. Propagation of the species is by rooted suckers or spring layering.

1 Chaenomeles japonica, Maule's quince, produces apple-shaped fruit which makes excellent jelly. 2 Chaenomeles lagenaria, the Japanese quince, will grow to 6–10 feet across. Grown on a wall it will flower from February to April.

## Choisya (choy-ze-a)

Named in honour of a Swiss botanist, Jacques Denys Choisy (*Rutaceae*). Mexican orange. A small genus, possibly of one species only, *C. ternata*, a hardy evergreen flowering shrub which can be used as a specimen plant or for hedging purposes. It was introduced from Mexico in the early nineteenth century. It makes a rounded bush 4–6 feet in height with fragrant white flowers in May and often spasmodically again in summer and autumn.

**Cultivation** *C. ternata* will grow in any ordinary soil, including those containing chalk or lime. It will thrive near the sea, but usually requires a sheltered position. In the north of England it should be planted against a wall. Plant out in October or March, adding peat and leafmould to the soil. Prune after the first flush of flowers is over, simply shortening the straggling shoots. It can be grown in pots in a compost of equal parts of peat, loam, leafmould and sand. Pot up in September or October and water only sparingly until March, after which give plenty of water. Put the pots in a cool greenhouse from September to May and have them out of doors for the rest ρf the time. Propagate from cuttings 3 inches long, taken from March to June and put into well-drained pots of sandy soil under a bell-jar or in a propagating frame at a temperature of 55–65°F (13–18°C), or taken from August to September and rooted in a cold frame.

## Cistus (sis-tus)

From the Greek *kistos,* a rock rose (*Cistaceae*). Rock Rose. A genus of evergreen shrubs, hardy and half-hardy, from southern Europe. They are good plants for the small garden if protected; few survive really hard winters except in the milder counties. All flower in June and July. Individual flowers are fleeting but are produced abundantly in long succession.

**Species cultivated** *C. × aguilare,* 6 feet, white flowers with brown blotches, a strong growing hybrid; var. *maculatus,* crimson blotches. *C. albidus,* 5 feet, rosy-white, hardy. *C. bourgeanus,* 2 feet, flowers white, small. *C. canescens,* 4 feet, leaves grey, flowers lilac; var. *albus,* flowers white. *C. × corbariensis,* 3 feet, white flowers, hardy. *C. crispus,* 2 feet, rosy-red flowers, fairly hardy. *C. × cyprius,* gum cistus, 6 feet, white flowers with maroon blotches, hybrid; var. *albiflorus,* flowers lacking blotches. *C. × florentinus* 3 feet, white flowers, hybrid. *C. × glaucus,* 3–4 feet, flowers white, large. *C. ladaniferus,* 4 feet, also known as the gum cistus, white flowers with crimson blotches; var. *albiflorus,* yellow blotched. *C. laurifolius,* 6 feet, the hardiest white flowered species; var. *decumbens,* the perpetual rock rose, flowers similar to those of *C. cyprius,* but borne continuously, plant

Choisya ternata is one of the few Mexican shrubs that can be grown in the open in the south-east of Britain. It was introduced in 1825 and the fragrant flowers are plentifully produced in April and May. It is known as the Mexican orange blossom

denser, of dwarf habit. *C. × laxus,* 3–4 feet, flowers white, yellow centred. *C. loretii,* 1½–2 feet, large white flowers with crimson basal blotches. *C. palhinhaii,* 1½–2 feet, white. *C. × platysepalus,* 2–3 feet, flowers white with yellow basal blotches. *C. populifolius,* 6 feet, white; var. *lasiocalyx,* larger flowers. *C. × pulvreulentus,* 2 feet, flowers rosy-pink. *C. × purpureus,* 3–4 feet, reddish pink flowers with chocolate blotches, a beautiful but tender plant. *C. salvifolius,* 2 feet, white; var. *prostratus,* prostrate in habit. *C. × skanbergii,* 4 feet, almond pink flowers, a hybrid. *C. symphytifolius,* 5–6 feet, flowers magenta. *C. × verguinii,* 2–3 feet, white with maroon basal blotches. *C. villosus,* 2–3 feet, flowers magenta; var. *albus,* white. Among the cultivars 'Elma' grows to 6 feet and has very large white flowers; 'Pat', 4 feet, has 5 inch wide white,

maroon-blotched flowers, and 'Silver Pink' is a fine hardy hybrid, 2½ feet tall.

**Cultivation** The hardy kinds will grow in almost any soil, but all do best in light, well-drained soils in a fairly sheltered position. The dwarf kinds are good rock garden shrubs; all do well on a hot, sunny bank. The only pruning needed is the cutting out of any parts of the plant killed by hard weather, and the removal of seed-heads. Plants benefit from some protection in severe winters. Propagation is by sowing seeds in sandy soil in a frame or unheated greenhouse in March, pricking out into small pots and planting out in June, or by taking cuttings in September, 4 inches long, rooting them in pots of sandy soil placed in a cold frame or greenhouse. Where there is the risk of established plants being killed by frost it is wise to root a few cuttings for planting out in late spring.

## Columnea (kol-um-ne-a)

In honour of an Italian nobleman, Fabius Columna, author of the earliest botanical book illustrated with copper

plates, published in Naples in 1592 **1**
(*Gesneriaceae*). Evergreen trailing sub-
shrubs for stove or warm greenhouses,
principally from Mexico and Costa Rica.
They are particularly suited for culture
in hanging baskets, which gives the
long growth a chance to develop fully
and the bold, tubular blossoms to be
displayed properly.

**Species cultivated** *C. banksii*, scarlet
flowers, early summer. *C. gloriosa*,
scarlet and yellow flowers, summer; var.
*purpurescens*, purple foliage, scarlet and
yellow flowers, summer. *C. magnifica*,
scarlet flowers, early summer. *C. microphylla*, scarlet and yellow flowers,
summer. *C. schiedeana*, scarlet flowers,
summer.

**Cultivation** Columneas require an open
and well-drained compost; John Innes
No. 1 is suitable. Temperatures: 65–70°F
(18–21°C) spring to autumn, 60°F (16°C),
(55°F (13°C) positive minimum) from
autumn through to spring. Water freely
and maintain humid conditions during
the warm season, much less so during
the cool, darker months. Propagation is
by cuttings of shoots taken in the latter
half of April and rooted in a warm frame
at 65°F (18°C) with bottom heat. Repot
at the end of March.

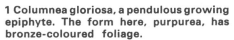

**1 Columnea gloriosa, a pendulous growing
epiphyte. The form here, purpurea, has
bronze-coloured foliage.**
**2 Cistus × cyprius albiflorus, a hardy,
vigorous rock rose growing to 6 feet.**
**3 C. × cyprius with crimson basal blotch-
ed petals. The high Award of Garden Merit
was given in 1926 by the RHS.**

## Cornus (kor-nus)

The Latin name for the cornelian cherry *(Cornaceae)*. Dogwood, cornel. Decorative deciduous and evergreen trees, and herbaceous plants. The often showy flowers' of several kinds are in reality bracts of the insignificant true flowers. The genus is now often split into genera *Cornus, Thelycrania, Chamaepericlymenum, Benthamia* and *Benthamidia*, here given as synonyms.

**Species cultivated** *C. alba* (syn. *Thelycrania alba*) (D), thicket-forming shrub with red stems to 10 feet; vars. *sibirica*, smaller, brighter red branches; *spaethii*, handsome golden-variegated form; *variegata*, white variegated form. *C. alternifolia argentea* (D), 18–10 feet, silver-variegated leaves, USA. *C. amomum* (D), 8–10 feet, shoots purplish in winter, flowers yellowish-white, fruits pale-blue, USA. *C. baileyi* (D), shrub to 10 feet, white berries, good autumn colour, USA. *C. canadensis* (syn. *Chamaepericlymenum canadensis*), herbaceous, running carpeting plant with large white flowers, May–June, and red berries. *C. capitata* (E), tree to 30 feet or more, sulphur-yellow bracts, June and July, followed by large crimson strawberry-like fruit, hardy only in the milder west, Himalaya. *C. controversa*, (syn. *Thelycrania controversa*) (D), tree to 30 feet, with tiers of horizontal branches and white petalous flowers in July; var. *variegata*, white variegation, Japan, China. *C. florida* (syns. *Benthamia florida, Benthamidia florida*) (D), American flowering dogwood, wide spreading tree to 20 feet, large white or pink bracts in May, good autumn foliage; var. *rubra*, red bracts, eastern USA. *C. hemsleyi* (D), shrub or tree to 20 feet, clusters of small white flowers, July, China. *C. kousa* (syns. *Benthamia japonica, Benthamidia kousa*) (D), shrub or small tree to 20 feet, showy creamy-white bracts in June, followed by strawberry-like fruits, Japan, Korea; var. *chinensis*, a better garden plant, China. *C. macrophylla* (D), tree to 30 feet or more, clusters of small creamy-white flowers, July and August, Himalaya, China, Japan. *C. mas* (D), cornelian cherry, shrub or small tree to 25 feet, small yellow flowers in February on leafless branches followed by edible red fruits; vars. *elegantissima*, leaves variegated yellow and pink; *macrocarpa*, larger fruits; *variegata*, leaves pronouncedly margined with white, Europe. *C. nuttallii* (D), Pacific dogwood, shrub or small tree to 20 feet, large cream coloured bracts, later tinged pink, in June, red and gold foliage in autumn, western USA. *C. obliqua* (D), similar to *C. amomum*, berries blue or white, North America. *C. officinalis* (D), tree-like to 25 feet, otherwise similar to *C. mas*, flowers yellow, fruits red, Korea. *C. paucinervis* (D), 6–8 feet, clusters of creamy, white flowers, July and August, fruits black, China. *C. racemosa* (syn. *C. candidissima*) (D), 8–12 feet, flowers

1 Cornus sibirica the Westonbirt Dogwood, provides welcome colourful stems in winter after the leaves drop. The shoots can reach 6 to 10 feet when grown in ordinary soil. 2 Cornus sanguinea, Common Dogwood, in flower.

creamy-white, June and July, fruits white, good autumn colour, North America. *C. rugosa* (D), 6–10 feet, flowers white, June, fruits pale blue, North America. *C. sanguinea* (syn. *Thelycrania sanguinea*) (D), common dogwood, shrub to 6 feet, with red and purple leaves in autumn, Europe, including British Isles. *C. stolonifera* (D), suckering shrub to 8 feet, purplish-red shoots, small dull white flowers; var. *flaviramea*, the yellow-barked dogwood, yellow shoots, USA. *C. walteri* (D), tree 25–30 feet, flowers white, June, fruits black, China.

2

Cultivation The herbaceous *C. canadensis* thrives in moist acid, sandy or peaty soil among shrubs, a good carpeting plant. *C. alba*, *C. sanguinea* and *C. stolonifera* which do well on pool margins, should be cut back to the ground to produce fresh coloured stems. This does not apply to *C. alba spaethii*.

The larger tree-like kinds need a choice sheltered position.

Propagation of spreading kinds is by division, though *C. canadensis* comes well from seed. The tree-like species can be raised from seed, which may not germinate until the second season. Cuttings can also be rooted.

## Corokia (kor-o-ke-a)

From the Maori name for the plant, *korokia (Cornaceae)*. A small genus of slow-growing evergreen shrubs from New Zealand and the Chatham Islands, one or two rather hardier than once thought, though benefiting from a sheltered position or mild climate.

Species cultivated *C. cotoneaster*, 6–8 feet, spoon-shaped leaves on very contorted stems, tiny star-like yellow flowers, summer, followed by orange-red berries. *C. buddleioides*, 6–8 feet, attractive willow-like foliage, less hardy. *C. macrocarpa*, 10 feet or more, leaves silvery below, flowers small, yellow, June, fruits orange, hardy only in the milder climates, Chatham Islands. *C. virgata*, 6–8 feet, bronze leaves, small yellow starry flowers, summer, followed by orange-yellow berries.

Cultivation The corokias will succeed in ordinary light well-drained, even poor soil. A position sheltered by a wall is ideal, though there is a good deal of

wind hardiness particularly with *C. cotoneaster* and *C. virgata*. Plant out autumn or spring. Propagate by cuttings, preferably taken with a heel, in July, and stuck in sandy soil in a well-drained pan under a bell-jar or in a frame. Layer suitable shoots in autumn.

1 The strawberry-like fruits of Cornus kousa, that was given an Award of Merit by the RHS in 1958. 2 The flowers of Cornus mas, the Cornelian cherry, produced in February, followed by red berries ¼ inches long. 3 The white bracts and inconspicuous flowers of Cornus kousa, a Japanese tree up to 20 feet

1 Cotinus coggygria foliis purpureis a shrub grown for its rich foliage tints. 2 C. coggygria, from south Europe, the Venetian sumach or Smoke Tree, so called because of the plume-like inflorescences

drainage is essential. The easiest method of propagation is by digging up rooted suckers and transplanting them in autumn, though cuttings of semi-ripe wood will root in a cold frame in summer, or young shoots may be layered in spring. Seed gives good results, but the seedlings vary slightly, and specially good forms should preferably be propagated by using suckers, cuttings or layers.

## Cotinus (kot-i-nus)

From the ancient Greek name for the wild olive *(Anacardiaceae)*. Shrubs with yellow wood and milky sap, closely related to plants of the genus *Rhus* and sometimes placed in that genus. Two species are commonly grown, each requiring plenty of space for full effect.
**Species cultivated** *C. americanus* (syn. *Rhus cotinoides)*, to 20 feet, small inconspicuous flowers borne in large panicles at the ends of shoots, brilliant autumn leaf colouring. *C. coggygria* (syn. *Rhus cotinus),* smoke tree, wig tree, Venetian sumach, to 10 feet, bears numerous branched hairy flower panicles, pale pink or brownish at first, later turning smoke-grey, hence the names smoke tree, wig tree; vars. *atropurpurea,* leaves and inflorescences rosy purple; *foliis purpureis,* leaves rich plum-purple; *foliis purpureis* 'Notcutt's Variety', darker leaves, the finest form.
**Cultivation** A sunny position is desirable, and any soil is suitable, although these shrubs do better on light soils. Good

## Cotoneaster (ko-to-ne-as-ter)

From the Latin *cotoneus,* quince, *aster,* likeness, referring to the resemblance *(Rosaceae).* A genus containing many species of evergreen and deciduous shrubs, natives of Europe, northern Asia (except Japan), North Africa, varying in size from prostrate plants to near trees 30 feet or more in height. They are mainly grown for their brightly coloured (usually red) fruits in autumn, but some have worthwhile flowers, usually borne in May or June, and some deciduous species show good autumn colouring of the leaves in favourable places. Some are useful hedge plants. Except where stated, all have white flowers.
**Species cultivated** *C. acutifolius* (D), 10–12 feet, flowers pinkish, fruits black, good autumn colour; var. *villosulus,* leaves larger. *C. adpressus* (D), 1–1½ feet tall, up to 5 feet across, useful for covering spaces in rock garden, fruits red, leaves turn red in autumn; var. *praecox* ('Nan-Shan'), 2 feet, larger

orange-red fruits. *C. affinis* (D), 12–15 feet, fruits purplish-black; var. *bacillaris*, leaves glabrous, fruits black. *C. ambiguus* (D), 6–8 feet, fruits purplish-red, good autumn leaf colour. *C. amoenus* (E), 3–5 feet, compact habit, red fruits. *C. bullatus* (D), 10–12 feet, flowers rosy-white, handsome red fruits; var. *floribundus*, flowers and fruits more freely produced, good autumn leaf colour. *C. buxifolius* (E), spreading shrub, 1–2 feet, spreading, orange-red berries. *C. congestus* (E), creeping, congested habit, fruits red. *C. conspicuus* (E), 4–5 feet, spreading, arching habit, flowers freely produced, fruits bright red; var. *decorus*, more prostrate. *C. cooperi* (SE), 10–20 feet, fruits bright red. *C. × cornubia* (D), 20–25 feet, vigorous, large bright red fruits borne so freely as to weigh down the branches. *C. dammeri* (E), prostrate, rooting branches, good for covering banks, rocks etc., fruits coral-red. *C. dielsianus* (D), 8 feet, flowers pinkish, fine scarlet berries, good autumn colour in leaves; var. *elegans*, leaves smaller,

fruits coral-red. *C. distichus* (SE), 5–8 feet, flowers tinged pink, fruits orange, persistent. *C. divaricatus* (D), 6–7 feet, pink flowers, bright red fruits, good autumn colour. *C. × exburyensis* (E), tall shrub, fruits apricot-yellow, persistent. *C. foveolatus* (D), 6–8 feet, flowers pink, fruits black, large leaves colouring well in autumn. *C. franchettii* (E), 8 feet, poor flowers but handsome brilliant scarlet fruit. *C. frigidus* (D), to 30 feet, tree or shrub, quick growing, vigorous, very fine bright red fruit; var. *fructoluteo*, yellow fruit. *C. glaucophyllus* (E), 6 feet, orange fruits; var. *vestitus*, taller, fruits colouring in December. *C. harrovianus* (E), 6 feet, arching habit, fruits red, colouring in December. *C. hebephyllus* (D), 6–8 feet, arching habit, dark red fruits. *C. henryanus* (E), 12 feet, fruits rich crimson. *C. horizontalis* (D), 5 feet, distinctive herringbone branching, small box-like leaves colouring in autumn, pinkish flowers, red berries, covers wall without nailing, very useful in north aspect; var. *variegatus*, leaves edged

1 Cotoneaster conspicuus, a wide spreading shrub reaching 4 to 5 feet. An Award of Merit was given in 1933.
2 Cotoneaster horizontalis.
3 Cotoneaster horizontalis in flower; these are eagerly visited by honey bees.

white. *C.* × *hybridus pendulus* (E), prostrate or can be trained to weeping tree shape, bright red fruits. *C. integerrimus* (D), 5–6 feet, flowers pink, fruits red, rare native shrub. *C. lacteus* (E), 12 feet, large leaves, red fruits, late. *C. lindleyi* (D), 10–12 feet, long arching branches, fruits black. *C. lucidus* (D), 8–10 feet, flowers pink and white, fruits black, good autumn colour. *C. melanocarpus* (D), 6 feet, flowers pink, fruits black, leaves colour well; var. *laxiflorus*, larger leaves. *C. microphyllus* (E), 4–5 feet tall, up to 10 feet across, densely branched, good for banks or tops of walls, fruits, scarlet; vars. *cochleatus*, prostrate form; *thymifolius*, smaller leaves, rock garden. *C. moupinensis* (D), 10–12 feet, flowers rosy–white, fruits black, good autumn colour. *C. multiflorus* (D), 5–6 feet, arching habit, fruits bright red, ripening early. *C.* × *newreyensis* (D), 8–10 feet, fruits red. *C. nitens* (D), 5–6 feet, fruits black, good autumn colour. *C. obscurus* (D), 8–10 feet, flowers pinkish, fruits dark red, leaves yellowish below. *C. pannosus* (E), 8–10 feet, fruits dull red. *C. racemiflorus* (D), 6–10 feet, red fruits; var. *microcarpus,* smaller fruits. *C.* × *rothschildiana* (E), 6–10 feet, spreading, vigorous, yellow fruits. *C. rotundifolius* (SE), 6 feet, scarlet berries retained till spring. *C. salicifolius* (E), 15–16 feet, bright red fruits; vars. *floccosus*, narrower leaves, smaller fruits abundantly borne; *fructu-luteo*, fruits clear yellow. *C. serotinus* (E), 10 feet, berries bright red retained till April. *C.* 'St. Monica' (SE), 20 feet, hybrid with large red berries, good autumn leaf colour. *C. simonsii* (SE), 9 feet, fruits scarlet, suitable for unpruned hedge. *C. thymifolius* (E), prostrate, a dwarf, densefoliaged shrub, possibly a form of *C. microphylla. C. tomentosus* (D), 6–8 feet, large red fruits, leaves very white, woolly underneath. *C. turbinatus* (SE), 5–6 feet, leaves white below, fruits red. *C. wardii* (E), 6–10 feet, orange-red fruits. *C.* × *watereri* (E or SE), 20 feet, hybrid, heavy crops of scarlet fruits if unpruned, can be used as hedge.

**Cultivation** Cotoneasters will grow in any ordinary soil, and are tolerant of lime and acid soils. They are among the best shrubs for poor soils. Sunny positions suit them best, but they tolerate semi-shade, and *C. horizontalis* is good in a north aspect. Plant from October to February. Pruning should be confined to shortening ungainly growths and removing overcrowded or very old branches. Propagation is by seed sown out of doors in March, 1 inch deep, but some do not come quite true from seed, and for these cuttings should be inserted in sandy soil in a frame in September, or they can be layered in spring. Clipping cotoneaster hedges tends to remove flowering shoots, so it is best not to try for too neat a surface. Merely cut out overlong shoots.

## Cytisus (si-tis-us)

From the Greek *kytisos,* trefoil, a reference to the leaves of some species *(Leguminosae).* Broom. A genus of deciduous and evergreen shrubs and small trees, some tender, all very colourful and decorative, natives of Europe, particularly the Mediterranean region, some from Asia Minor.

**Species cultivated: Greenhouse** *C. canariensis* (E), the florists' 'genista', up to 6 feet, fragrant yellow flowers, spring and summer; var. *ramosissimus,* smaller leaves, longer flower racemes. *C. fragrans* (D), Teneriffe broom, 2–3 feet, fragrant, yellow flowers, summer; var. *elegans,* 4 feet, taller but with similar yellow flowers. Both grown as florists flowers. Both species are from the Canary Isles and are not hardy in Britain, except maybe in the most favoured spots where the pots can be stood out of doors in the summer.

**Hardy** *C. albus* (syn. *C. multiflorus*) (D), white Spanish broom, white Portugal

broom, 6–10 feet, white, May and June. *C. ardoinii* (D), about 6 inches, matforming, bright yellow, April and May. *C. austriacus* (D), 2–3 feet, bright yellow, July to September. *C. battandieri* (D), Moroccan broom, 10 feet, bright yellow, pineapple scented flowers in cone-shaped heads, May to July. Foliage soft, grey-green rather like that of a laburnum. Hardy in sheltered gardens, a good wall shrub. *C. beanii* (D), 6–18 inches, deep yellow flowers, June. *C.* × *burkwoodii* (D), 5–7 feet, cerise and maroon, May. *C.* × *dallimorei* (D), 6–8 feet, pink and crimson, May. *C. decumbens* (D), prostrate, bright yellow, May and June, rock garden. *C. grandiflorus* (D), woolly-podded broom, 8–10 feet, bright yellow, May, pods covered with grey woolly hairs. *C. hirsutus* (D), 1–3 feet, buff-yellow and brown, May to July; var. *demissus* (syn. *C. demissus),* prostrate, buff-yellow. *C.* × *kewensis* (D), prostrate, cream, April and May. *C. maderensis* (E), 15–20 feet, leaves silvery, flowers fragrant, bright yellow, May and June, hardy only in mild

**1 Cytisus × kewensis, a deciduous shrub for the rock garden or dry wall.**
**2 Cytisus × praecox, the Warminster Broom, flowers in May.**
**3 Cytisus × burkwoodii needs acid soil.**

places, otherwise needs conservatory protection; var. *magnifoliosus,* leaves larger, flower trails larger. *C. monspessulanus* (SE), Montpelier Broom, 8–10 feet, yellow, April to June, liable to frost damage except in milder areas. *C. nigricans* (D), 3–6 feet, yellow, late summer. *C.* × *praecox* (D), 4–6 feet, cream, May. *C. procumbens* (D), 2 feet, yellow, May to July. *C. purgans* (D), 3–4 feet, usually leafless, flowers fragrant, yellow, April and May. *C. purpureus* (D), purple broom, 1½–2 feet, purple, May and June; var. *albus,* white. *C. ratisbonensis* (D), 3 feet, bright yellow, May and June. *C. scoparius* (D), common broom, Scots broom. 5–10 feet, bright yellow, May and June, native plant; vars. *andreanus* 6 feet. *C.* × *versicolor* (D), 2–3 feet, buff and

pinkish-purple, May and June.
**Named cultivars** All deciduous, include 'Cornish Cream', 6–7 feet, creamy-yellow; 'Donard Seedling', 6–8 feet, red, streaked yellow; 'Dorothy Walpole', 6–7 feet, rich crimson; 'Enchantress', 5–6 feet, pink; 'Goldfinch', 4–5 feet, lemon-yellow and cream; 'Hillieri', 2–3 feet, yellow and bronze, fading to pink, May and June. 'Johnson's Crimson', 5–6 feet, carmine and red; 'Lady Moore', 6–7 feet, red, buff and rose; 'Lord Lambourne', 6–7 feet, crimson and cream; 'C. E. Pearson', 6–7 feet, apricot, yellow, red, pink; 'Peter Pan', 1–1½ feet, crimson; 'Porlock', 6–8 feet, fragrant cream, early-flowering, hardy in the south. Cultivars of *C. scoparius* include 'Criterion', 6–7 feet, red and lemon-yellow; 'Diana', 6–7 feet, yellow and primrose; 'Firefly', 6–7 feet, crimson and yellow; 'Golden Sunlight', 6–7 feet, rich golden-yellow.
**Cultivation** Brooms are always grown in pots until they are big enough to plant in their permanent positions, because they do not transplant easily.

They thrive best in a sunny, open, well-drained position and do very well in poor, stony, dry soils. The smaller kinds are ideal for rock gardens and the taller growing ones are elegant enough to use as specimen shrubs. Pruning consists in cutting back old shoots immediately after flowering to the base of promising new ones. Never cut into old wood, as the broom does not break readily to produce new growth from the old wood. If shrubs become leggy at the base it is often better to replace the plant by a young one than try to cut it back. The hardy species can be propagated from seed sown out of doors in March or April but hybrids do not come true from seed and stock of these is increased by cuttings taken in July or August and put into a sandy compost and potted up into sand and loam once they are rooted. Grafting is possible and should be done in March or April, when the named varieties can be grafted on to laburnum stocks and kept in a temperature of 60°F (16°C) until the

**1** A seedling Cytisus scoparius, the common yellow or Scots broom. **2** Cytisus battandieri, from Morocco is doubtfully hardy. **3** Cytisus scoparius, the influence of which is to be seen in many of today's popular hybrids and cultivars.

union is complete.

The greenhouse kinds are grown in pots in a compost of 2 parts of loam, 1 of peat, 1 of sharp sand. Pot in May or June. Prune after flowering, cutting flowered shoots to within 2 inches of their bases. Keep pruned plants in a temperature of 50–55°F (10–13°C) to encourage new growth; after repotting place pots out of doors in a sunny place to ripen the growth. Bring them into the greenhouse again in October. Water freely June to November, moderately at other times. Feed when in flower. They are usually propagated by cuttings taken in spring and put into a propagating frame in a temperature of 75–80°F (24–27°C). Seed of the species can be sown in a temperature of 65–70°F (18–21°C) in March.

# -D-

## Daphne (daf-nee)

Named in commemoration of Daphne who in Greek mythology was pursued by Apollo and after praying for help was transformed into a laurel bush *(Thymelaeaceae)*. A genus of deciduous and evergreen shrubs notable for their fragrant flowers, widely distributed, many of them wild in Europe and two of which are native plants.

**Species cultivated** *D. alpina* (D), 6–18 inches, flowers white, May and June. *D. arbuscula* (E), dwarf, almost prostrate, rosy-pink flowers, June. *D. aurantiaca* (E), 2–2½ feet, flowers yellow, May. *D. blagayana* (E), 9–12 inches, semi-prostrate branches ending in clusters of richly scented cream flowers, March and April, good for the rock garden; spreads by its underground stems. *D. × burkwoodii* (syn. *D.* 'Somerset') (D), 3 feet, hybrid, quick-growing, flowers pale pink, May and June, very free flowering. *D. caucasica* (D), 4–5 feet, white flowers, May and June. *D. cneorum* (E), garland flower, 9–12 inches, fragrant pink flowers, May; vars. *album,* white; *eximia,* more prostrate; *pygmaea,* prostrate; *variegatum,* leaves cream-edged. *D. collina* (E), 15–18 inches, purplish-rose flowers, spring and early summer; var. *neopolitana,* 2–3 feet, rosy-pink. *D. genkwa* (D), 2–3 feet, lilac-blue, April and May, often difficult to establish. *D. giraldii* (D), 1½–2 feet, flowers yellow, June, berries bright red. *D. gnidium* (E), flax-leaved daphne, 2 feet, white, June to August. *D. × houtteana* (D or SE), leaves purplish, flowers reddish-purple, April, hybrid. *D. hybrida,* (syn. *D. dauphinii*) (E), 3–4 feet, pinkish-purple, almost continuously in flower, hybrid. *D. laureola* (E), spurge laurel, 3 feet, a native woodland species, slightly fragrant, green flowers, February and March. *D. mezereum* (D), the native mezereon, 4 feet, rich pinkish-purple flowers, February and March, scarlet autumn berries; vars. *alba,* white flowers, March, yellow berries; *grandiflora,* autumn-flowering; *rosea,* flowers rose-pink. *D. odora* (E), 2–3 feet, white, purple-marked flowers, January to March, rather tender, and frequently grown in a greenhouse where its blossoms escape the frost; var. *aureomarginata,* leaf margins variegated yellow, a hardier form. *D. oleoides* (E), 1½ feet, flowers variable, white to purplish, May and June. *D. pontica* (E), 2–3 feet,

yellowish-green flowers, April. *D. retusa* (E), 1–1½ feet, slow-growing, dense habit, good for the rock garden, white flowers touched with purple, May. *D. × rossettii* (E), 1½–2 feet, flowers pink, but not often produced, hybrid. *D. sericea* (E), 1–2 feet, rosy-pink, May and June. *D. tangutica* (E), 4–5 feet, rosy-purple, March and April.

**Cultivation** Most daphnes like rich loam or sandy peat and fail in hot dry con-

1 Daphne laureola, the Spurge Laurel, is a native woodland shrub. 2 Daphne mezereum flowers in February and March.

ditions; *D. mezereum* and *D. × neopolitana* like lime, the others need a lime-free soil. Some, e.g. *D. blagayana* and *D. retusa*, are at their best among stones in rock gardens. Propagation is by seed sown as soon as it is ripe for such easily grown species as *D. mezereum*, but *D. blagayana*, *D. cneorum*, *D. laureola*, *D. retusa* and *D. pontica* can be propagated by layering in autumn and the rarer species can be grafted on to stock of *D. mezereum* or *D. laureola,* depending on whether they are deciduous or evergreen. Grafting needs to be done in a greenhouse where a temperature of 55°F (13°C) can be maintained, in March.

## Daphniphyllum (daf-nee-fil-um)

From the Greek *Daphne* and *phyllon,* leaf *(Euphorbiaceae).* Hardy evergreen shrubs bearing large rhododendron-like leaves.

**Species cultivated** *D. humile,* 1½–2 feet, flowers inconspicuous, fruits blue-black, Japan. *D. macropodum* (syn. *D. glauces-*

*cens)*, 8–10 feet, slow-growing, striking plant with pale green leaves, glaucous on the lower surface, giving a white effect, China, Japan, Korea.

**Cultivation** These plants will tolerate limy or chalky soils and shade and are grown mainly for their handsome foliage and berries. The flowers are unisexual, carried on different plants and thus it is necessary to plant both forms for good berries to be produced. Plant in November. Propagation is from cuttings of the ripened wood, rooted under cloches or in a frame in July.

---

**Desfontainea** (des-fon-tain-e-a)
Commemorating a French botanist, René Louiche Desfontaines *(Logani-aceae)*. An evergreen flowering shrub, somewhat tender, first introduced in the middle of the nineteenth century. A good plant for west Scotland, Ireland and maritime south-west counties. The only species is *D. spinosa,* 6–10 feet. The leaves are holly-like and the general habit of the shrub is stiff; the flowers are tubular in shape, scarlet and yellow, and are borne in late summer over a long period. This is a striking and magnificent shrub when established.

**Cultivation** *Desfontainea spinosa* dislikes lime and needs a good loam. It does particularly well on Cornish granite soil. Plant in October, November or April. The only pruning needed is to take out dead or unwanted pieces of wood. The plant can be grown under glass in tubs or borders, in a compost of equal parts of loam, peat and sand with some charcoal. Pot or plant in March or April and water moderately during the summer, reducing water in the winter. Propagation is by cuttings in spring in a temperature of 55–65°F (13–18°C).

---

1 Daphniphyllum macropodum, a hardy evergreen that tolerates alkaline soil.
2 Desfontainea spinosa, a late flowering somewhat tender evergreen from Chile and Peru, that reaches 6 to 10 feet.

2

1 Desmodium spicatum, a hardy deciduous shrub reaching 6 to 8 feet, flowering
in September and October. It was introduced from China in 1896. 2 Deutzia
gracilis, a shrub that reaches 3 to 4 feet
and flowers in June.

## Desmodium (dez-mo-de-um)

From the Greek *desmos*, a bond, a
reference to the united stamens
*(Leguminosae)*. Hardy and greenhouse
shrubby perennials and sub-shrubs, one
greenhouse kind, *(D. motorium)*, displaying a curious example of animated
leaves.

**Species cultivated:** Greenhouse *D. motorium* (syn. *D. gyrans*), telegraph plant,
2–3 feet, flowers violet or mauve,
summer. In sunshine, particularly, when
the temperature is above 72°F (22°C),
the leaflets move round in all directions.
At night they droop.

**Hardy** *D. canadense*, tick trefoil, 3 feet,
purple flowers, July and August, a
hardy perennial dying down each year
and breaking again from ground level.
*D. tiliaefolium*, shrubby, 3–5 feet, pale
lilac flowers, August and September.

**Cultivation** The tender species needs a
winter temperature of 55–65°F (13–18°C),
and a compost of equal parts of good
loam, peat and sand. The hardy kinds
should be planted in March in sunny
borders; they are propagated by division
in March. *D. motorium* is raised from
seed sown in a temperature of 75–80°F
(24–27°C) in early spring, or by cuttings
rooted in sandy peat in a propagating
case in spring.

## Deutzia (doyt-se-a)

In honour of Johann van der Deutz,
a Burgomaster of Amsterdam, a patron
of botany *(Saxifragaceae)*. Deciduous,
hardy, free-flowering shrubs, useful out
of doors and for forcing for conservatory
decoration. They come mainly from
China and other Far Eastern countries.
**Species cultivated** *D. × candelabrum*,
4–5 feet, white flowers, June, similar
to *D. gracilis*, but hardier, hybrid. *D.
chunii*, 5 feet, flowers pink outside,
white within, July. *D. compacta*, 5–6 feet,
fragrant white flowers, July. *D. discolor*,
4–6 feet, large flowers, white, pink
flushed on the outside; var. *major*,
larger flowers. *D. × elegantissima*,
4–6 feet, rose-pink, June, hybrid; var.
*fasciculata*, flowers bright pink. *D.
glomeruliflora*, 5–6 feet, flowers large,
white, May and June. *D. gracilis*, 4–5
feet, Japanese snowflower, white flowers,
June. This is the species usually grown
under glass, when it flowers in April and
May. *D. hookeriana*, 4–6 feet, flowers
white, late June. *D. hypoglauca*, 7–8 feet,
leaves white below, flowers white, June.
*D. × kalmiaeflora*, 5–6 feet, flowers
white, carmine flushed, June. *D. longifolia*, 4–6 feet, large clusters of lilac-
pink flowers, June; var. *veitchii*, 4–6 feet,
probably the most popular pink-flowered

kind. *D. × magnifica*, 8 feet, a hybrid,
vigorous in growth, double white
flowers, June; vars. *eburnea*, flowers
single, white; *latiflora*, large single
flowers; *longipetala*, single flowers with
long narrow petals. *D. monbeigii*, 4–6
feet, leaves white underneath, flowers
white, starry, June. *D. ningpoensis*, 6–7
flowers white, July. *D. pulchra*, 7–8 feet,
flowers white in long trails, May and
June. *D. × rosea*, 4 feet, pinkish flowers,
June, hybrid; vars. *campanulata*, white;
*carminea*, 4 feet, rose-carmine flowers;
*grandiflora*, flowers large white, flushed
pink; *venusta*, flowers large, white.
*D. scabra* (syn. *D. crenata*), 7 feet, white
flowers, June; vars. *candidissima*, pure
white, double; *macrocephala*, larger
flowers, July; *plena* ('Pride of Rochester')
double, flushed rosy-purple outside;
*watereri*, single white flowers tinted
carmine. *D. setchuenensis*, 6 feet, slow-
growing, white flowers, June to August;
var. *corymbiflora*, larger leaves and
flowers. *D. sieboldiana*, 3–4 feet, starry
white fragrant flowers, June. *D.
staminea*, 4–5 feet, flowers white, June.
*D. vilmoriniae*, 8–10 feet, quick growing,
flowers white, June.

**Cultivation** Deutzias prefer a good loam
soil but will grow in most soils. It is
essential to encourage well-ripened wood

each year to ensure free flowering. Remove old worn-out wood once flowering is over, to a point where young shoots are developing, but do not shorten shoots generally as this results in loss of flower. Feeding with a mulch of old manure helps to ripen the wood and enrich the soil. Propagation is from cuttings in May or June or in July when the wood is firmer. Pinch out the tips of growth the following season to encourage bushy growth.

When *D. gracilis* is to be forced, pot up rooted cuttings into a compost of 2 parts of loam, 1 part of decayed manure and sand, in October or November. Keep in a cold greenhouse or frame throughout the winter, giving the plants little water. Start watering more in March when the plants respond to a minimum temperature of 55–60°F (13–16°C), and will flower in April and May. After three years or so plants should either be discarded or planted out of doors for a year before repotting.

## Elaeagnus (el-e-ag-nus)

From the Greek *elaia,* an olive tree, *agnos,* a willow-like plant *(Elaeagnaceae).* Hardy deciduous and evergreen decorative shrubs with insignificant, but fragrant, silver-coloured flowers, resembling small fuchsias.

**Species cultivated** *E. angustifolia* (D), oleaster, 15–20 feet, branches spiny, silvery, willow-like leaves, fruits large, oval, silvery-amber, southern Europe and western Asia; var. *orientalis,* larger leaves. *E. commutata* (syn. *E. argentea*) (D), silvery berry, up to 10 feet, silvery leaves, silvery-yellow, fragrant flowers, May, southern North America. *E.* × *ebbingei* (E), up to 10 feet, handsome hybrid *(E. glabra* × *E. pungens),* silvery-green foliage, flowers small pendent, silvery-white, fragrant. *E. glabra* (E), up to 15 feet, narrow silvery leaves, Japan. *E. macrophylla* (E), 10 feet, strong grower, round silvery leaves, yellow, fragrant flowers, October and November, Japan. *E. multiflora* (D), up to 10 feet, flowers creamy, April and May, leaves silvery beneath, deep orange

1

2

1 Deutzia 'Magician', a hybrid of Deutzia longifolia.
2 Elaeagnus grow well on a dry bank.

1 Elaeagnus pungens, the type, will grow to 15 feet. It is not as handsome as its variegated leaf varieties.
2 Elaeagnus pungens aereo-variegata has gold-splashed leaves.
3 Enkianthus campanulatus, a shrub growing to 8 feet that requires lime-free soil. Light shade is tolerated.

edible fruit, Japan, *E. pungens* (E), up to 15 feet, silvery white fragrant flowers, October and November; *E. umbellata* (D), 15 feet, strong growing and spreading, flowers creamy-white, May, fruit silvery, becoming deep red, Himalaya.

**Cultivation** Plant the deciduous species from October to December, and the evergreen species in April or September. All thrive in dryish, ordinary soil either in an open, exposed situation, if hardy, and in a warm climate or indoors, if tender. Propagation is by cuttings placed in sandy soil in a cold frame in September, by layers in spring, or by seed sown in March in boxes of light soil in a temperature of 55°F (13°C).

### Enkianthus (en-ke-an-thus)

From the Greek *enkuos*, enlarged, *anthos*, a flower, possibly a reference to the rounded, bell-shaped flowers *(Ericaceae)*. A small genus of deciduous shrubs for a lime-free soil. The drooping urn-shaped flowers are interestingly veined, and during the autumn months the whorls of the leaves are beautifully coloured.

**Species cultivated** *E. campanulatus*, 6–8 feet, erect habit, flowers sulphur-yellow, veined bronze-crimson, May, leaves richly coloured in the autumn, Japan. *E. cernuus*, 6–8 feet, cream, May, Japan; var. *rubens*, deep red flowers, fine

autumn colour. *E. chinensis* (syn. *E. sinohimalaicus*), up to 20 feet, salmon-red flowers, May and June, western China. *E. perulatus* (syn. *E. japonicus*), 4–6 feet, white flowers, May, autumn leaves bright scarlet, Japan.

**Cultivation** Plant in dappled shade in early autumn or in April. The soil must be lime-free and some leafmould or peat should be dug in to retain moisture. Propagation is by cuttings of firm shoots taken in the spring and inserted in sandy soil in gentle heat, or by seed sown in peaty soil in the spring.

---

## Erica (er-e-ka)

From the Greek *ereike*, the name for heath or heather (*Ericaceae*). A large genus of evergreen, hardy and greenhouse flowering shrubs from Africa and Europe. The majority are compact, dwarf-growing, but some species attain the height of small trees. Most species require a lime-free soil, although *E. carnea* and its varieties, *E. × darleyensis*, *E. mediterranea*, *E. terminalis* and the tree heath, *E. arborea*, are to a varying degree tolerant of chalky soil. Hardy heaths are most effective when grouped together and thrive better than when dotted about singly. They are excellent plants for suppressing weeds.

1 **Erica tetralix, the Cross-leaved Heath, flowers freely from June to October.**
2 **Erica cinerea coccinea, a form of the native Grey Heath, Scotch or Bell Heather, that flowers in June and July.**

---

By making a careful selection it is possible to have heathers in flower in the garden almost throughout the year, provided there is sufficient space for a comprehensive collection.

**Species cultivated:** Hardy *E. arborea,* tree heath, 10–20 feet, panicles of fragrant white flowers, April and May, grey foliage, hardy only in the south and west, Mediterranean; var. *alpina,* 6–8 feet, similar, but hardier, Spain. *E. australis,* Spanish heath, 6–8 feet, rosy-red, April and May, rather tender; 'Mr Robert' is a fine white variety. *E. canaliculata,* 12–18 feet, flowers white, March to May, South Africa, hardy only in the south-west, where it may be damaged in severe winters. *E. carnea,* dwarf to 18 inches, winter-flowering, central Europe; vars. *gracilis,* rose-pink, compact; *praecox rubra,* rose-red, early; *vivellii,* carmine, dwarf, later-flowering, winter foliage bronze. *E. ciliaris,* Dorset heath, 9–18 inches, rosy-red, branching spikes, June to October, south-west Europe and south-west England; var.

*maweana,* larger flowers. *E. cinerea,* bell or Scotch heather, also known as fineleaved or twisted heather, 9–24 inches, branching, rosy-purple, June to August, western Europe and British moorlands; vars. *alba,* white; *alba major,* white, taller; *atropurpurea,* bright purple; *coccinea,* dwarf, scarlet; *fulgida,* dwarf, scarlet; *rosea,* rose-pink. *E. × darleyensis* (syn. *E. mediterranea hybrida*), 1½–2 feet, rosy-lilac, November to May, an easily grown hybrid (*E. carnea × E. mediterranea*). *E. lusitanica* (syn. *E. codonodes*), Portuguese heath, up to 10 feet, white, tinged pink, slightly fragrant, March and April, rather tender, south-west Europe. *E. mackaiana* (syn. *E. mackayi*), 1–1½ feet, rosy crimson, July to September, western Ireland, north-western Spain; var. *plena,* double flowers. *E. mediterranea,* 6–10 feet, hardiest of the tree heaths, rosy-lilac, honey-scented flowers, March to May, western Europe; vars. *alba,* white; *hibernica,* dwarfer, more compact; *superba,* pink, more compact. *E. pageana,* 1 foot, rich yellow, March and April. South Africa. *E. × praegeri* (syn. *E, tetralix praegeri*), 1–1½ feet, pale pink, June to October, hybrid. *E. scoparia,* 10 feet, flowers tiny, greenish, May and June, western Mediterranean, Madeira; var. *minima* (syns. *pumila, nana*), 1½–2

1 Erica carnea alba flowers profusely
from December to April on 12 inch stems.
2 Erica hyemalis from South Africa.

feet, dwarf form. *E.* × *stuartii,* 9–12
inches, deep rose, June to September,
natural hybrid, Galway. *E. terminalis*
(syn. *E. stricta*), Corsican heath, 5–8
feet, rose-pink, urn-shaped, June to
September, western Mediterranean. *E.
tetralix,* cross-leaved heath, 12–18 inches,
rose-pink, June to October, Europe, including Britain; vars. *alba,* white;
*lawsoniana,* dwarf, pink; *mollis,* grey
leaves, white flowers; *rosea,* rose-pink.
*E. umbellata,* 1 foot, cerise-pink, summer,
hardy in the south and west only, Spain,
Portugal, North Africa. *E. vagans,*
Cornish heath, 2–3 feet, wide spreading
habit, rosy-lilac, July to October, south-
west Europe, including Cornwall; vars.
*grandiflora,* rose-red; *kevernensis,* rose-
pink; *kevernensis alba,* white; *rubra,*
rosy-red. *E.* × *veitchii,* 3–6 feet, white,
fragrant, February to April, hybrid tree
heath. *E.* × *watsonii,* 12–18 inches,
rosy-red, July to September, natural
hybrid, Cornwall. *E.* × *williamsii,* 12–18
inches, leaves tipped gold, rosy-pink
flowers, late summer to autumn, natural
hybrid, Cornwall.

44

1 Erica cinerea 'Golden Hue'; the foliage turns red in winter.
2 Erica carnea, the winter-flowering heath, forms hummocks of colour from December to April. It received the RHS Award of Garden Merit in 1924.

**Cultivars** include: *E. carnea* 'Cecilia M. Beale', white; 'James Backhouse', early, taller; 'King George', deep pink, dwarf; 'Prince of Wales', rose pink: 'Queen Mary', deep rose-red; 'Ruby Glow', dark red, dark foliage; 'Springwood', white, tall, early; 'Springwood Pink', rose-pink; 'Winter Beauty', rose-pink, very early. *E. ciliaris* 'Stoborough', white. *E. cinerea* 'C. D. Eason', deep pink. *E. darleyensis* 'George Rendall', deeper coloured flowers; 'Silberschmelze', white flowers. *E. mediterranea* 'Brightness', dwarf, rose-pink; 'W. T. Ratcliff', white. *E. tetralix* 'Mary Grace', bright pink flowers, silvery foliage; 'Pink Glow', pink flowers, grey foliage. *E. vagans* 'Lyonesse', pure white; 'Mrs D. F. Maxwell', deep cerise. *E. × watsonii* 'Dawn', spreading habit, later flowering; 'H. Maxwell', taller, flowers clear pink. Many more are offered in specialist's catalogues.

**Greenhouse** *E. × cavendishiana (E. abietina × E. depressa)*, 4 feet, yellow, May. *E. elegans*, 2 feet, red, May, South Africa. *E. gracilis*, 1–1½ feet, rose-purple in terminal clusters, September to December, South Africa. *E. hyemalis*, winter heath, 1½ feet, rose-tinted white, December to March, South Africa. *E.*

*persoluta*, 1–3 feet, rosy-red, March to May, South Africa.

**Cultivation** For the hardy species a well-drained soil containing plenty of peat or leafmould is required and it should be lime free for all except *E. carnea, E. × darleyensis* and *E. mediterranea*, although *E. arborea* and *E. terminalis* may tolerate a little lime in the soil, but do better where it is absent. Plant deeply in April and May or in October and November. Heathers like an open sunny position and the best results are obtained by starting with small, really young plants, which will quickly get established. Old woody layers will not prove satisfactory. To avoid a patchy look, always plant in groups of one variety and set them fairly close together—about 15 inches apart if they are low-growing or 2 feet apart if you are planting the larger, tree heaths.

A generous topdressing of granulated peat or leafmould in the spring may be advisable where the soil is poor and light, but it is not essential on reasonably fertile soil. Plants should be clipped over lightly after they have flowered; this will keep them compact and they will live longer. Propagation is by small cuttings inserted in sandy peat in pots in July or August with gentle bottom heat; in hot weather they will need frequent overhead spraying. Plants may also be propagated by division in October, or by layering young growths in the spring, scooping out the soil round the plants, pressing the growths back into the dish-like depression so formed and filling up the centre with light, sandy soil. The shoots will root into this.

With the greenhouse species treatment is as follows: Repot autumn and winter-flowering plants in March, summer flowering plants in September. The compost should consist of 2 parts of fibrous peat and 1 part of lime-free silver sand. Pot firmly. Water carefully at all times keeping the soil moist, but not wet. Maintain a minimum winter temperature of 40°F (4°C). Propagation of greenhouse species is by cuttings about 1 inch long inserted in sandy peat in a propagating frame in the spring with a temperature of about 65°F (18°C).

## Eriobotrya (er-e-o-bot-re-a)

From the Greek *erion*, wool, *botrys*, a bunch or cluster, referring to the downy clusters of flowers *(Rosaceae)*. A small genus of east Asian shrubs and small trees of which one is cultivated. This is *E. japonica* (syn. *Photinia japonica*), the loquat, a slightly tender evergreen flowering shrub from China. This reaches between 10–30 feet in height and, particularly after a hot summer, produces intermittently from autumn to spring, white or yellowish-white fragrant flowers, reminiscent of those of hawthorns. The edible fruits, about the size of a green walnut, are borne in bunches and are downy, pale orange-red in colour. The fruits rarely ripen in the open in England, but the leaves, dark glossy green, up to 1 foot long, woolly beneath, make it a striking shrub. It is grown in the open in sheltered south-western gardens but elsewhere requires the protection of a south-facing wall.

**Cultivation** Plant in the early autumn or in the spring in a light, loamy soil. It may be grown against the back wall of a cold or slightly heated, sunny, lean-to greenhouse, where it should be watered moderately during the winter and freely from April onwards. Syringe with water during hot weather. Prune straggling shoots in April. Propagation is by seed sown in spring or autumn in pots of light soil, or by cuttings of firm shoots in August inserted in pots of sandy soil, both placed in a cold greenhouse or frame.

1 Eriobotrya japonica, the Loquat, a slightly tender evergreen shrub from China. The fruit is edible but rarely ripens in the open in England.
2 Escallonia 'Peach Blossom' grows to 6 feet and is suited to coastal gardens.
3 Escallonia 'Apple Blossom', a compact growing evergreen shrub. It grows to 4 feet and flowers in June.

## Escallonia (es-kal-o-ne-a)

Commemorating Senor Escallon, Spanish traveller in America *(Saxifragaceae)*. Glossy-leaved shrubs, mostly natives of Chile, the majority of which are evergreen and many of which are hardy in the southern counties and by the sea. The shelter of a south-facing wall helps in many districts.

**Species cultivated** *E. × edinensis* (E or SE), 6 feet, rosy-pink, summer, hybrid. *E. × exoniensis* (E) 12–15 feet, white and rose, summer, hybrid. *E. illinita* (D), 10–12 feet, white, June to August. *E. × ingramii* (E), 12 feet, rose-pink, summer, hybrid. *E. × iveyi* (E), 10–12 feet, white, late summer to autumn, hybrid. *E. × langleyensis* (E or SE), 6–10 feet, rosy-carmine flowers, summer, does well against a north wall, hybrid. *E. leucantha* (E), 12–15 feet, flowers pure white in 1 foot long spikes, July. *E. macrantha* (E), 6–10 feet, fragrant crimson flowers, June, used as a hedge in south-western counties. *E. montana* (E), 5–6 feet, compact habit, flowers white, summer. *E. montividensis* (E), 10–12 feet, white, summer, needs wall protection. *E. × newreyensis* (E), 10 feet, white, pink flushed, summer, hybrid. *E. organensis* (E), 4–6 feet, rosy-red, summer. *E. punctata* (E), 6–10 feet, deep crimson,

Eucryphia 'Nymansay', so called because it was a chance hybrid at Nymans, Sussex. This hardy evergreen shrub is quick growing. It bears large, white flowers in August.

July and August. *E. pterocladon* (E), 8–10 feet, white, fragrant, June to August, Patagonia. *E. revoluta* (E), 15–20 feet, grey foliage, pink to white flowers, July to September. *E. rubra* (E), 12–15 feet, red, July and August; var. *pygmaea*, 1–2 feet, suitable for rock garden. *E. virgata* (syn. *E. philsippiana*) (D), 6–8 feet, white, June and July, the hardiest of all species, but not suitable for chalky soil. *E. viscosa* (E), 8–10 feet, flowers white in drooping spikes, June to August.

Escallonias hybridise easily and several good named cultivars are even more vigorous and hardier than the parent plants. They include 'Apple Blossom' (E), 4 feet, soft pink flowers, June, compact growth; 'C. F. Ball' (E), 6 feet, bright carmine-red flowers, June to August, large leaves, especially attractive against a wall; 'Donard Beauty' (E), 4–5 feet, rosy-red, summer; 'Donard Radiance' (E), 4–5 feet, deep pink, July and August; 'Donard Seedling' (E), 5 feet, white and pale pink

flowers, summer, a particularly hardy hybrid; 'E. G. Cheeseman' (E), 8–10 feet, large, bell-like cherry-red flowers, summer; 'Gwendolyn Anley' (E), 5–6 feet, blush pink, June and July; 'Peach Blossom' (E), 5–6 feet, summer; 'Pride of Donard' (E), 5–6 feet, rich red, May to July; 'Slieve Donard' (E), 5–6 feet, apple-blossom pink, summer; 'William Watson' (E), 4 feet, red, summer. Others, varying in height, flower colour, time of flowering and vigour, are listed in nurserymen's catalogues.

**Cultivation** Escallonias do best in rich, well-drained soil in sheltered positions, against walls, or in southern counties in the open. Plant during October and November, but in uncertain districts, subject to cold winds, plant in March. Light pruning only is needed in spring to maintain shape. Propagation is from cuttings made from short sideshoots in August and inserted round the edge of a pot of sandy compost. In general the hybrids are sturdier than the species.

## Eucryphia (u-krif-e-a)

From the Greek *eu*, well, *kryphia*, a covering, probably referring to the cap that covers the flower buds *(Eucryphiaceae)*. A genus of four species of trees and shrubs evergreen or semi-evergreen, those kinds grown in the British Isles usually remaining shrubby, with large white snowy flowers in late summer.

**Species cultivated** *E. billardieri* (syn. *E. lucida*) (E), shrub or small tree, fragrant pendent flowers, June and July, hardy only in the mildest districts, will grow on chalk, Tasmania. *E. cordifolia* (E), tree to 70 feet in very mild conditions, or large shrub, flowers August, suitable for alkaline soils, Chile. *E. glutinosa* (syn. *E. pinnatifolia*) (D), erect-growing shrub, flowering freely, July and August, leaves colouring brilliantly in autumn, needs acid soil, Chile. *E. × hillieri (E. billardieri × E. moorei)* (E), tall shrub, pendent, cup-shaped flowers, summer, hybrid, hardier than *E. moorei*. 'Winton' is the best form, hardy in the south. *E. × intermedia* (E), 8–10 feet, hybrid between *E. glutinosa* and *E. billardieri*, vigorous shrub, flowers up to 2 inches across, August and September. *E. moorei* (E), small tree, solitary flowers, 1 inch wide, autumn, tender except in the mildest counties, Tasmania. *E. × nymansensis* (E), tall, quick-growing shrub, hybrid between *E. glutinosa* and *E. cordifolia*, flowering August and September, the best form of which is 'Nymansay'.

**Cultivation** The two hardiest are *E. glutinosa* and *E. × nymansensis*; the former needs moist, acid soil with plenty of leafmould, while the latter will grow on soils containing lime. Plant in early autumn or spring, choosing a protected site where the roots will be cool and shaded. Propagation is by seed sown in peaty soil in spring; the forms of *E. nymansensis* from late summer cuttings, or long shoots may be layered.

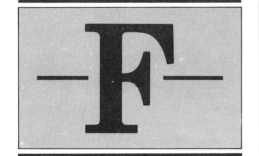

## Fatsia (fat-se-a)

From the Japanese *fatsi*, the name for *F. japonica (Araliaceae)*. A genus of two species of evergreen, slightly tender shrubs, related to *Aralia,* with large and striking leaves like a seven-pointed star. There are but two species, of which the only one likely to be found in cultivation is *F. japonica* (syns. *Aralia sieboldii* and *Aralia japonica*), rice paper plant, fig-leaf palm, false castor-oil plant, a native of Japan, 6–15 feet tall, with dark shining leaves which branch out on long stalks from the main stem, and are quite often up to a foot or more across. The variety *variegata* has white tips to the leaf lobes. Both bear many-branched heads of milk-white flowers in rounded clusters in October and November, followed by black fruits.

**Cultivation** *Fatsia japonica*, a useful late-flowering evergreen, can be grown out of doors in a partially shaded position, protected from wind. Plant out in May, allowing sufficient room as it is a strong-growing plant. It makes a good house plant when young, particularly in spacious surroundings; it is ideal for public buildings and spacious conservatories. Pot up in the spring in a compost of 2 parts of sandy loam, 1 part of leaf-mould, sand and old dry manure; water regularly during the summer months but moderately only from September to March. It should be kept just free from frost, though, when grown out of doors, it will stand a good many degrees of frost without severe injury.

## Forsythia (for-si-the-a)

Named in honour of the King's gardener, William Forsyth, 1737–1804, who was the head gardener of the Chelsea Physic Garden *(Oleaceae)*. A small genus of hardy, showy, deciduous shrubs flowering in spring. Except for one species *(E. europaea)* which is a native of south-eastern Europe, they are all from eastern Asia.

**Species cultivated** *F. europaea,* 4–6 feet, flowers pale creamy yellow, February and March. *F. giraldiana,* 6–8 feet, pale yellow, February and March. *F.* ×

**1 Fatsia japonica has ball-like heads of creamy flowers in autumn.**
**2 Forsythia 'Beatrix Farrand', a modern cultivar with large flowers.**

*intermedia,* 6–10 feet, a hybrid of upright habit, rich yellow flowers, March; vars. *densiflora,* more compact, flowers paler; *primulina,* pale yellow; *spectabilis,* flowers larger, bright yellow; *vitellina,* erect habit, flowers deep yellow; 'Arnold Dwarf' is a cultivar which is 2–3 feet in height only, but with a spread of 6 feet or more and thus has some value as a ground-cover shrub; its flowers are small, yellowish-green. 'Arnold Giant' is much taller, with very large, rich yellow flowers. 'Beatrix Farrand' is a modern cultivar with large flowers, orange at the throat; 'Lynwood' has even larger flowers, with broader petals. *F. ovata*, 4–5 feet, primrose-yellow, February and March; var. *robusta*, taller, larger flowers; 'Spring Glory' is a free-flowering cultivar with bright yellow flowers. *F. suspensa*, golden bell, 8–10 feet, taller when trained, golden yellow, March and April; vars. *atrocaulis*, lemon-yellow; *fortunei*, stiffer habit, arching stems; *sieboldii*, more slender, arching branches. *F. viridissima*, 5–8 feet, bright yellow, April; var. *bronxensis*, 12–15 inches, dense, twiggy habit, pale yellow flowers.

**Cultivation** Ordinary garden soil, and almost any position suits these accommodating, tough shrubs. *F. suspensa* is suitable for training against a wall or may be planted at the top of a bank and its shoots allowed to trail down. The more slender variety, *atrocaulis*, may be trained over an archway. Forsythias, in general, are easy to manage if they are pruned as soon as flowering is over, because the flower buds for the following year develop on the side-shoots of the old branches. Cut the old wood back to allow for new wood to be formed. Propagation is by cuttings from young shoots in June put in a sandy frame or pot, or of the matured wood, made about 1 foot long and rooted out of doors in late autumn. Young plants of forsythia can be forced in a warm greenhouse, potted in John Innes potting compost No. 1 and brought indoors in November.

**Fothergilla** (foth-er-gil-a)
Commemorating Dr John Fothergill, 1712–1780, who made a remarkable collection of North American plants in Essex *(Hamamelidaceae)*. American wych hazel. A small genus of hardy flowering shrubs. The branches resemble fluffy bottle brushes because the stamens of the flowers are very prominent, the petals being absent. The leaves colour brilliantly in the autumn.

**Species cultivated** *F. gardenii* (syn. *F. alnifolia*), 5 feet, whitish stamens, April and May; var. *glaucophylla* has glaucous leaves. *F. major*, 6–7 feet, the best known species, pinkish-white flowers with yellow stamens, April and May. *F. monticola,* slow-growing to 5 feet, creamy white flowers, April and May.

**Cultivation** Provide the fothergillas with a sandy peat in semi-shade and give them an annual mulch of leafmould to keep the roots cool. Choose a site away from the early morning sun so that the flowers will not be damaged by frost and east winds. No pruning is needed other

1 **Forsythia spectabilis has large deep yellow flowers in March.**
2 **Fothergilla major, a popular shrub reaching 6–7 feet, has white bottle-brush-like flowers, in April and May.**

than to remove old branches occasionally, to keep the bushes open. Propagation is by layering the ends of the branches in autumn or by cuttings taken with a heel of old wood in July or August, inserted out of doors and protected with a cloche. Seed is slow to germinate but may be sown in gentle heat in spring.

---

### Fuchsia (fu-sha)

Commemorating Leonard Fuchs, sixteenth-century German botanical writer and professor of medicine *(Onagraceae)*. A genus of about 100 species of shrubs mostly for the greenhouse, a few hardy. Most of the fuchsias grown today are hybrids, of which thousands have been raised in the past 120 years or so, and more and more make their appearance each year. A typical fuchsia flower consists of the tube and sepals, usually of one colour, the petals (corolla), usually differing in colour from the tube and sepals (if the colours are the same, the variety is known as a self-coloured variety) and the protruding stamens and style. When describing the colours of fuchsia flowers it is conventional to give that of the tube and sepals (t and s) first, followed by that of the corolla (c). Double and single flowered varieties are available and the modern trend is to produce larger flowered varieties.

**Hardy species cultivated** Some of these may be killed to the ground in cold weather but produce new growth again in spring. *F. excorticata*, tree to 40 feet in its native habitat, a tall shrub in the milder counties of Great Britain, elsewhere a low bush, not reliably hardy, flowers 1 inch long, calyx yellow, sepals violet and green, New Zealand. *F. × exoniensis*, 6 feet, resembles *F. magellanica*, one of its parents, but with larger flowers, hybrid. *F. magellanica* (syn. *F. macrostemma*), 6–20 feet, the scarlet and purple flowered 'typical' fuchsia, graceful in growth; vars. *alba*, pale pink; *gracilis* (syn. *F. gracilis*), more slender; *g. variegata*, leaves silver, pink and rose; *riccartonii*, scarlet and violet purple, used as a hedge plant in mild localities; *versicolor*, leaves grey-green and slightly variegated, South America. *F. parviflora*, prostrate, calyx crimson, petals coral-red, Mexico, hardy in mildest areas. *F. reflexa*, similar to *F. parviflora*, flowers cerise.

**Hardy cultivars** 'Caledonia', reddish cerise and reddish violet, free-flowering, lax habit; 'Chilleton Beauty', white edged pink and violet-mauve, vigorous habit; 'Corallina', scarlet and reddish-purple, vigorous, lax habit; 'Dunrobin Bedder', scarlet and purple, dwarf; 'Madam Cornelissen', crimson and white, semi-double; 'Mrs Popple', scarlet and purple, free-flowering; 'Mrs W. P. Wood', pink and white, free-flowering; 'Tom Thumb', cerise and mauve, dwarf;

'Tresco', scarlet and deep purple.

**Cultivation** These hardy or near hardy kinds need a deep rich soil and a well-drained position. Plant in autumn or spring and cut back old growth in February close to the base of the plant. They may require some protection in winter in the form of ashes or peat litter. Propagation is from seed or cuttings as for the tender types.

**Greenhouse species** Only the expert

1 Fuchsia 'Mrs Popple', a free-flowering hardy cultivar, has scarlet and purple flowers.
2 Fuchsia fulgens, a greenhouse species, has long coral-scarlet flowers.
3 Fuchsia 'Burning Bush' looks effective when planted in a large container. The pale yellow-green foliage, with red veins and stems is a good foil for the coral-magenta flowers.
4 Fuchsia 'Beauty of Bath' has semi-double flowers in white and pink.

2

3

4

and collector grows the species as they are far superseded by the named varieties, but several species are worth cultivating. *F. corymbiflora*, 4–6 feet, long, deep red flowers, Peru. *F. fulgens*, 3–4 feet, long coral scarlet flowers, Mexico. *F. procumbens*, trailing, calyx orange-yellow, sepals violet and green, stamens red and blue, fruits large and red, New Zealand; can be grown out of doors in very mild districts. *F. serratifolia*, 6–8 feet, pink, scarlet and green waxy flowers, winter, Peru. *F. simplicicaulis*, 12 feet, crimson flowers, autumn, Peru. *F. triphylla*, 1–1½ feet, cinnabar red flowers, West Indies. *F. triphylla* has given rise to a range of long-flowered, red-bronze-leaved hybrids, including 'Mantilla', carmine, and 'Thalia', a variety over a hundred years old with flame flowers and rich reddish foliage. Other species are listed by specialist growers.

Among the named cultivars the range of colour and flowering time is so wide that it is possible, by selection of variety and growing habits, to ensure a long display of flower. So many are available that it is possible to give a selection only here.

**Bush trained varieties** 'Burning Bush', pale yellowish-green foliage with red veins and stems, coral-magenta flowers; 'Beauty of Bath', semi-double pink, white and carmine flowers; 'Glitters', a single, waxy, orange-red; 'Mission Bells', cyclamen-pink and heliotrope, semi-double, calyx reflexed; 'Mrs Lovell Swisher', ivory and pink; 'Party Frock', rose tube, blue corolla and pink; 'Pink Favourite', rose-pink self; 'Swanley Gem', an old variety, single, violet and scarlet; 'Swingtime', rich red and white; 'Texas Longhorn', a giant flower, up to 8 inches across, not everyone's favourite, red and white; 'Topaz', light coral and violet; 'Vanessa', double, pale carmine and lilac.

**Cascade fuchsias** 'Angel's Flight', pink and white rather a long flower; 'Cara Mia', semi-double, shrimp-pink and white; 'Falling Stars', coral with blood-red tube; 'Fort Bragg', a recent introduction with double flowers of lilac with a rose tube; 'Golden Marinka', grown for its golden foliage, flowers deep red, semi-double; 'Marinka', semi-double, red, 'Red Ribbons', white with deep red spreading corolla; 'Red Spider', single crimson and deep rose, a tiny edging of crimson on the corolla.

**Standards** 'Angela Leslie', two tones of pink, double; 'Blue Lagoon', double flowers, very abundant, bright red tube, deep bluish-purple corolla; 'Bravado', large red and periwinkle-blue; 'Cascade', single, white and carmine; 'Citation', single, rose and white; 'Court Jester', red shrimp-pink and white; 'Pink Flamingo', pink and white; 'Pink Quartet', double, tube deep pink, corolla paler; 'Red Ribbons', red and white; 'Tennessee Waltz', rose and mauve.

**Fan training varieties** 'Curtain Call', carmine tube and sepals, deep rose corolla with darker flecks, double; 'Flirtation Waltz', white and pink, rather frilly corolla; 'Mission Bells', semi-double, violet and cyclamen; 'The Doctor', single, flesh-pink and orange-red.

**Cultivation** Fuchsias need a minimum winter temperature of 45–50°F (7–10°C) and can be used out of doors in summer as dot plants in bedding schemes, or for ribbon effects (varieties such as 'Tom Thumb'), to decorate loggias or as room plants. Window boxes look decorative when filled with such varieties as 'Benitchea', 'Evening Sky', 'Santa Lucia', 'Siena Blue', 'Tinker Bell', because they cascade slightly over the sides of the box.

Start plants into growth in February by syringeing daily and 'stop' them frequently during spring to encourage bushiness or for training as required. Water moderately, feed once the flower buds show, remove seed pods to prolong the season and dry off somewhat after flowering in the sun to ripen the wood. A compost of 2 parts of fibrous loam to 1 part of well-decayed manure and leaf-mould with a good handful of sand per bushel of the mixture is suitable. Prune in February. Propagation is by seed sown in spring in a temperature of up to 70°F (21°C) but it is more usual to propagate by cuttings. Take young shoots 2–3 inches long in spring and insert with bottom heat of 60°F (16°C) reducing it to 50–60°F (10–16°C) about 3 weeks later. Pot up the cuttings, pinching in between shifts, as required.

If you are buying new plants, make sure that they are planted out some time in late May to give them a chance to become well established before they have to stand up to their first winter. Plant them with the crown about 4 inches below the surface.

Keep a watch for capsid bugs which attack growing tips and young foliage.

**Training fuchsias** Stopping during the spring is required, whatever, form the plants are to take, but if they are destined to be standards they must, from the beginning, be confined to a single stem and all sideshoots rubbed away, until the main stem is 3½ feet high. Then all the sideshoots that grow from this head must be stopped.

To form a bush or pyramid, every sideshoot should be stopped at the third joint until enough branches are produced.

Fan training combines the two ideas, laterals are trained in to a frame and sideshoots pinched out. It takes eighteen months to produce a good trained form and there is no short cut, but the finished article is something of immense charm and fascination.

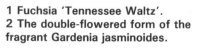

1 Fuchsia 'Tennessee Waltz'.
2 The double-flowered form of the fragrant Gardenia jasminoides.

# G

**Gardenia** (gar-dee-nee-a)
Honouring Dr Alexander Garden, an eighteenth-century botanist from South Carolina *(Rubiaceae).* A genus of evergreen flowering shrubs from tropical Asia and tropical Southern Africa, suitable for a warm greenhouse. Most species have sweetly scented flowers.

**Species cultivated** *G. amoena,* 3–5 feet, white with purple markings outside, June. *G. jasminoides,* Cape jasmine, 2–6 feet, white, fragrant flowers, summer. This is the chief kind found in cultivation and although it normally flowers from June onwards, it can be forced into flower at other times of the year, including winter, to produce a long succession of bloom. Its double-flowered form, *florida,* is the most popular. The flowers bruise particularly easily; var. *fortuniana* has larger flowers than the type. *G. thunbergia,* to 15 feet, pure white flowers, January to March. There are some named hybrids available from trade lists.

**Cultivation** Warmth and plenty of water are needed when gardenias are coming into flower; a minimum temperature of 55°F (13°C) for winter flowering, rising to 70–80°F (21–27°C) with sun heat for summer flowering. A compost of 1 part of loam, 1 part of peat and 1 part of well-rotted manure and some charcoal is suitable. The manure can be substituted by peat and leafmould. Propagate in February or March by cuttings taken with a heel and inserted in a propagating frame with bottom heat of 70–80°F (21–27°C).

Pinch back the shoots once a few inches of growth has been made. Pot up into 5 or 6 inch pots to flower as one-year old plants. Prune them to shape when 12 months old and pot into larger pots if required. Young plants always flower better than older ones and so a good supply of cuttings should be maintained if possible.

**Garrya** (gar-e-a)
Commemorating Nicholas Garry, Secretary of the Hudson's Bay Company in the nineteenth century, who assisted David Douglas on his plant-hunting expeditions in North America *(Garryaceae).* Silk tassel bush. A small genus of evergreen shrubs producing outstandingly attractive catkins, particularly on the male plants.

The showy, silvery-green catkins of the male form of Garrya elliptica are produced early in the year. This is a good plant usually grown on a wall

**Species cultivated** *G. elliptica,* 6–12 feet, silver-green catkins, up to 1 foot long develop in January and drape the male plant for several weeks. Female plants are rarely seen but nurserymen stock them; they are less attractive at catkin time but carry long clusters of black fruits in autumn where both forms are planted. *G. × thuretii,* 10–20 feet, a hybrid of garden origin, remarkable for its rate of growth and a first-class wind break. Its leaves are dark glossy green, about 5 inches long; it rarely flowers.

**Cultivation** Not particular about soil, *G. elliptica* thrives best against a wall, even a sunless one. *G. × thuretii* can be grown as a windbreak in maritime regions and warm districts. Propagation is from cuttings of matured wood made in August, about 4 inches long and inserted in sandy soil in a cold frame or under a cloche. Shoots can be pegged down and layered in September and severed the following April for planting out in permanent positions.

**× Gaulnettya** (gawl-net-e-a)
From *Gaultheria* and *Pernettya,* the parents of this bigeneric hybrid *(Ericaceae).* An evergreen shrub of dense habit, a hybrid between *Gaultheria* 'Shallon' and *Pernettya mucronata.*

**Species cultivated** × *G. wisleyensis,* 1–2 feet, sometimes catalogued as 'Wisley Pearl', leaves dark and leathery, about 1 inch in length, white flowers on short sprays in the leaf axils in early summer followed by ox-blood red berries freely-borne in autumn. This hybrid occurred naturally at the Royal Horticultural Society's garden at Wisley, nearly 40 years ago. × *G. oaxacana,* a pink-flowered bigeneric hybrid, has been found in Mexico but is probably not in cultivation in this country.

**Cultivation** In common with most ericaceous plants, *G. wisleyensis* likes a lime-free soil and does best in a semi-shaded position, where its roots are cool. Propagation is by cuttings taken in August and inserted in sandy peat in a closed frame. Alternatively the shoots can be layered in the late summer.

## Gaultheria (gawl-thee-re-a)

In honour of Dr Gaultier of Quebec, physician and botanist in the eighteenth century *(Ericaceae)*. A genus of hardy and tender evergreen shrubs, sometimes prostrate, with small heath-like flowers but grown mainly for their autumn fruits.

**Species cultivated** *G. antipoda*, to 4 feet, flowers white, June, fruits red or white, New Zealand. *G. cuneata*, 9 inches, white flowers, June, fruits first blue then white, China. *G. forrestii*, 3 feet, white flowers, small bright blue fruits, China. *G. fragrantissima*, 4 feet or more, white or pink flowers, spring, violet-blue fruits, Himalaya. Hardy only in mild areas. *G. hookeri*, 3–6 feet, pink flowers, spring, violet fruits, Himalaya. Hardy in mild districts. *G. itoana*, 4–6 inches, white flowers, spring, white fruits. *G. miqueliana*, 6–9 inches, white flowers, June, white or pink fruits, Japan. *G. nummularioides*, 4–6 inches, dense tufted trailing growth, flowers white or pink, fruits blue-black, Himalaya. *G. procumbens*, partridge berry, creeping wintergreen, 2–6 inches, prostrate, white or pinkish flowers, red fruits, North America. *G. shallon*, 2–6 feet, usually less, pinkish white flowers, early summer, rather more conspicuous than in other species, followed by blue-black or dark purple fruits, North America. *G. trichophylla*, 4–6 inches, white or pinkish flowers, May, blue fruits, China. *G. veitchiana*, 1–3 feet, flowers white, May, fruits dark blue, China. *G. wardii*, 2–3 feet, flowers white, May and June, fruits blue, Tibet. Liable to frost damage.

**Cultivation** A peaty, sandy soil, free from lime is necessary. The smaller species are suitable for moist pockets in the rock garden or for associating with heathers and rhododendrons. They are not suitable for colder districts and exposed gardens. Plant either in autumn or spring. Propagation is by the removal of rooted offsets in spring or from seed for the rarer kinds, sown in autumn as soon as the fruits have matured. Sow in peaty sand in a cold frame or out of doors.

## Genista (jen-is-ta)

Possibly from the Celtic *gen*, a small bush *(Leguminosae)*. Broom. Highly ornamental deciduous or practically leafless, pea-flowered shrubs of diverse

**1** × **Gaulnettya wisleyensis.**
**2 Gaultheria shallon**, a hardy, evergreen shrub from North America.

and June, south-east Europe. *G. lydia*, 2 feet, bright yellow, May and June, south and eastern Europe, Syria. *G. monosperma*, 2–4 feet, white, spring, southern Europe, North-west Africa, half-hardy. *G. pilosa*, 6 inches, deep yellow, June, a good native rock garden shrub. *G. radiata*, 1½–2½ feet, yellow flowers, June, Europe. *G. sagittalis*, 1 foot, golden yellow, June, south-east Europe. *G. scorpius*, 5–7 feet, golden-yellow, May to July, southern Europe, half-hardy. *G. silvestris*, 4–6 inches, yellow flowers, June, spiny in growth; var. *pungens* (syn. *G. dalmatica*), Dalmatian broom, even more spiny, Balkans. *G. tinctoria*, dyer's greenweed, dyer's greenwood, 1–2 feet, deep yellow, June to September, Europe including Britain; vars. *anxatica*, dwarf form; *elatior*, 4–5 feet, erect-growing, golden yellow flowers; *flore-pleno (plena)*, double flowers; *humilior*, purple stems, deep yellow flowers. 'Royal Gold' is a 3 feet tall cultivar, compact in habit, with golden-yellow flowers. *G. villarsii*, 6–9 inches or almost prostrate, yellow, June and July, Balkans. *G. virgata*, Madeira broom, 6–12 feet, golden yellow, June, Madeira.

**Cultivation** Plant the hardy genistas from October to March in light soil, and sunny positions, preferably from pots. Prune to shape or to remove dead branches after flowering. Propagation is from cuttings, taken with a heel, made from young sideshoots in April or August; they will root in a sandy compost in a frame with good light and air. The true species are best increased from seed sown in February under glass or March and April out of doors. The half-hardy species may be grown in pots in the frost-proof greenhouse or conservatory. John Innes potting compost is suitable; little heat is required, merely protection from frost.

habit, three of which are native plants. They are mostly hardy and excellent for dry banks, the taller kinds for shrub borders and the low-growing ones for rock gardens.

**Species cultivated** *G. aethnensis*, Mount Etna broom, 6–12 feet, golden-yellow flowers, July and August, rush-like growth with inconspicuous leaves, fast growing, Sardinia and Sicily. *G. anglica*, petty whin, needle furze, 1–2 feet, spiny shoots, yellow flowers, May and June, native. *G. cinerea*, 3–7 feet, long, whippy branches tipped with butter-yellow flowers, July onwards, Spain, south-west Europe, North Africa. *G. delphinensis*, 1–2 inches, prostrate, bright yellow,

1 Genista villarsii, an almost prostrate Broom from the Balkans.
2 Genista sagittalis, another dwarf broom, bears golden flowers in June.
3 Genista cinerea, one of the taller growing Brooms, may reach 7 feet. It flowers from July onwards.

July and August, southern France. *G. falcata*, 1–2 feet, golden-yellow, summer, Spain and Portugal. *G. hispanica*, 2–3 feet, Spanish broom, Spanish gorse, spiny shrub, golden-yellow flowers May and June, south-west Europe. *G. horrida*, 1–2 feet, very spiny shrub, yellow, July to September, Spain, France. *G. januensis*, Genoa broom, 1 foot, yellow, May

# H

**Hamamelis** (ham-a-me-lis)
From the Greek *hama*, together, and *mela*, fruit; flowers and fruit are present on the plant at the same time. (*Hamamelidaceae*). Witch- or wych-hazel. A small genus of attractive, hardy, deciduous shrubs, mostly flowering in winter or early spring, and mostly having yellow flowers with long thin, twisted petals, giving a spidery appearance,

which are seldom affected by frost.

**Species cultivated** *H. japonica,* up to 10 feet, yellow, slightly fragrant flowers, late December to February, Japan; vars. *arborea,* to 20 feet, vigorous, with darker flowers and purple calyces, *flavo-purpurascens,* petals reddish, *zuccariniana,* to 20 feet, lemon-yellow flowers. 'Carmine Red' and 'Copper Beauty' are two cultivars with names descriptive of the flower colours. *H. mollis,* 10–15 feet, the most popular species, yellow flowers, the narrow petals of which are not twisted but have hooked ends, December to February. The primrose fragrance of the flowers is particularly evident when a spray is brought indoors. The foliage has good yellow and reddish autumn tints, China; vars. *brevipetala,* petals shorter, orange, *pallida,* sulphur yellow. *H. vernalis,* 6–8 feet, yellow flowers, January and February, spreads by suckers, North America. *H. virginiana,* 8 feet, Virginian witch-hazel, the source of medicinal witch-hazel and pharmaceutical bay rum, flowers small, yellow, borne in autumn before the foliage falls, the leaves turn a good golden-yellow before dropping, Eastern North America.

**Cultivation** Plant in autumn where there is sufficient space and, if possible, an evergreen background so that the beauty of the flowers can be appreciated. If possible choose a rich loam, although these shrubs are not fussy about soil. Most species are slow growing. Propagation is interesting. *H. virginiana* is reproduced from seed sown in April, and grown on in pots to provide stocks on which to graft the Chinese and Japanese kinds. Grafting is carried out in spring under glass. Self-sown seedlings of most species are sometimes found, but take a couple of years to appear and are not always true to type. All species can be layered at the end of the summer. Cuttings have the reputation of being almost impossible to root.

## Hebe (hee-be)

From the Greek, *hebe,* small *(Scrophulariaceae).* A genus of about 140 species of evergreen flowering shrubs, mostly natives of New Zealand, some hardy, some tender, formerly included in the genus *Veronica.* The tender sorts are the better plants, and although they may be killed or damaged by frost, they root so easily from cuttings and grow so quickly that losing a shrub need not be a disaster. Some, such as *H. armstrongii, H. buchananii* and *H. cupressoides,* have very tiny, overlapping leaves, resembling those of conifers, and are known as 'whipcord hebes'. These have small, insignificant white flowers, but make good foliage shrubs.

**Species cultivated** *H. albicans,* 2 feet, white flowers, summer. *H. angustifolia,* 3–6 feet, pale lilac, summer. *H. anomala,* 3–4 feet, small bright green leaves, white

Hamamelis mollis pallida, a sulphur-yellow form of the Chinese Witch-hazel.

flowers, hardy in south-west, July to September. *H. armstrongii,* to 3 feet, tiny, cypress-like leaves, white flowers, July. *H. brachysiphon,* (syn. *H. traversii)* 5 feet, sometimes more, white flowers, June-July. *H. buchananii,* 2 feet, tiny leaves, white flowers, June and July. *H. carnea,* 3–4 feet, flowers pink fading to white, May to August. *H. catarractae,* 1–2 feet, white or blue flowers, July to September; var. *diffusa* less tall, mat-forming, white, purple-veined flowers. *H. colensoi,* 1–2 feet, small leaves, white flowers, July and August; var. *glauca,* glaucous-blue leaves. *H. cupressoides,* 4–5 feet, cypress-like leaves, mauve flowers, June-July. *H. darwiniana,* 2–3 feet, small leaves, white flowers, July-August. *H. elliptica,* 5–6 feet, or more, mauve, July and August, the commonest species, used for hedging near the sea; var. *variegata,* leaves edged with cream. *H. gracillima,* 3–4 feet, lilac, July and August; *H. hulkeana,* 4–6 feet, flowers pale lavender in panicles up to 1 foot long, May and June, needs wall protection. *H.* × *lindsayi,* 1–2 feet, pink flowers, summer, hybrid. *H. macrantha,* 2 feet, large

white flowers, summer. *H. parviflora,* 4–6 feet, lilac-flushed white flowers, July and August. *H. pinguifolia,* 1–1½ feet, small leaves, white flowers, June and July; vars. *carnosula,* 2–2½ feet, white June and July; *pagei,* 1 foot, white flowers, June and July. *H. salicifolia,* 5–10 feet, narrow leaves, lilac-tinged flowers, June to August. *H. speciosa,* 4–5 feet, purplish flowers, July to September, tender, parent of various hybrids. *H. subalpina,* 2–2½ feet, small leaves, white flowers, June and July. *H. vernicosa,* 1½–2 feet, tiny leaves, lavender flowers, June and July. Cultivars include 'Alicia Amherst', purple, summer, slightly tender; 'Autumn Glory', 1½–2 feet, deep violet, summer to winter, hardy; 'Bowles's Variety', 3–4 feet, white flowers, June-July; 'Carl Teschner', 9–12 inches, dense spreading habit, violet flowers, July and August; 'Diamant', 3–4 feet, bright crimson, summer, slightly tender; 'Ettrick Shepherd', 2 feet, violet, summer, moderately hardy; 'Hidcote', 3–4 feet, pale lilac, summer, hardy; 'Hielan Lassie', 2 feet, violet-blue, summer, hardy; 'La Seduisante', 4 feet, crimson, summer, slightly tender; 'Marjorie', 3 feet, violet, July to September, hardy; 'McEwanii', 1 foot, bright blue flowers, summer; 'Midsummer Beauty', 3–5 feet, flowers lavender in long spikes, July to Sep-

tember, hardy, one of the best; 'Mrs E. Tennant', 2½–3 feet, light violet, July to September, hardy; 'Purple Queen', 4 feet, rich purple, summer, slightly tender; 'Simon Delaux', 3–4 feet, rich crimson, summer, slightly tender.

**Cultivation** These shrubs are not fussy about soil, and will succeed in chalky soils. The slightly tender kinds thrive near the sea and one or two are used for making seaside hedges. Little pruning is required unless bushes become straggly, when they may be cut back in April. The dwarf species grown for foliage effect may be lightly trimmed over after flowering to remove spent flower heads. Propagation is from cuttings taken after the plants have flowered. These root very easily, even in water but, preferably, dip the cut end in rooting powder then insert round the edge of a pot filled with 3 parts sand (by bulk), 2 parts peat and 1 part soil. Once rooted, pot individually, using John Innes No. 2. It is advisable always to take cuttings of tender kinds and winter them in a frame for replacements.

1 Hebe macrantha grows up to 2 feet and has large white flowers in summer.
2 Hebe 'Carl Teschner', a dense plant of spreading habit has violet flowers.
3 Hebe 'Midsummer Beauty' has long spikes of lavender flowers in late summer.
4 Hebe pinguifolia 'Pagei' is a good form of the white flowered bush.
5 Hebe 'Autumn Blue' a popular and hardy cultivar with deep violet flowers.
6 Hebe armstrongii, one of the 'Whipcord Hebes', has conifer-like foliage.

# Hydrangea (hi-drain-gee-a)

From the Greek *hydor*, water, *aggeion*, a vessel, referring to the shape of the seed capsule *(Saxifragaceae)*. A genus of shrubs, mostly deciduous, many hardy, but some needing greenhouse conditions, some climbing by aerial roots like ivy, most with showy flowerheads. In some species some of the florets, usually those round the edge of the flowerhead, are sterile and larger than the fertile florets.

**Species cultivated** *H. anomala,* climber to 40 feet, flowers yellowish-white, June, slightly tender. *H. arborescens,* 3–4 feet, dull white flowers, July and August; var. *grandiflora,* all flowers sterile, borne in large clusters, a much better plant than the type. *H. aspera,* 6–8 feet, large leaves, large sterile flowers, blue or white, June and July; var. *macrophylla,* fertile flowers porcelain-blue, sterile flowers lilac-pink. *H. bretschneideri,* to 10 feet, white flowers, turning pink with age, July. *H. heteromalla,* to 10 feet, white flowers, June and July. *H. intermedia,* 3–4 feet, pink flowers, summer. *H. involucrata,* 1½–3 feet, flowers white or bluish-white, fertile flowers blue or lilac, outer sterile, somewhat tender; var. *hortensis,* flowers double. *H. macrophylla* (syn. *H. hortensis*) common hydrangea, 3–8 feet or more, outer sterile flowers pink or blue, inner fertile flowers pink or blue, July to September; vars. *hortensia,* all flowers sterile, in rounded heads, *maculata* (syn. *H. m. variegata*), leaves broadly margined with white, *mariesii,* flowerheads flat, outer sterile flowers very large, 2–3 inches across, rosy-pink, *mariesii alba,* flowers white, *rosea,* outer sterile flowers with toothed margins. There are many cultivars (see below). *H. paniculata,* 6–10 feet, flowerheads pyramidal, held upright, outer sterile flowers white, fertile flowers yellowish-white, summer to autumn; var. *grandiflora,* flowers nearly all sterile, white, turning pink with age, in heads 1 foot or more tall. *H. petiolaris* (syn. *H. scandens*), self-clinging climber to 60 feet, white flowers in flattish heads, early summer. May be grown as a shrub. *H. quercifolia,* 5–6 feet, leaves lobed, flowers white in pyramidal heads up to 1 foot tall. *H. sargentiana,* 6–10 feet, velvety leaves, flattish flowerheads, outer sterile flowers white, inner fertile flowers bluish, July and August, needs shade and protection from wind. *H. serrata,* 3–4 feet, outer sterile flowers white, pink or bluish, inner fertile flowers blue or white, July and August;

1 A Lace Cap Hydrangea, H. macrophylla.
2 Hydrangea macrophylla 'Hamburg' has deep pink or purple flowers in full heads. It flowers in August.
3 Hydrangea sargentii bears flat flowerheads; the outer flowers are sterile. The leaves are smooth and velvety.
4 Hydrangea macrophylla mariesii.

1 The Common Hydrangea, H. macrophylla, so often called H. hortensis, has many cultivars.
2 Hydrangea paniculata has pyramidal flowerheads which are held upright.
3 Hydrangea macrophylla rosea. The outer flowers are sterile in many species as in 4 H. macrophylla lilacina and 5 H. serrata rosa alba (overleaf).
6 A striking shrub growing up to 8-9 feet, Hydrangea villosa has hairy leaves and sterile outer flowers of lavender and inner, fertile ones of clear porcelain blue.
7 The large leaves and large sterile flowers of Hydrangea aspera. The shrub reaches 6-8 feet and the flowers are mauve-blue or white in June.

var. *rosalba,* outer flowers white or pink. toothed, larger. 'Grayswood' is a cultivar with inner flowers blue, outer white, changing to crimson. *H. villosa,* 8–9 feet, leaves very hairy, outer sterile flowers lavender, inner fertile flowers porcelain-blue, August. *H. xanthoneura,* 6–15 feet, flowers creamy white, June; var. *wilsonii,* outer sterile flowers white, turning deep pink with age.

Cultivars of *H. macrophylla* may be divided into two classes, the 'hortensias with globular heads, mainly of sterile flowers, sometimes known as mophead hydrangeas, and the 'lace-caps', with flat heads of flowers, the outer flowers sterile, the inner fertile. 'Hortensia' cultivars include 'Alpengluhn', clear rich red; 'Altona', deep rose, serrated petals, vigorous; 'Ami Pasquier', rich crimson; 'Atlantic', blue; 'Benelux', deep blue with white eye; 'Deutschland', pink or blue, large fringed florets; 'Generale Vicomtesse de Vibray', sky-blue; 'Hamburg' deep pink or purple; 'Madame F. Travouillon', several shades on same plant; 'Montgomery', soft pink or light blue; 'Pia', dwarf variety, 12–

4

5

15 inches tall; 'Soeur Thérèse', creamy-white, vigorous; 'Westfalen', dwarf, rich crimson or violet. The above are a few only of the hundred or more varieties offered by nurserymen. 'Lace-cap' cultivars include 'Blue Wave', violet fertile florets, dark blue sterile flowers; 'White Wave', large white florets.

**Cultivation** In reasonably sheltered gardens, the common hydrangea with its great trusses of blue, pink or white flowers, can be grown in the open. It is equally attractive as a greenhouse plant. Out of doors the bushes will go on growing for years, reaching heights of 8 feet or more. Indoors, the plants, carrying one truss of bloom, can be put into an ordinary 6-inch pot and rather bigger plants can be grown satisfactorily in tubs.

Outdoor plants need to be thinned as soon as they have finished flowering. The strongest growing shoots are left to make the flowers for the next year, and those that have borne flowers can

be cut back to make a shapely bush. These shoots will flower again off the old wood, but the new growth will make the bigger trusses. Hydrangeas in pots or tubs should have the old wood cut back and be stood out of doors until late autumn. The new wood must be well matured or the plants will not flower satisfactorily the next year. They should be kept in a cool but frost-proof greenhouse during the winter and watered moderately only until April and then more liberally. For early flowers, in the heated greenhouse, the temperature should be raised to around 60°F (16°C). In the cold greenhouse, the blooms will appear about June. Varieties which give blue flowers on acid soils are usually pink or reddish-pink on alkaline soils, although occasionally, even on chalky soils, hydrangeas may bear blue flowers without any special treatment of the soil. Normally, however, the pink flowers can be turned blue by adding aluminium sulphate or one of the commercial blueing preparations

to the soil. White flowers are not affected by the treatment.

A cold spring may mean loss from frost of the terminal buds on the outdoor plants and this in turn means no flowers. In an unexpectedly hard winter, like that of 1963, the bushes may be destroyed. It is always worthwhile taking cuttings from your favourite bushes in August and to keep them under cold, but frost-proof conditions, for planting out the following spring if needed. Frost, in fact, is the great enemy and if you live in an area susceptible to this weather hazard you need to give consideration to this fact. It is a waste of time, for instance, trying to plant out a hydrangea originally bought as a pot plant as it is unlikely that it will survive. You should stick to the hardier garden varieties.

Propagation is by cuttings, which are taken from the ends of the non-flowering shoots, with two or three pairs of leaves. They should be inserted singly in small pots filled with sandy soil,

**1**

with a pinch of silver sand in the hole before the cutting is inserted. When the pot is well filled with roots, transplant to a bigger pot containing John Innes potting compost. During the rooting period, they should be kept in a shaded frame.

**Hypericum** (hi-per-ik-um)
Possibly from the Greek *hyper*, over, *ereike*, heath *(Guttiferae* or *Hypericaceae)*. St John's Wort. A large genus of annuals, herbaceous perennials, sub-shrubs and shrubs, mainly hardy, widely spread throughout the northern hemiphere, many species and hybrids grown in our gardens for their attractive, usually yellow flowers, with numerous

**1** On limy or chalky soils hydrangeas usually produce pink or red flowers. This can be corrected by dressings of sulphate of aluminium, sulphate of iron, or alum.
**2** Hypericum 'Hidcote' has flowers up to 3 inches across, in late summer.
**3** Hypericum olympicum is a sub-shrub with large yellow flowers in August.
**4** The fruits and flowers of Hypericum elatum 'Elstead' in late summer.

stamens. The sub-shrubs and shrubs are mainly evergreen or nearly so.

**Species cultivated** *H. androsaemum,* tutsan, 1–3 feet, sub-shrub, flowers bright yellow, ¾ inch across, June to September, followed by conspicuous fruits first red, then black, native plant. *H.* × *arnoldianum,* 3–4 feet, flowers numerous, ½ inch or so across, yellow, hybrid. *H. calycinum,* Rose of Sharon, Aaron's beard, 1 foot, sub-shrub, trailing habit, often forming dense carpets, much used for ground cover on banks or under trees, flowers bright yellow, over 3 inches across, June to September, leaves often bronze in winter. *H. chinense,* 2–3 feet, flowers 2½ inches wide, bright yellow, August and September, hardy in the south. *H. coris,* 6 inches, sub-shrub, leaves heath-like, flowers ¾ inch across, golden yellow, summer, plant sometimes succumbs to severe frosts. *H. dyeri,* 3–4 feet, shrub, flowers yellow, to 1½ inches wide, summer. *H. elatum* (SE), 4–5 feet, shrub, flowers yellow, 1 inch across, summer, not quite hardy in cold gardens. *H. empetrifolium,* 1–1½ feet, sometimes prostrate shrub, flowers golden-yellow, ½–¾ inch across, July to September, half hardy except in the south; var.

*prostratum,* 2 inches, mat-forming plant, flowers orange-yellow, June to August, rock garden. *H. fragile,* 4–6 inches, flowers yellow, 1 inch across, July and August, rock garden. *H. frondosum* (D), 3–4 feet, shrub, leaves bluish-green, flowers orange-yellow, to 2 inches across, July and August. *H. galioides,* 2–3 feet, sub-shrub, flowers yellow, July to October. *H. hircinum,* stinking St John's Wort (SE), 2–4 feet, sub-shrub, flowers bright yellow, July to September; var. *pumilum,* dwarf, compact variety. *H. kalmianum* (SE), 2–3 feet, shrub, flowers bright yellow, to 1 inch across, August. *H. kouytchense* (SE), 3–4 feet, shrub, narrow leaves, sometimes turning bronze in autumn, flowers golden-yellow, to 2 inches across, June to October. *H.* × *moserianum,* 15–18 inches, shrub, flowers rich yellow, to 2½ inches across, July to October, excellent ground cover plant, hybrid; var. *tricolor,* leaves variegated white and pink on green. *H. napaulense,* prostrate shrub, stems

to 2 feet long, flowers golden, summer. *H. olympicum,* 1–1½ feet, sub-shrub, flowers yellow, to 2 inches across, July and August. *H. patulum,* 1–3 feet, shrub, flowers bright yellow, to 2 inches across, July to October, hardy in the south; vars. *henryi,* leaves colour well in autumn, larger flowers, hardier; 'Hidcote', to 6 feet, flowers to 3 inches across, the finest variety; *uralum,* 2–3 feet, flowers to 1 inch across. *H.* × *penduliflorum,* 4–5 feet, shrub, drooping habit, flowers yellow, 2–2½ inches across, summer to early autumn, hybrid. *H. polyphyllum,* almost prostrate, herbaceous, stems to 1 foot long, flowers golden yellow, sometimes splashed with scarlet, to 2 inches across, July to September, rock garden; var. *sulphureum,* flowers sulphur-yellow. *H. prolificum,* 3 feet or more, flowers yellow, to 1 inch across, July to September. *H. repens,* 3 inches, herbaceous perennial, trailing, heath-like foliage, flowers yellow, summer, rock garden. *H. reptans,* 3 inches, shrub, leaves colour well in autumn, flowers rich yellow, to 1¾ inches across, June to September, rock garden. H. 'Rowallane Hybrid', 5–8 feet, shrub, flowers rich yellow, to 2½ inches across, summer, one of the finest hypericums, but needs a sheltered situation except in the mildest counties. *H. trichocaulon*, 3 inches, trailing shrub, flowers red in bud, pale yellow when open, July and August, rock garden. Other species and hybrids may be offered by nurserymen from time to time.

**Cultivation** Hypericums do well in ordinary garden soil, especially if it is well drained. With the exception of *H. androsaemum* and *H. calycinum*, they should be planted in sunny positions. The less hardy kinds do better if given the protection of a wall or fence. Plants should be set out in autumn or spring. *H. calycinum* and *H. moserianum* will benefit from hand pruning, cutting the plants hard back in March to promote new growth; other species require little pruning other than the removal of frost-damaged shoots in spring. *H. calycinum* is easily propagated by division in spring; other species may be increased by seed, or by cuttings taken in late summer and rooted in sandy soil in a cold frame.

Hypericum or St. John's Wort is an easy shrub to grow for both its flowers and fruit.

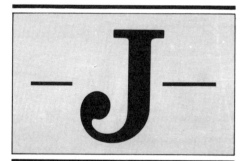

## Jacobinia (jak-o-bin-e-a)

From Jacobina, in South America, near Bahia. A genus of some 40 species of showy herbs and shrubs, from the hotter parts of America and first introduced in the mid-eighteenth century (*Acanthaceae*). Stove flowering plants of easy cultivation, but which become weedy unless correctly pruned and cared for.

**Species cultivated** *J. carnea*, flesh pink, 3–4 feet, August–September. *J. chrysostephana*, 3 feet, yellow, winter. *J. ghiesbreghtiana* (syn. *Justicia ghiesbreghtiana*), 1½–2 feet, scarlet, December. *J. pauciflora* (syn. *Libonia pauciflora*), 2 feet, scarlet tipped yellow, winter. *J. suberecta*, 1 foot, bright scarlet, summer, low, spreading habit and excellent for a hanging basket in the warm house.

**Cultivation** Pot in March–April in equal parts by volume of loam, leafmould, peat and sand. Stand in a well lit stovehouse from September–June with a temperature of 55–65°F (13–18°C). Water moderately September–March, freely at other times. Pinch tips of young shoots between May–August, to encourage bushy growth.

The scarlet flowers of the Brazilian Jacobinia coccinea appear in February.

Stand in sunny frames, June–September, and apply liquid fertiliser twice a week to plants in flower. Prune shoots to within 1 inch of the base after flowering. Propagate by cuttings of young shoots placed in sandy soil under a hand light in a temperature of 75°F (24°C) between March and July.

# K

**Kalmia** (kal-me-a)
Commemorating Peter Kalm, 1715–1779,
a Finnish pupil of Linnaeus *(Ericaceae)*.
These are evergreen and, rarely, deciduous shrubs with dark, glossy leaves and
exquisitely shaped waxy flowers. They
thrive in an acid soil in dappled shade.
**Species cultivated** *K. angustifolia*, sheep
laurel, 3 feet, crimson, early summer.
There are three varieties: *nana*, a dwarf;
*rosea*, with pink flowers, and *rubra*, red
flowers. *K. carolina*, 3 feet; this is
similar to *K. angustifolia*, the only
difference being in the leaves, which are
downy on the undersides. *K. cuneata*, 4
feet, white, June–July. This species is
deciduous or partially evergreen. *K.
hirsuta*, 2 feet, purplish, summer, difficult
to cultivate in the British Isles. *K.
latifolia*, calico bush, mountain laurel,
6–10 feet, clear pink, June. This beautiful
species is the most popular, growing to
the size of a small tree in favourable
districts, but it is slow growing, so is
usually seen as a shrub. There is a
dwarf variety, *K. l. myrtifolia. K. poli-
folia*, 2 feet, rosy-lilac, late spring.
**Cultivation** Plant in the autumn or spring
in a shady part of the garden; they are
particularly suitable for woodland planting and like a soil that is lime-free and
well supplied with peat, sand and
leafmould. They are also suitable for
growing in the greenhouse in the winter
in a temperature of 55°F (13°C), being
stood out of doors in the summer. The
compost should contain sand, peat and
leafmould. No pruning is necessary.
Propagate by layering in spring, or take
cuttings in early summer and root them
in a cold frame in sandy peat. Keep
shaded. Seeds may be sown in pans in a
cold frame in spring or autumn, using a
sandy peat compost.

**Kalmiopsis** (kal-me-op-sis)
A kalmia-like shrub, hence the name
kalmia, and *opsis*, from the Greek,
meaning like or similar to *(Ericaceae)*.
This choice, evergreen shrub is perfectly
hardy and was introduced into this
country in the twentieth century. It likes

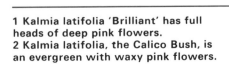

1 Kalmia latifolia 'Brilliant' has full
heads of deep pink flowers.
2 Kalmia latifolia, the Calico Bush, is
an evergreen with waxy pink flowers.

a sunny position but will tolerate slight shade. Only one species is grown, *K. leachiana,* which grows to just over 1 foot in height. The bright purplish-pink flowers are produced from March to May.

**Cultivation** The soil should be a sandy peat with leafmould added, and free from lime. Plant in either autumn or spring and do not prune. This dwarf shrub may be propagated by cuttings taken in the summer and inserted in sandy soil, kept close until rooted, by layering, and by seed if obtainable.

## Kolkwitzia (kolk-witz-e-a)
Named after a German professor of botany, Professor R. Kolkwitz *(Caprifoliaceae).* This charming deciduous shrub deserves to be better known. It has abelia-like flowers in pale pink with a yellow throat which are produced in early summer. It is justly called the beauty bush. The only species cultivated is *K. amabilis,* which is a shrub of 5 feet in height or more. Some forms seem to be more free-flowering than others, so be certain to acquire a bush propagated from a good form.

**Cultivation** Plant in full sun in a warm situation in the autumn or spring. It is a shrub that likes warmth and good soil. Pruning is not necessary, but remove the flower heads after blooming. Propagate by cuttings of half-ripe shoots in July, or well-ripened growth in October. Root the cuttings in a cold frame in a sandy compost.

1 **Kolkwitzia amabilis, the Beauty Bush**
2 **Lavendula, known as lavender.**

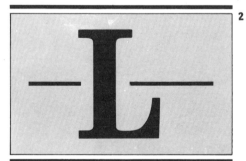

## Lavandula (lav-an-du-la)
From the Latin *lavo,* to wash, since the Romans and Greeks used lavender in their baths *(Labiatae).* Lavender. A genus of about 20 species of shrubs, sub-shrubs and herbaceous perennials from the Mediterranean area, the Canary Isles and India. All have very fragrant foliage and the common lavender, grown in this country for four centuries, has a great deal of old world charm. Until recently the dried flowers were sold in the streets of London. They are tiny, in shades of purple and lavender, and are clustered on spikes which stand up

above the grey-green foliage. Lavenders are often used to make low-growing hedges. Commercially, the flowers of *L. spica* and *L. vera* yield an essential oil, distilled for perfume. The flower spikes are also gathered and dried for their scent, usually being made up into small sachets, used for scenting bed linen etc.

**Species cultivated** *L. dentata,* to 3 feet, flowers lavender-blue, July and August, Spain, Mediterranean region, not fully hardy, needs winter protection. *L. lanata,* to 2 feet, leaves and stems woolly white, flowers violet, July to September, Spain, not fully hardy. *L. pedunculata,* 1½–2 feet, violet-purple, summer, Spain, Portugal, not fully hardy. *L. spica* (syn. *L. officinalis*), common lavender, 4 feet, purple, mid to late summer, Mediterranean area; vars. *alba,* white flowers; *compacta,* a low-growing variety; *rosea,* flowers lilac-pink, *nana alba,* 1 foot, dwarf, white flowers; *L. stoechas,* 1 foot, light green leaves, dark purple flowers, summer, south-west Europe. *L. vera* (syn. *L. spica vera*), Dutch lavender, 2 feet, dense habit, wide silver leaves, flowers pale blue on long spikes, July–August, Mediterranean area.

**Named cultivars** The following are garden varieties of the species *L. spica:* 'Baby Blue', 1½ feet, makes a dwarf, rounded shrub and flowers over a long period; 'Folgate', 1½ feet, good variety for hedges, with soft lavender flowers;

'Grappenhall Variety', 3 feet, strong grower; 'Gwendolyn Anley', 1½ feet, good scent, the delicate lavender flowers are slightly pink; 'Hidcote', 1–1½ feet, deep purple-blue, makes a good hedge; 'Nana Munstead Dwarf', 1 foot, compact dwarf with lavender-blue flowers; 'Twickle Purple', 2–3 feet, flower spikes bright purple, standing out at an angle instead of upright.

**Cultivation** Choose an open position, dry and sunny, and plant in the autumn or spring. A light soil suits lavenders best, in fact, in heavy wet soils they are liable to die out in the winter. After flowering, trim the bushes, avoiding cutting into the old wood. Lavender hedges are apt to get bare at the base unless they are trimmed in the spring. If the flower spikes are wanted for drying, gather them as they come into flower. Lavenders are propagated easily from cuttings taken with a heel in August and rooted in a cold frame or taken in October and rooted out of doors in a sheltered place. It is also possible to divide well-grown plants in the spring.

Those that are not fully hardy should be given some protection in winter or grown in the alpine house or cold greenhouse, with sufficient heat only to keep out frost.

For hedging purposes set the plants 9 to 12 inches apart, depending on height.

1 'Hidcote', a deep purple-blue form of Lavandula spica, useful for low hedges.
2 Lavandula spica, the Common Lavender does well in hot, dry situations.
3 A robust Privet, Ligustrum lucidum is a late-flowering evergreen.

### Ligustrum (li-gus-trum)

Possibly from the Latin *ligo*, to bind, the twigs being used for tying *(Oleaceae)*. Privet. A genus of about 50 species of shrubs or small trees, deciduous or evergreen, natives of the Old World. *L. vulgare*, the common privet, is a ubiquitous plant, used in gardens throughout the country for hedging. In cold winters the leaves of evergreen species may turn dull brownish-green and eventually drop. The fact that one or two kinds make fast-growing hedging plants has tended to obscure the value of other kinds as handsome flowering shrubs in their own right. Privets, in general, are vigorous plants requiring a good deal of food. The panicles of small white or occasionally yellowish flowers, which appear in June and July, have an unusual and not unpleasing scent, which is often missed because the plants, particularly those used for hedging purposes are closely clipped, thus removing the flowering shoots.

**Species cultivated** *L. acutissimum* (E), 5–6 feet, branches spreading, flowers white in nodding clusters, China. *L.*

*chenaultii* (D), to 10 feet or more, leaves up to 9 inches long, flowers white in long clusters, a very handsome species, China. *L. compactum* (SE), shrub or small tree, to 30 feet in nature, leaves to 5 inches long, flowers creamy-white in large panicles, China, Himalaya. *L. confusum* (E or SE), 10–15 feet, flowers pure white, borne in large panicles, fruits purplish-black, to ½ inch long, freely borne and striking, Himalaya, tender except in the mildest counties. *L. delavayanum* (E), to 6 feet, spreading habit, flowers white with violet anthers, June, China. *L. insulare* (SE), similar to *L. vulgare*, but with larger flower spikes and fruits, origin uncertain. *L. japonicum* (E), 6–8 feet, leaves oval to 4 inches long, flowers white, borne in large panicles, late summer, Japan; vars. *macrophyllum,* leaves much larger; *rotundifolium,* leaves rounded, dark green, slow-growing, compact variety. *L. lucidum* (E), 15–30 feet, flowers white in panicles to 8 inches long and wide, late summer, China; vars. *excelsum superbum,* leaves edged and splashed with deep yellow and cream; *latifolium,* leaves larger than the type; *tricolor,* leaves with a broad white border, pink when young. *L. obtusifolium* (D), 6–10 feet, flowers white in nodding clusters, Japan; var. *regelianum,* less tall, branches horizontal, leaves turn rosy-purple in autumn. *L. ovalifolium* (E or SE), 12–15 feet, leaves oval, flowers dull white, unpleasantly scented, the best hedging privet, Japan; var. *aureo-marginatum,* golden privet, leaves with wide golden margins, less vigorous, suitable for low hedges. *L. quihoui* (D), 8–10 feet, flowers white in panicles up to 1½ feet long,

September and October, one of the best flowering species, China. *L. sinense* (D or SE), Chinese privet, 10–12 feet, white flowers in short panicles, very freely borne, another fine flowering species, China; var. *variegatum,* leaves variegated grey-green and white. *L. vulgare* (SE), common privet, 8–10 feet, flowers dull white, heavily fragrant, in short spikes, often used for hedging, though

---

1 A good bush of Ligustrum ovalifolium aureum, the golden-leaved Privet. The leaves may be either completely yellow; or they may have green centres.
2 Ligustrum ovalifolium, the Privet commonly used for hedges, has white, sweetly-scented flowers in summer. But if left unpruned it will reach a large size.
3 The black fruits of Ligustrum vulgare, the partially evergreen common Privet which particularly thrives on chalk.

not as good as *L. ovalifolium* for this purpose, Britain, Europe, North Africa; vars. *fastigiata,* upright form; *xanthocarpum,* yellow berries.

**Cultivation** Privets will grow in any soil and position. The evergreen species can be planted at any time between October and April, the deciduous from October to March. If grown as specimen shrubs, the deciduous kinds are pruned in the autumn, and the evergreen species in the spring. When grown for hedging purposes, plants 1–3 feet high are put in 1½–2 feet apart during the autumn or winter and cut back hard after planting to encourage a good strong framework from low down on the plants. Established hedges are clipped over once or twice as necessary during the summer. Propagation is by tip cuttings during the summer, by hardwood cuttings out of doors in the autumn, or by seed sown in October, the young plants being transplanted a year later.

# M

**Mahonia** (ma-ho-ne-a)
Commemorating Bernard McMahon,
1775–1816, an American horticulturist
*(Berberidaceae).* At one time the
mahonias were included in the same
genus *(Berberis)* as the barberries. The
chief distinguishing character of these
evergreen shrubs is the pinnate leaf
(lacking in *Berberis*) and the fact that
the leaves are spiny, while the branches
lack spines. When *M. aquifolium* was
first introduced from North America in
1823, it had a great vogue and plants
were sold for £10 each. Now in certain
coverts in southern England the plant
has naturalised itself, easily ousting
native woodland undershrubs.
**Species cultivated** *M. aquifolium,* to 4
feet, leaves with 3–7 pairs of leaflets,
yellow flowers in winter, bluish fruits
(this is called the holly-leaved barberry

1 The long racemes of sweetly scented
flowers of Mahonia japonica.
2 The leaves of Mahonia bealei colour
well in autumn.
3 The blue-black berries of Mahonia
aquifolium are glaucous.

and, quite wrongly, the Oregon grape),
North America. *M. bealei,* to 6 feet,
pinnate leaves with 5–9 pairs of leaflets,
6-inch racemes of yellow flowers in
winter held more or less erect, China.
*M. fortunei,* 6 feet, 3–8 pairs of leaflets,
racemes of yellow flowers 6 inches long,
China. *M. haematocarpa,* 4–6 feet, 2 or 3
pairs of narrow leaflets, flowers yellow
in short, few-flowered inflorescences,
fruits scarlet, New Mexico, California.
*M. japonica,* much like *M. bealei,* but the
long racemes are lax and the flowers are
pendent and sweetly scented, winter,
Japan; var. *trifurca,* leaflets sea-green,
flowers in erect spikes. *M. lomariifolia,*
6–12 feet, 10–20 pairs of sea-green rigid
leaflets, flowers deep yellow, in erect
racemes to 10 inches long, with up to 250
flowers per raceme, November and
December, Formosa, Yunnan, the finest
of the genus and one of the most striking
of all flowering shrubs. *M. nepalensis,* to
10 feet, 5–11 pairs of leaflets, racemes of
yellow flowers 1 foot long, Himalayas. *M.
nervosa* (true Oregon grape), to 2 feet,
3–9 pairs of leaflets, leaves to 18 inches
long, racemes of yellow flowers 8 inches
long, North America. *M. nevinii,* similar
to *M. haematocarpa* but with smaller
leaves and black fruits, California. *M.
pinnata,* to 16 feet, similar to *M. aquifolium,* but more handsome, racemes of
yellow flowers not confined to the top of

a branch (not hardy in the north) southern North America and Mexico. *M. repens*, less than 1 foot, 2–4 pairs of leaflets, racemes of yellow flowers, 3 inches long, fruit black, North America; var. *rotundifolia*, 2–3 feet, leaves bluish-green, spineless. *M. trifoliolata*, to 8 feet, 1 pair of leaflets, plus one terminal leaflet, glaucous white in colour, flowers in short corymbs, yellow, Texas, Mexico. *M.* × *wagneri*, 5–8 feet, similar to *M. aquifolium*, but with 7–11 pairs of leaflets.

**Cultivation** Though *M. aquifolium* is not in any way particular about soil or situation, some of the others are not so accommodating and most need a well-drained growing medium and a sunny aspect. *M. fortunei, M. fremontii, M. pinnata* and *M. trifoliata* are hardy in milder sections only and even there should be given the protection of other shrubs or trees or of a wall. Elsewhere they do better in a cold greenhouse, where they can be protected from frost. Propagation is from seed sown in a frame in spring, suckers detached from the parent plant in autumn or spring or half-ripe cuttings rooted in sandy peat under glass.

---

### Melianthus (may-li-an-thus)

From the Greek *meli*, honey, *anthos*, flower, referring to the honey-filled calyces *(Melianthaceae)*. A genus of 8 species from the Cape of Good Hope of semi-woody, evergreen shrubs; the alternate, pinnate leaves produce a disagreeable smell when bruised. The flowers are followed by fruits which are winged, inflated capsules containing black seeds. *M. major* is also found in India.

**Species cultivated** *M. comosus*, 4 feet, leaves 6 inches long, orange, red-spotted flowers, summer. *M. major*, 7–10 feet, the most ornamental species, with attractive foliage, the leaves up to 1 foot or more in length, flowers red-brown in summer, hardy, given protection in favourable situations, but tender elsewhere. *M. minor*, 2–4 feet, downy young

1 Mahonia aquifolium has deep yellow flowers during the winter months.
2 Melianthus major, a native of the Cape of Good Hope, can be grown out of doors in mild localities in Britain.
3 Melicope ternata is a graceful shrub with large shining leaves. The creamy-white flowers are insignificant.

---

leaves, dull red flowers, early summer.

**Cultivation** Although *M. major* may be grown out of doors in the milder counties, this and other species are more likely to be seen in representative collections of greenhouse shrubs. *M. comosus* and *M. minor* are occasionally grown in sub-tropical bedding schemes. They are best grown out of doors in rich loamy soil and the roots should be protected with bracken litter in winter. Under glass they should be grown in a compost of 2 parts of loam and 1 part of leafmould and sand and the pots should be given a sunny position. Pot in late winter or spring. Maintain a minimum winter temperature of 40–50°F (4–10°C). Propagation is by seeds sown in a temperature of 65–75°F (18–24°C) in late winter or early spring, or in a slightly lower temperature in late summer. Cuttings, taken in spring, will root in a propagating case with bottom heat.

## Melicope (mel-e-co-pee)

From the Greek *meli,* honey, and *kope,* cutting or division, in reference to the nectary having notched glands *(Rutaceae).* A genus of some 20 trees and shrubs ranging from tropical Asia to Australasia and Polynesia. One only of the two New Zealand species and a hybrid appear to be cultivated. Both are half hardy and can be grown out of doors only in the mildest parts of the British Isles.

**Species cultivated** *M.* × *mantellii,* a hybrid from the species described below, which is perhaps slightly hardier. It has smaller leaves, is more slender in its habit of growth and is not as handsome as its parent. *M. ternata,* the wharangi, an elegant shrub from 6–10 feet tall in cultivation. The flowers are insignificant but it has handsome, shining foliage, the leaflets of which are borne in threes.

**Cultivation** *M. ternata* should be given a deep soil liberally supplied with humus, while *M.* × *mantellii* is less demanding and will grow in most well-drained soils. Both will tolerate considerable shade and can be grown under woodland conditions. Propagation is by seed, or semi-hardwood cuttings which should be inserted in sand in a frame or greenhouse with gentle bottom heat.

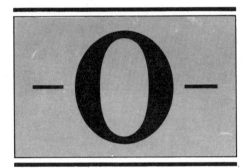

## Osmanthus (oz-man-thus)

Derived from the Greek *osme,* fragrance, and *anthos,* flower, most of the species having fragrant flowers *(Oleaceae).* Fragrant olive. A genus of evergreen shrubs and small trees, numbering about 15 species, some half-hardy only, those grown in the open in the British Isles being of Asiatic origin, cultivated for their fragrant flowers and evergreen leaves.

**Species cultivated** *O. armatus,* 10–15 feet, large, holly-like, leathery leaves, clusters of creamy-white flowers, September, China. *O. delavayi* see Siphonosmanthus, *S. delavayi. O. forrestii,* 10–25 feet, ivory-white, fragrant flowers in clusters, October and November; a slow-growing, large-leaved species, similar to *O. armatus,* but less hardy, China. *O.* × *fortunei,* to 10 feet or more, leaves holly-like, rounded, flowers white, fragrant, autumn, hybrid. *O. fragrans,* shrub or small tree, flowers very fragrant, summer to autumn, China, Japan, suitable only for the milder

**Osmanthus armatus is a handsome evergreen shrub with toothed, holly-like leaves. It has small white flowers in September, followed by dark violet fruits.**

counties. *O. ilicifolius* (syn. *O. aquifolium*), 10–15 feet, narrow, holly-like leaves, clusters of white, fragrant flowers, autumn; a slow-growing shrub of compact rounded habit, Japan; vars. *aureomarginatus,* leaves with deep yellow margins; *latifolius variegatus,* leaves broader than in the type, variegated silver; *myrtifolius,* leaves spineless; *purpurascens,* growths purple at first, later flushed with purple; *rotundifolius,* leaves rounded in outline, spineless; *variegatus,* leaves with creamy-white edges. *O. serrulatus,* similar to *O. forrestii,* but habit more compact, leaves smaller.

**Cultivation** These handsome shrubs like a loamy soil and a sheltered, sunny border, or, particularly in less favoured areas, can be grown against a wall facing south or west. Plant in September, October, or April. Little pruning is necessary, although plants may be trimmed to shape in April or May. *O. ilicifolius* is sometimes used as a hedge and may be clipped into formal hedge shapes in April or May. In most parts of the country, except in the south and west, osmanthus do better in the unheated greenhouse or conservatory, where they may be grown in large pots

or tubs, in a compost made up of 2 parts of sandy, lime-free loam and 1 part of leafmould and sand. The containers may be placed out of doors from June to September, in a sunny place, but should be kept under glass between September and June, in a minimum temperature of 40–45°F (4–7°C). Water the plants freely from spring to autumn, but moderately only at other times. Propagate by seed sown in sandy peat in a cold frame in spring or autumn, or by cuttings taken in summer. These should be of firm young shoots which should be inserted in sandy peat in a cold frame.

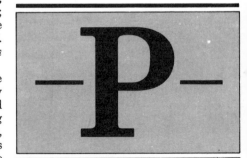

## Pernettya (per-net-e-a)

Commemorating A. J. Pernetty (1716–1801), who wrote a book on the Falkland Islands *(Ericaceae).* This genus of 20 species of hardy evergreen shrubs is largely American, but some are Tasmanian and New Zealand plants.

They are berry-bearing shrubs closely allied to the gaultherias. Indeed, a natural bigeneric hybrid occurred at the Royal Horticultural Society's Garden, Wisley, between *Gaultheria shallon* and *Pernettya mucronata* (see x Gaulnettya).
**Species cultivated** *P. ciliata,* 1–2 feet, leaves narrow, to 1 inch long, flowers white flushed pink, fruits dark reddish-brown, Mexico. *P. mucronata,* the species most commonly grown, makes a low-growing evergreen spreading shrub to about 3 feet, which has small white, heath-like flowers, in May–June, followed by marble-like berries, white, pink, red or purplish in colour, which persist all winter. Native of the area around the Magellan Straits, it is the hardiest of all South American shrubs which can be grown in the open in the British Isles. Some good varieties are the following: *alba,* white berries, deepening to pale pink; 'Bell's Seedling', large dark red berries; 'Davis's Hybrids', fruits large, many colours, *lilacina,* lilac berries; *thymifolia,* small-leaved, male, no berries. *P. prostrata,* 6 inches, growths prostrate or nearly so, flowers white, May–June, fruits blue-black, poisonous, Venezuela to Chile; var. *pentlandii,* somewhat more erect, fruits jet black.
**Cultivation** The pernettyas prefer a peaty, acid soil, well-drained, and can be planted in autumn or spring. They are generally hermaphrodite but in order to get a really good crop of berries, it is best to plant them in groups of three or

1 A shrub useful for good effective berries is Pernettya mucronata. Its small heath-like flowers are white and come in May and June.
2 The berries of Pernettya mucronata come in a range of colours.

four. Propagation is by seed, sown ¼ inch deep in peaty soil out of doors in autumn, by layering in spring, or by suckers when available. Plants make decorative specimens when grown in pots in the cold greenhouse or conservatory in a mixture of 2 parts of peat, 1 part of leafmould and sand. They should be potted up in October or November and watered moderately only. After the fruits have shrivelled, plant the specimens out of doors.

---

**Philadelphus** (fil-a-del-fus)
An ancient Greek name meaning brotherly love *(Saxifragaceae).* Mock orange; often erroneously referred to as syringa, the botanical name for the lilacs. Well known for the powerful fragrance of some kinds, this genus of 75 species of hardy deciduous shrubs from northern temperate regions of North America, Asia and southern Europe, supplies some of the most valuable garden plants. The most popular ones are nearly all hybrids, and the earliest cross, which was between *P. coronarius* and *P. microphyllus,* was made by the famous French nurseryman Victor

Lemoine of Nancy, in about 1883. In modern jargon this would be called a 'breakthrough', and it certainly opened the way to some splendid new cultivars. 'Manteau d'Hermine' and 'Virginal', two of Lemoine's early crosses, are still in demand, the first growing to about 4 feet, a very good height for today's small gardens, and the second being still the best double-flowered hybrid. A particularly good quality of the mock oranges is their habit of flowering in June and July when the first great flush of flowering shrubs is over.
**Species cultivated** *P. argyrocalyx,* 6–8 feet, graceful spreading habit, flowers white, 1¼ inches across, July, New Mexico. *P. x burfordensis,* to 10 feet, erect habit, flowers large, cup-shaped, with conspicuous yellow stamens, June, hybrid. *P. californicus,* 8–10 feet, flowers fragrant, white, 1 inch across, borne in panicles of up to 20, June, California. *P. coronarius,* flowers creamy white, scented, about 1 inch across, June, southeastern Europe. *P. coulteri,* rose syringa, 5–6 feet, flowers borne singly, very fragrant, to 1¼ inches wide, white spotted purplish-red at the base of the petals, July, slightly tender, Mexico; parent of many purple-blotched hybrids. *P. delavayi,* 10–15 feet, large white flowers, very fragrant, June, China. *P. x falconeri,* 8–10 feet, flowers slightly fragrant, white, to 2 inches across, petals narrow, June, hybrid. *P. x insignis* ('Souvenir de Billiard'), 10–12

feet, white, fragrant, July, hybrid of doubtful origin. *P.* x *lemoinei*, 6 feet, white, very fragrant, June, hybrid, numerous named varieties. *P. lewisii*, 8–10 feet, white, very floriferous, scentless, June to July, western North America. *P. microphyllus*, 4–5 feet, white, very fragrant, June, western North America. *P. pekinensis*, 6–8 feet, flowers slightly fragrant, yellowish-white, to 1 inch wide, borne in racemes, May–June, northern China, Korea; var. *brachybotrys*, flowers creamy white, to 1½ inches across. *P. pubescens*, to 15 feet or more, flowers white, slightly fragrant, 1¾ inches wide, south-eastern United States; var. *intectus*, flowers borne more freely, more fragrant. *P. purpurascens*, 10–12 feet, white and violet-purple, June, China. *P. satsumanus*, 6–8 feet, erect habit, flowers white, slightly fragrant, borne in racemes, June,. Japan. *P.* x *splendens*, spreading habit, flowers large, white, borne in clusters, June, hybrid. *P. verrucosus*, to 9 feet, flowers white, slightly fragrant, to 1 inch across, June, origin uncertain. Cultivars include 'Avalanche', masses of small fragrant flowers on arching shoots; 'Beauclerk', large white flowers, cerise in the centre; 'Belle Etoile', large white flowers, flushed maroon in the centre, scented; 'Manteau d'Hermine', creamy-white, double fragrant; 'Sybille', white with purple centre and very strong scent; 'Virginal', double white, fragrant. A number of others will be found in nurserymen's catalogues.

**Cultivation** Any ordinary good soil is suitable, and a sunny aspect is best. Prune immediately after flowering quite drastically, cutting out all the flowered shoots back to the old wood, and leaving plenty of room for the new shoots to spread and ripen. This method keeps the shrubs within bounds and gives great showers of fine blossoms on the year-old wood. Propagation is from firm young cuttings placed in sandy soil, and a temperature of 55°F (13°C) from April onwards. Suckers are also sometimes available, and may be detached. Seed is an unreliable method of increase with the hybrids.

The Philadelphus, erroneously known as 'Syringa' is one of the most popularly grown flowering shrubs. It produces arching branches of pure white flowers in late May.
1 The form of the shrub Philadelphus, or Mock Orange, is squarish with long arching branches.
2 A cultivar of Philadelphus which has single, white, fragrant flowers.
3 Philadelphus × lemoinei has very fragrant white flowers in June.
4 Philadelphus 'Avalanche' has numerous smallish white flowers which are particularly fragrant and come on well-arched branches.
5 Philadelphus 'Beauclerk' is a cultivar with large white dark-centred flowers in mid-summer.
6 The double-flowered Philadelphus 'Bouquet Blanc' has fragrant flowers in clusters, along the arching branches.

## Pieris (pe-er-is)

From *Pieria*, the abode of the Muses in Greek mythology *(Ericaceae)*. A genus of 10 species of hardy evergreen shrubs or small trees, with racemes of small waxy, white flowers, looking like lilies of the valley, sometimes faintly tinted with pink. They are related to *Andromeda* and *Lyonia* and are natives of North America, China, Japan and the Himalaya. They flower very freely under the right conditions. Some kinds are grown as much for the brilliant red tints of their young growths in spring, which look like red shuttlecocks at the ends of the shoots, as for their flowers.

**Species cultivated** *P. floribunda* (syn. *Andromeda floribunda*), 4–6 feet, numerous erect panicles of flowers in March and April, south-eastern United States; var. *grandiflora*, flower panicles longer. *P. formosa* (syn. *Andromeda formosa*), 8–12 feet, or up to 20 feet in the milder parts of Britain, young growths scarlet, flowers in erect panicles, April and May, spreads by suckers, eastern Himalaya; var. *forrestii*, 8–10 feet or more, but up to 50 feet in circumference in maturity, young growths more brilliant in colour, flowers larger, in larger, pyramidal panicles. There are various forms, including 'Wakehurst Form', varying in the intensity of colouring of the young growths. P. × 'Forest Flame', is a hybrid between *P. formosa forrestii* and *P. japonica*, probably about 10 feet tall, of dense habit. The young growths are bright red, the flower buds are pink, opening to cream. *P. japonica* (syn. *Andromeda japonica*), similar to *P. floribunda*, but to 10 feet, foliage more attractive, flowers larger, borne in numerous drooping racemes, March and April, Japan; var. *variegata*, slow-growing, leaves variegated creamy-white. *P. taiwanensis*, 3–8 feet, perhaps more in the milder counties, young leaves brightly coloured, flowers in semi-upright panicles, March to May, Formosa. There is a species at present offered under the collector's number F. 8945, which grows 10 feet tall and has brightly coloured young growths, the colour persisting until early summer. The flowers are borne in panicles from March to June.

**Cultivation** A peaty acid soil in a moist, but well-drained position is preferred in a lightly shaded border or in woodland with shelter from cold winds. Plant in autumn or early spring. Little pruning is necessary except to remove straggling shoots immediately after flowering, and to encourage natural shape. If the weather is dry water the plants freely in the summer. Propagation is by seed sown in sandy peat November or March in a cold frame, by layering shoots in early autumn, by offsets (suckers), or by cuttings taken with a heel and rooted in a sand/peat mixture in pots in a cold frame in August–September.

Pieris may also be grown in large pots or other containers such as tubs, in the cold greenhouse, placing the containers in a shady situation out of doors from June until November. A suitable soil mixture consists of peat, leafmould and sharp sand in equal parts. Water the plants freely from spring to autumn, but moderately only in winter.

## Pyracantha (pire-a-kan-tha)

From the Greek *pyr*, fire, and *akanthos*, a thorn, alluding to the brilliant colour of the berries and the spines, hence the common name firethorn *(Rosaceae)*. A genus of 10 species of evergreen shrubs mostly from China, related to *Crataegus*, with clusters of white flowers in early summer, followed by the colourful berries. They are effective as specimens in a border, but are more often grown as wall shrubs where they grow taller. They

5

6

are also used as hedge plants.

**Species cultivated** *P. angustifolia* (syn *Cotoneaster angustifolia*), 8–10 feet narrow leaves, grey beneath, orange berries, China. *P. atalantioides* (syn. *P gibbsii*), 15–18 feet, of erect habit, with deep red berries, persisting till the following spring, China; var. *aurea*, has rich yellow berries. *P. coccinea*, tree to 15 feet or more, or leafy shrub, fruits bright red, south-eastern Europe, Asia *lalandii* is a popular variety with large orange-red berries. *P. crenulata*, 8–10 feet, a variable species; the form *flava* with yellow berries is the most popular Himalaya. *P.* x *watereri*, 8–10 feet, a free-flowering hybrid bearing an abundance of bright red berries.

**Cultivation** Pyracanthas are easily grown in ordinary garden soil, particularly on chalk. They are good plants for town gardens in sun or shade. Plant in autumn or spring; no pruning is necessary unless they are used for hedging purposes or trained against a wall, when trimming should be done in July or early August. Propagation is by cuttings taken in July or August, about 4 inches long, with a heel, and inserted in sandy soil in a propagating frame without heat or by hardwood cuttings taken in the autumn and placed in a cold frame.

1 Pieris japonica (syn. Andromeda japonica) has creamy-white flowers in profuse, drooping racemes.
2 The young leaves of Pieris formosa forrestii are shining rose-red and look like shuttlecocks held at the ends of the branches in spring.
3 The yellow-fruited Pyracantha atalantioides.

1 Pyracantha rogersiana is as attractive in flower as in berry. The flowers are held in a profusion of creamy white in summer.
2 Pyracantha coccinea lalandii is a vigorous form, growing to a small tree and bearing brilliant orange fruits in the autumn and winter.

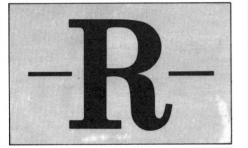

# R

## Rhododendron (ro-do-den-dron)

From the Greek *rhodon*, rose, and *dendron*, tree. Possibly the first true rhododendron to be so named was *R. ferrugineum*, the alpenrose, or *rose des alpes (Ericaceae)*. This is a large genus, with up to 600 species, ranging from prostrate alpine plants to tree-like specimens, some with enormous leaves. It includes those plants which were at one time described under the genus *Azalea* and others which were once included in the genus *Rhodora*. There are both evergreen and deciduous species and hybrids. One point which they have in common is that they will not tolerate lime in the soil, except for those mentioned below. The greatest number of species has been introduced from

western China, Tibet, north-western India and Burma; there are also a few from Java and Malaysia, which require warm greenhouse conditions when grown in cold climates. As there are probably well over 200 species and many hundreds of hybrids in cultivation, it is possible here to describe a selection only, under the main headings.

3 The genus Rhododendron has wide variation in habit, from sizable trees and large shrubs to low-growing species.

These are: *rhododendron section* species cultivated: hardy; tender; hybrids, hardy; *azalea section* species cultivated: hybrids, deciduous, mollis, Ghent, occidentalis, double mollis,

75

double Ghent, Knap Hill and Exbury hybrids, evergreen hybrids. Those readers who require further details of species and hybrids in cultivation should refer to specialist works on the genus *Rhododendron* and to the catalogues of nurserymen who specialise in the genus.

## Rhododendron section

All the species or varieties in this section are evergreen, including both the hardy and tender species, as well as the hybrids.

**Hardy species cultivated** *R. aberconwayi,* 4–5 feet, small, dark green leaves, white flowers, saucer-shaped, tinged pink, with red spots, in May, Yunnan. *R.*

*ambiguum,* 5–6 feet, leaves slender-pointed, dark green, aromatic, flowers small, funnel-shaped, yellow, spotted green, in clusters, early May, western China. *R. arboreum,* 30–40 feet, leaves dark green, wrinkled, up to 8 inches long, silvery beneath, flowers blood-red, bell-shaped, from January to March; there are white and pink forms, Himalaya. Should be given the protection of trees; young plants do not produce flowers. *R. augustinii,* 6–10 feet, leaves dark green, narrow, tapering, small clusters of flowers in variable shades of lilac, blue and mauve, May, China; needs woodland protection. *R. auriculatum,* 10–20 feet, light green,

12-inch long leaves, flowers large, white, fragrant, borne in a loose truss in July and August, even later, China; it does not start to flower until reaching maturity. *R. calophytum,* 10–15 feet, light green, down-curving, 12-inch long leaves, large trusses of white or pink-flushed flowers, with a maroon blotch at the base, March and April, China, Tibet. *R. calostrotum,* 1–2 feet, attractive grey foliage, flowers large, flat, rosy-purple, May and June, Burma; forms a neat bushy shrub for the rock garden. *R. campylocarpum,* 5–8 feet, dark green, slightly glaucous leaves, 4 inches long, flowers yellow, bell-shaped, April and May, Sikkim; starts to flower when

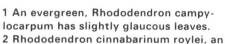

1 An evergreen, Rhododendron campy-locarpum has slightly glaucous leaves.
2 Rhododendron cinnabarinum roylei, an evergreen with bell-shaped flowers.
3 Rhododendron 'Seven Stars'.
4 Rhododendron wardii.
5 The tubular flowers of R. keysii.
6 Rhododendron 'Elizabeth'.
7 Rhododendron 'China'.
8 Rhododendron williamsianum grows in a distinctive rounded form.

quite young. *R. dauricum* (SE), 4–5 feet, flowers bright rosy-purple, in terminal clusters, January to March, northern Asia. *R. falconeri*, 15–25 feet, taller in the wild, dark green leaves up to 12 inches long, heavily veined, with the underside heavily covered with rusty brown, woolly hair, large, rounded trusses of waxy yellow flowers in April, Himalaya; for a position sheltered from wind which is liable to ruin the large leaves. *R. fargesii*, 10–15 feet, dark green leaves, glaucous beneath, medium-sized trusses of cup-shaped flowers, varying from white to pink, very free-flowering, in March and April, China. *R. ferrugineum*, alpine rose, 3–4 feet, of spreading habit, small, glossy green leaves, thickly covered with rust-coloured scales, flowers small, pink to crimson, June, central European Alps; tolerates lime. *R. fictolacteum*, 15–40 feet, dark green, 12-inch long leaves, heavily brown-felted beneath, trusses of creamy-white flowers with a crimson blotch, April and May, China. *R. griersonianum*, 5–8 feet, leaves up to 8 inches long, slender and woolly beneath, vivid scarlet heads of flowers, June, borne on quite young plants when happily established, Yunnan. *R. haematodes*, 3–4 feet, a bushy shrub, small, dark green leaves, brown-felted beneath, flowers brilliant blood red, funnel-shaped, May, Yunnan; although dwarf it is slow to start flowering. *R. hirsutum*, alpine rose, 3–4 feet, similar to *R. ferrugineum*, but the growths are more hairy, flowers dull rose-pink, June; grows on limestone

formations in the southern central European Alps. *R. impeditum*, 1 foot, forming a twiggy mound covered with small pale purplish-blue flowers in May, western China; a good rock garden plant. *R. lutescens*, 5–6 feet, slender-pointed leaves, bronze-red in the young stage, flowers yellow, funnel-shaped, March, China; of willowy habit, it is a delightful shrub for a light woodland. *R. orbiculare*, 4–6 feet, compact, dome-shaped habit with handsome rounded leaves, glaucous beneath, flowers small, bell-shaped, rose-pink, March and April, China; the blooms are susceptible to spring frost. *R. ponticum*, 12–20 feet, long dark, glossy green leaves, flowers mauve to lilac-pink, May and June, Spain, Asia Minor; makes an excellent hedge or screen, widely naturalised in Britain. *R. racemosum*, 4–5 feet, roundish, leathery leaves up to about 2 inches long, glaucous beneath, flowers small, pale to bright pink, freely produced, April and May, western China. *R. sinogrande*, 20–30 feet, the largest-leaved of all rhododendrons, each sometimes up to 2½ feet long and 1 foot broad, shiny dark green above, pale buff beneath, creamy-white flowers borne in large trusses in April, China, Burma, Tibet; for semi-shade and shelter from strong winds. *R. yakusimanum*, 2½–3 feet, young growths covered in silvery hair, dark green leaves covered with brown felt beneath, bearing a mass of pink, cup-shaped flowers, becoming white, May, Japan.

**Tender species cultivated** *R. bullatum,* up to 10 feet, flowers white, or white flushed pink, fragrant, April and May, China. *R. edgeworthii,* 6–10 feet, flowers large, white, occasionally flushed pink, fragrant, April and May, Himalaya. *R. elliottii,* 8–12 feet, flowers large, brilliant red, tubular, May and June, India. *R. lindleyi,* 5–6 feet, with trusses of large, trumpet-shaped, fragrant, white or cream flowers with a yellow blotch, April and May, Himalaya. *R. maddenii,* 6–9 feet, flowers large, white, flushed rose-pink, trumpet-shaped, sweetly fragrant, June and July, Himalaya. *R. megacalyx,* 10–15 feet, flowers large, white, funnel-shaped, drooping, with a nutmeg scent, April and May, Burma. *R. nuttallii,* up to 30 feet, flowers large, trumpet-shaped, fragrant, white, flushed yellow, April and May, Bhutan.

**Hardy hybrids** These hybrids range from those of dwarf and medium habit, suitable for a small garden, to those which eventually develop into large shrubs or trees suitable for a spacious woodland setting. The diversity of colour and form of the individual flowers are remarkable. The choice of varieties runs into hundreds, and the following is a small selection only of leading hybrids, which flower in late May and early June unless otherwise stated. 'Beauty of Littleworth', a tall shrub with large white, crimson-spotted flowers, April;

'Blue Peter', medium height, with lavender-blue flowers with a deeper blotch; 'Britannia', medium height, with trumpet-shaped, glowing scarlet-crimson flowers, slow-growing; 'Cynthia', medium height, flowers rosy-crimson in large heads; 'Faggetter's Favourite', medium height, with scented, coral-pink and cream flowers; 'Goldsworth Orange', medium height, pink in the bud stage, opening to pale orange; 'Lady Chamberlain', up to 8 feet, with long, waxy, orange-yellow pendent bells, flushed pink; 'Lavender Girl', medium height, pale lavender; 'Loder's White', medium height with large trusses of blush-pink flowers fading to white; 'May Day', up to 8 feet, bright scarlet; 'Mother of Pearl', makes a large shrub, pearly-white, a sport of 'Pink Pearl'; 'Mrs G. W. Leak', medium height, pale pink flowers with a large, distinct purple-brown blotch; 'Nobleanum', up to 15 feet, but slow-growing, with small trusses of rosy-scarlet flowers in January and February; 'Pink Pearl', a large shrub with elegant heads of bright pink flowers freely borne; 'Susan', up to 8 feet, with large trusses of lavender-blue flowers with deeper markings; 'Yvonne', tall-growing, with large bells of blush-pink, fading to white.

## Azalea section

This section contains a considerable number of species, both evergreen and deciduous, from North America, Japan, China, eastern Europe and Asia Minor. There are also innumerable hardy colourful hybrids, mainly raised in Belgium, Holland, England and Japan. Tender varieties grown under glass are popular when forced for Christmas flowering.

**Species cultivated** *R. arborescens* (D), 8–15 feet, flowers fragrant, white with conspicuous bright red filaments, June and July, North America. *R. calendulaceum* (D), up to 10 feet, flowers orange-red and yellow, June, North America. *R. indicum* (E), 3–6 feet, of spreading habit, flowers large, salmon-red, June, Japan (not to be confused with the so-called Indian azalea, *R. simsii,* which is forced by nurserymen for winter flowering); vars. *balsaminaeflorum*, double, salmon-pink, dwarf; 'Hakatashiro', ivory-white. *R. kaempferi* (SE), 6–8 feet, free-flowering, flowers brilliant orange-red, June, Japan; cultivars are 'Daimio', salmon-pink, June and July; 'Mikado', apricot-salmon, June and July. *R. luteum* (syn. *Azalea pontica*), 8–12 feet,

1 The decorative young leaves of Rhododendron macabeanum.

2 The leaves of some Rhododendrons have undersides with rust-coloured hairs.

3 A tender species of Rhododendron, R. superbum.

4 Rhododendron obtusum.

5 R. simsii, the Indian Azalea.

6 The Japanese, or Kurume, Azaleas.

5

4

6

the common hardy azalea, flowers very fragrant, yellow, May, the leaves turn to glorious shades of crimson, pink, purple and orange before they fall in the autumn, Asia Minor and eastern Europe. *R. mucronatum* (syn. *Azalea ledifolia*) (E), 6–10 feet, white flowers, May, Japan. *R. nudiflorum* (D), 3–6 feet, flowers pink or whitish, fragrant, in clusters, May, North America. *R. obtusum* (E or SE), about 2 feet, of low-spreading habit, with small leaves, bearing a mass of small magenta-crimson flowers, May, Japan; vars. *coccineum,* scarlet; *splendens,* rose-pink. *R. occidentale* (D), 8–10 feet, flowers fragrant, white with a yellow blotch, June, North America. *R. reticulatum* (syn. *Azalea rhombica*) (D), up to 20 feet, flowers light purple, April and May, Japan. *R. schlippenbachii* (D), 5–15 feet, large pale rose flowers in April and May, the 5-leaved whorls turn to shades of orange, yellow and crimson in the autumn, Japan, Korea; extremely beautiful, but liable to damage by late frost. *R. simsii* (known as *Azalea indica* in the nursery trade) (E), up to 5 feet, usually much less when grown as a pot plant for winter decoration, flowers rosy-red to dark red, China; there are numerous named hybrids in shades of scarlet, salmon, rose, magenta and white. *R. vaseyi* (D), 8–15 feet, white or light pink flowers in April and May, North America. *R. viscosum* (D), 6–8 feet, flowers white, honeysuckle-shaped, fragrant, July, North America.

### Deciduous hybrid azaleas

Hardy, hybrid azaleas are unsurpassed for brilliance and diversity of colour in the spring and early summer. Autumn colour of foliage is often splendid.

**Mollis hybrids** These grow 4–5 feet tall, and bear large trusses of scentless flowers, of almost translucent texture, which start to open in early May, before the leaves unfold. They include 'Anthony Koster', rich yellow, flushed orange; 'Christopher Wren' (syn. 'Goldball'), bright orange; 'Dr M. Oosthoek', deep orange-red; 'Emile Liebig', light salmon-orange; 'Golden Queen', golden-yellow; 'Mrs A. E. Endtz', deep yellow; 'Snowdrift', white with yellow markings which deepen to orange.

**Ghent hybrids** These reach 6–8 feet tall, and have elegant, tubular, honeysuckle-shaped fragrant flowers, which open in late May and early June when the leaves have developed. They include 'Bouquet de Flore', salmon-pink with an orange blotch; 'Coccinea Speciosa', brilliant orange-flame; 'Gloria Mundi', deep orange-red; 'Nancy Waterer', golden-yellow; 'Pucella' (syn. 'Fanny') magenta-pink, the top petals blotched with orange; 'Unique', large, clear orange-yellow.

**Double Mollis and double Ghent hybrids** These are 5–8 feet tall, with fragrant flowers in late May and June. Cultivars include 'Aida', rose-pink with deeper

flush; 'Byron', white, tinged rose; 'Norma', bright rose; 'Phidias', cream, flushed rose.

**Azalea occidentalis hybrids** *(R. occidentale)* Plants in this group grow up to 10 feet tall, and have large trusses of fragrant flowers from mid-May to early June, in delicate shades of pink, cream or white flushed with pink. Among those available are 'Delicatissimum', cream with a pink blotch; 'Exquisitum', cream with a pink flush, later flowering; 'Graciosum', pink with an orange spot; 'Irene Koster', rose-pink, later flowering; 'Magnificum', cream, flushed pink; 'Superbum', pink, blotched apricot.

**Knap Hill hybrids and Exbury hybrids** These grow 4–8 feet tall. They are two

1 Exbury hybrid Azaleas, such as this apricot seedling, have been evolved at the Exbury estate, Hampshire, over a large number of years.
2 One of the hybrid 'mollis' Azaleas.
3 Rhododendron (Azalea) 'Blue Diamond'.

splendid strains which have been evolved over the years at the Knap Hill Nursery near Woking, Surrey, and at the Rothschild's estate at Exbury, near Southampton. Leading nurserymen offer numerous named varieties as well as plants raised from seed collected from selected, outstanding plants. The flowers are in shades of apricot, flame, pink, crimson, orange, yellow and cream, from early May to mid-June. Double-flowered varieties are also now available. Some good varieties are: *Exbury hybrids* 'Balzac', red and flame; 'Caprice', deep pink; 'George Reynolds', large deep yellow flowers; 'Hotspur', orange-red; 'Kathleen', salmon-pink and orange; 'Royal Lodge', deep vermilion-scarlet; 'White Swan', white with yellow flare. *Knap Hill hybrids* 'Gog', orange-red; 'Harvest Moon', pale yellow; 'Home-bush', rose-pink; 'Persil', white and yellow; 'Satan', blood-red; 'Seville', deep orange.

### Evergreen hybrid azaleas

The heights of these range from 2–6 feet. They were mainly raised by plant breeders in Japan and in Europe. Some start to flower in April but the majority are at their best in May when they are profusely covered with bloom.

**Kurume varieties** Outstanding Kurume varieties growing about 2–3 feet, include: 'Addy Wery', deep vermilion-red; 'Benegiri', bright crimson; 'Hatsugiri', crimson-purple; 'Hoo' (syn. 'Apple Blossom'), white, tinged pink; 'Kirin', deep rose, shaded silvery-pink; 'Ukamuse', vermilion and salmon-pink. Many other evergreen hybrid azaleas, derived from various crosses, are available.

**Cultivation** *Rhododendron section* Plant in autumn or early spring in a lime-free, moist soil containing plenty of leaf soil or peat. The majority like cool conditions for the roots and prefer light shade to full sun, although some of the hybrids flower freely in a sunny position, provided that the soil does not dry out. A top dressing each year in early spring, with leaf soil, garden compost, or old manure will help to provide nourishment for these hungry shrubs, as well as helping to retain moisture in the soil. The most effective way is to plant them in groups, where space permits, rather than singly. By this means the plants themselves provide better shade for their roots. Tender species may be grown in large pots or containers under glass, or in the greenhouse border. Repotting is necessary about every three or four years. A minimum winter temperature of 50°F (10°C) is sufficient, except for the

1 The Kurume Azaleas are evergreen and are of Japanese origin. 'Hinodegiri' has red flowers in May.
2 The Knaphill strain of Azalea was developed at Woking. Azalea 'Daybreak' has orange flowers.
3 Knaphill type, Azalea 'Silver Slipper'.

most tender which require 65°F (18°C). Most of those described above may be grown out of doors in mild, frost-free, sheltered gardens in the west of the British Isles.

Propagation is by the following methods. Seed can be sown in pans containing sandy, moist peat and placed in a propagating frame or greenhouse with a temperature of 55–60°F (13–16°C), the seed being lightly covered with sharp sand. Cuttings, preferably with the aid of mist, can be rooted in sandy peat with gentle bottom heat in a propagating frame. Take cuttings of nearly ripe shoots with a heel from mid-June to mid-July. Small-leaved varieties can be rooted without heat, but the larger the leaf the more difficult is the variety to root, and warmth is necessary. Cuttings of fully ripe wood may be taken during November and December of small-leaved varieties and rooted in a cold frame. Layering is best done in early spring, although it can be done at any time of the year, and roots are usually formed comparatively quickly. Aerial layering is useful where a shrub is too tall to provide layers at ground level. Grafting is done in December and January in a warm greenhouse with a moist atmosphere.

*Azalea section* The first essential for azaleas is a lime-free soil and they grow best in a sandy loam containing plenty

of leaf soil or peat, even a trace of clay, but they dislike a heavy wet soil or being baked dry at the roots in summer. They will flower well in full sun, provided that the roots remain reasonably moist and cool, and when grown in an open sunny position the colours are often more intense and the attractive bronze tint to the young leaves in spring is more pronounced, whereas in partial shade this may be absent. Nevertheless azaleas are admirable for a woodland garden in dappled·shade and the trees not only provide a beautiful setting, but afford

The hardy hybrid Rhododendrons range from small shrubs to near trees in height.
1 Rhododendron 'Mermaid'.
2 Rhododendron 'Queen Wilhelmina'.
3 Rhododendron 'Susan' has mauve flowers.
4 Rhododendron quinquefolium, from Japan, has broad bell-shaped white flowers and deciduous pale green leaves.
5 Rhododendron xanthostephanum, an evergreen with yellow flowers.
6 Rhododendron 'Red Carpet'.
7 Rhododendron 'Lord Swaythling'.

5

6

7

be used sparingly, if at all.

Azaleas make most decorative plants when grown in a tub, large Provence pot or fibre-glass container (beware of cement containers because of the lime content) on a terrace, or a patio or in a cold greenhouse. The container must have a layer of crocks over the drainage holes in the bottom. Use a compost consisting of equal parts of a lime-free loam and moist peat, to 2 parts of leaf soil, 1 part of old farmyard manure and 1 part of coarse silver sand to assist drainage. The compost must never be allowed to dry out or the azalea will soon show signs of distress. In such containers they may be grown in districts where the soil is chalky or limy, but they must be watered with rainwater if the tap water is normally 'hard', otherwise they will soon look sickly.

*Tender azaleas* The winter-flowering, pot-grown, azaleas—so-called *A. indica* —make admirable house plants if they can be grown in a room with a moderate temperature and not placed near a radiator where the atmosphere would be far too hot and dry. Use a similar compost to that recommended for other azaleas and spray the plants overhead with tepid water when in the bud stage, otherwise the buds may shrivel and not develop. After flowering, the plants should be kept in a cool place and in mid-May they can be planted out, or the pots plunged, in the open garden in a partially shaded place for the summer. In September the plants should be lifted, repotted and placed in a cool, but sunny room or greenhouse. In November give warmer conditions, about 60°F (16°C), to bring the plants gently along into flower.

Propagation by seed is a ready means of increase, in fact self-sown seedlings appear frequently among established plants. Sow the seed thinly in a pan or box on the surface of sandy peat from mid-January to mid-February and cover it with only a light sprinkling of silver sand. Place in a temperature of about 60°F (16°C) and keep moderately moist. Freshly harvested seed may germinate within a matter of days. Cuttings of firm shoots, about 3 inches long, taken with a heel, should be inserted in sandy soil in a propagating frame from June to November with a temperature of about 50°F (10°C). Hormone rooting compounds may be used if desired and mist propagation is useful for rooting azalea cuttings. Layering is an easy method which may be carried out at almost any time of the year, although the early spring is probably the best period to do this. Grafting is done by nurserymen, usually from January to March, in warm greenhouse conditions. By doing the work early in the year once the stock and scion are united the plant has the remainder of the summer to make growth before the winter.

some protection to the blooms which may otherwise be damaged by late spring frosts.

Azaleas associate well with maples *(acers)*, hardy heathers, kalmias, enkianthus and small-growing shrubs in the rhododendron section of the genus, all of which thrive in an acid or lime-free, well-drained soil. The maximum effect is obtained by planting in groups, even of three, if space does not permit for more liberal planting. As they can be lifted with a good ball of soil attached to the roots, planting may be done at any time

during the dormant season from late October to about mid-March. Well-budded young plants will usually flower quite happily the first season after being planted. A mulch each autumn of leaf soil, moist peat, or garden compost will keep the shrubs in good condition and farmyard manure, spread at any time from autumn to early spring around the plants, makes a first-class feed, far better than quick-acting fertilisers, which should be avoided. Poultry manure should not be used. Wood ash contains a high proportion of lime, and this should

## Rosa (roh-sah)

A name of old and uncertain derivation, probably alluding to the prevailing flower colour. It has been suggested that it may have been derived from the Celtic *rhod,* red *(Rosaceae).* Rose. A large genus of over 100 (or, according to some botanists, about 250) species of perennial, prickly shrubs and climbers with odd-pinnate leaves and five-petalled flowers followed by red and yellow or black heps (or hips). With few exceptions they are deciduous and hardy in the British Isles, although the wild distribution covers temperate and subtropical regions of the northern hemisphere of North America and Eurasia.

The rose, often styled the 'queen of flowers' is the most long-esteemed genus of flowering shrubs. The cultivars run into many thousands. For convenience, the following three groups may be distinguished: wild species, old garden

**Rosa banksiae lutea is a climbing Rose best grown on a warm wall.**

roses and modern roses.

**Wild species group** These include their varieties and interspecific hybrids. The wild species bear single flowers in nature, although double-flowered sports are known for at least a third of the species and are best grouped here. The flowering season is short (June to July mainly) but followed by plentiful, often showy hips in autumn. Several are worth growing as specimen shrubs (e.g., *R. multibracteata* and *R. hugonis*), as climbers (e.g., *R. banksiae*), as hedges (e.g., *R. rubiginosa*), as carpeters (e.g., *R. luciae wichuraiana*).

**Old garden roses group** These are shrubs and some early climbers, distinguished by the same short flowering season as for species, but with larger, mostly double flowers. They are typified by the

gallicas with many-petalled, saucer-shaped flowers in pink, mauve or maroon or variously mottled. Like the species they suit the shrub garden, wild garden and the backs of borders.

**Modern roses group** These, for the most part, have a long flowering season or marked recurrence of flowering in the autumn. They are typified by the few-petalled conical bud of the hybrid tea, with clear unfading colours. They are *par excellence* the group for cut and exhibition blooms. It is rarely desirable to mix roses of the modern roses group in the same bed as roses of the wild species or old garden roses groups because of the clash of colours and different habit and pruning requirements.

**Species cultivated** The following consists of wild species, varieties and hybrids with Latinised names (wild species group), considered to be of garden merit. *R.* x *alba,* white rose of York, is an ancient descendant of *R. gallica* × *R. canina*, or allied species, and forms a handsome erect shrub with grey foliage and intensely fragrant white blooms. It is the prototype of the Alba group, of which var. *incarnata* 'Céleste' has blush-pink flowers. Others range from pure white to carnation pink, and from semi-double to full, with a flat or incurving centre. *R.* × *anemonoides*, anemone rose, is a hybrid of *R. laevigata* and *R. gigantea* probably, and forms a vigorous climber for a south wall. Flowers are large and pink; 'Ramona' is a cerise-flowered sport. *R. arvensis*, field rose, sprawls or rambles with clusters of small white flowers followed by tiny globular red hips; a common sight of English hedgerows. The wild musk rose of Shakespeare. Parent of some Ayrshire roses, Europe. *R. banksiae*, Banksian rose, is an exceedingly vigorous, sparingly armed, tender climber for a warm wall, with narrow pointed pale green leaflets in threes. The tiny clustered flowers are white and double in var. *banksiae (albo-plena)*; single in var. *normalis*; single yellow in var. *lutescens*

1 Rosa × anemonoides, the Anemone Rose, is a cross between R. laevigata and R. gigantea. It is a vigorous climber.
2 The profusely produced flowers of Rosa californica plena are deep pink.
3 In Europe other forms are most commonly budded on to the rootstock of the Dog Rose, Rosa canina.

and double yellow in var. *lutea*, central and western China. *R. blanda* forms a thicket of glaucous red, sparingly prickly stems bearing 2-inch diameter pink flowers. The probable parent of the Boursault roses; var. *amurensis* has double flowers, northern United States. *R. bracteata*, Macartney rose, is a tender, very prickly, evergreen climber for a warm wall only. The white flowers are 2–2¾ inches across, borne in midsummer and onwards. Parent of 'Mermaid', and the only species unaffected by black spot, China. *R. brunonii*, summer-flowering musk rose (commonly misnamed *R. moschata*, which see), is a climber with small white flowers in large trusses, borne in late June and July, Himalaya. *R. californica* forms a medium to tall shrub with pink flowers; var. *plena*, with profuse double flowers, makes a fine display, western United States. *R. canina*, dog rose, is the favourite understock in Europe and exists in many varieties and cultivars. It scores over some exotics in longevity and hardiness, and excels on heavy soils, Europe. *R. centifolia*, cabbage rose, or

1 Rosa chinensis minima 'Rouletti' is the parent of the miniature or fairy Roses. It is itself a sport.
2 Rosa ecae is a dainty shrublet with burnet-like foliage. The flowers are a bright buttercup-yellow.
3 Rosa damascena 'Hebe's Lip' is a variety of the Damask Rose with velvety, crimson petals.

Provence rose, is the rose beloved of early eighteenth-century painters and recognisable in many works of the Dutch masters. It is an early descendant of *R. gallica* with cup-shaped, full, intensely fragrant blooms of rich pink. The following sports have received Latinised names; others will be found with cultivar names among old garden group roses: var. *muscosa,* moss rose, with sepals and sometimes also stalks, and foliage covered in resin-scented branched glands like moss; var. *albo-muscosa,* white Bath, is a white sport of the preceding; var. *cristata* ('Chapeau de Napoleon') has the 'moss' on the exposed edges of the sepals only; var. *pomponia* is the dwarf 'De Meaux' and var. *parviflora,* the still smaller 'Burgundy Rose'; var. *variegata,* has petals striped pink and white, and var. *bullata,* has oddly crisped leaves like lettuce. *R. chinensis* (syn. *R. indica*), China rose, is not in cultivation, being a vigorous climber from central China, but is represented by dwarf cultivars from Chinese gardens with extremely profuse flowering from June up to the first frosts. All modern group roses showing this character owe it to *R. chinensis* through hybridisation begun early in the nineteenth century. 'Old Blush' has loose pink flowers 2–2½ inches in diameter; var. *semperflorens,* 'Crimson China', has smaller deep crimson flowers; var. *minima,* 'Rouletti', is the parent of the miniature or fairy roses—a perfect dwarf sport, and var. *viridiflora,* green rose, has purplish-green flowers of leaf-like petals, an oddity for the connoisseur. *R. cinnamomea,* cinnamon rose, is a medium-sized, sparingly armed shrub with cerise blooms up to 2 inches across; var. *plena* has small, compact double blooms and is very dwarf, Europe and north-western Asia. *R. damascena,* damask rose, typifies the old damask roses with erect habit and very double pink blooms with flat, incurving centres or sometimes a green 'eye' and narrow hips (when not sterile); var. *trigintipetala* with pink flowers provides the rose water and attar in south-eastern Europe; var. *semperflorens* is the autumn damask or 'Four Seasons Rose', perhaps the same as Pliny's 'Rose of Paestum', which has a second flowering season in the autumn; var. *versicolor,* York and Lancaster rose, has flowers of all pink, all white or parti-coloured, pink and white. *R. × dupontii* is probably *R. gallica × moschata* and forms a lax shrub with good greyish foliage and trusses of showy white single flowers. *R. ecae* is a dainty shrublet with burnet-like foliage and bright buttercup-yellow flowers on mahogany-red stems. Prefers a warm sheltered position, Afghanistan. *R. farreri* is represented in cultivation by var. *persetosa,* the threepenny bit rose, a broadly arching very bristly shrub with a profusion of tiny pink blooms, north-western China. *R. fedtschenkoana* has silvery foliage and white blooms in June and occasionally later in the season, Turkestan. *R. × felicita (R. sempervirens × chinensis),* 'Félicité et Perpétué', is a sprawling sub-evergreen rambler with profuse double white flowers. 'Little White Pet' is a dwarf sport of this. *R. filipes* is a vigorous climber with greyish foliage and trusses of white flowers 1 inch across. 'Kiftsgate' is the best garden cultivar, of enormous vigour and size, suitable for climbing over trees or covering walls and ruins, western China. *R. foetida,* Austrian briar, has bright green foliage and vivid buttercup-yellow 2–2½-inch blooms on a spreading untidy shrub. The heavy sweet scent is found repellent by some people; var. *bicolor,* Austrian copper, has the petals yellow above and scarlet below so that the overall effect is a unique orange-red; var. *persiana,* Persian yellow, is double yellow. All modern, bright yellow and bicolor roses are descendants of *R. foetida* through hybridisation begun about 1900, western Asia. *R. foliolosa* forms a low thicket of suckering stems with narrow foliage and pale pink, 1½-inch wide flowers, North America. *R. gallica,* French rose or Provins rose, is the predominant influence throughout the groups of old shrub roses. The wild species is a low to medium suckering shrub with 3–5 large dark green leaflets per leaf and solitary showy light crimson blooms 2–3 inches across, followed by squat broad red hips; var. *haplodonta* has simply serrate leaves and woolly styles. The cultivars show a range of doubleness and colours from pink to deep purplish maroon fading to bluish, and variously mottled, striped or spotted; var. *conditorum* has semi-double purple

blooms; var. *officinalis* is the 'Apothecary's Rose' or 'Red Rose of Lancaster', long esteemed by the herbalists, with large, loose, semi-double blooms of light crimson; var. *versicolor (Rosa mundi)* is a variegated sport of the preceding, its crimson flowers having splashes and stripes of white or pink, the best of the old variegated shrub roses, southern Europe to western Asia. *R. gigantea,* tea rose, is a vigorous but tender climber for a south wall, with very large (4–5 inch) creamy-white flowers. Crossed with *R. chinensis* to produce *R. × odorata,* this is one parent of the tea and hybrid tea roses, Burma and south-western China. *R. × harisonii (R. foetida × spinosissima),* 'Harison's Yellow', is the most popular cultivar of this parentage with semi-double bright yellow 2½-inch flowers in May. A hardy, trouble-free shrub. *R. hemisphaerica,* sulphur rose, has full, flat-topped sulphur-yellow blooms which blemish easily in wet weather. The

**1** Rosa filipes, a vigorous climber with greyish foliage and white flowers.
**2** Rosa × harisonii has semi-double bright lemon yellow flowers in May and June.
**3** Rosa hugonis is one of the most popularly grown yellow-flowered bush roses. It also blooms early in the summer.

foliage is blue-green. Of historical interest only. The single-flowered wild species, var. *rapinii,* is not in cultivation, western Asia. *R. × highdownensis* is a seedling, probably hybrid, from *R. moyesii,* and equally splendid with showy, soft crimson blooms followed by large, long waxy red hips. Makes a good specimen shrub 10 feet or more in diameter. *R. hugonis* forms a shapely large bush with solitary yellow blooms early in the season. Suitable as a specimen shrub, central China *R. kordesii* is a spontaneous tetraploid

from *R. rugosa* × *R. luciae wichuraiana* and parent of the hardy, recurrent Kordesii climbers. Foliage glossy, bright green, flowers light crimson, almost single. *R.* × *l'heritierana (R. chinensis* × *blanda ?)*, Boursault rose, bears semi-double mauve-pink flowers on wide-spreading purplish glaucous stems, almost devoid of prickles. *R. longicuspis* is a vigorous if somewhat tender climber up to 20 feet bearing a profusion of showy trusses of small white banana-scented flowers in midsummer, western China. *R. luciae* is a sub-evergreen climber with glossy bright green leaves and clusters of small white flowers in July and August; var. *wichuraiana*, memorial rose, has larger blooms and a more prostrate habit, ideal for carpeting embankments and rough ground. Parent of the wichuraiana ramblers, which inherit the superior, mildew-resistant foliage, eastern Asia. *R. macrophylla* forms a massive shrub topped with rich pink blooms followed by large flagon-shaped red hips in autumn, Himalaya. *R. moschata*, autumn musk rose, is exceptional in flowering in late summer, with trusses of white musk-scented blooms borne on a tall lax shrub. Roses under this name which flower in June to July are more correctly referred to *R.*

1 Rosa moyesii, grown mostly for its lantern-shaped hips, forms a large shrub and has blood-red flowers.
2 Rosa pomifera, the Apple Rose, has resin-scented leaves and bright pink semi-double flowers.
3 The pale yellow blooms of Rosa primula, from Turkestan and northern China, grow on a widely spreading shrub.
4 Rosa rugosa 'Sarah van Fleet'.

*brunonii* and its allies. *R. moyesii* forms a large shrub to 10 feet or more with few prickles, purplish canes, attractive dark leaves, 2-inch pink to blood-red flowers and 2–2½-inch shiny red hips. It makes a spectacular specimen shrub for floral and fruit display; 'Fred Streeter' and 'Geranium' are two selected cultivars; var. *fargesii* has smaller, almost round leaflets, western China. *R. multibracteata* bears trusses of small pink flowers on broadly arching stems in July. 'Cerise Bouquet' is a garden hybrid with semi-double flowers and unusual appearance, western China. *R. multiflora*, polyantha rose, is a vigorous sprawling shrub with large clusters of small white flowers. Important both as a rootstock for imparting maximum vigour and as a parent of garden polypom roses; var. *cathayensis* has single pink blooms; var.

*carnea* double pink; var. *platyphylla*, seven sisters rose, double purple flowers which fade through pink to nearly white; var. *nana* is dwarf, recurrent blooming and non-climbing. *R. carteri* which blooms from seed in 2–3 months is referable here; var. *watsoniana* is a curious chimaera with narrow crimped foliage rather like a Japanese maple, and small flowers, China and Japan. *R. nitida* forms a low ground cover of bristly suckering stems with distinctive purple-flushed foliage and narrow leaflets. Flowers deep pink, 1½–2 inches in diameter, eastern United States. *R. × noisettiana (R. moschata × R. chinensis)*, blush noisette, is a lax, tall-growing shrub with fairly double 2-inch pinkish white fragrant flowers in large terminal clusters from July onwards. Forerunner of the noisette roses. *R. × odorata (R. gigantea × R. chinensis)* is a rather tender shrub with semi-double fragrant blush flowers; the parent of tea and hybrid tea roses. 'Indica Major' is a hardy strain used as an understock. *R. × paulii (R. rugosa × R. arvensis)* forms a tangled thicket of prickly stems with 2½-inch white flowers in clusters. Suitable for the wild garden; var. *rosea* has pink flowers. *R. pendulina*, alpine rose, forms low thickets of freely suckering, almost unarmed reddish stems bearing 2-inch pink to crimson blooms and, later, bright red hips; var. *oxyodon* has rose flowers, central and southern Europe; var. *pyrenaica* is a dwarf carpeter for the larger rock garden. *R. × penzanceana (R. rubiginosa × R. foetida bicolor)* is the prototype of the Penzance briars, with sweetbriar-scented foliage and coppery pink flowers shading to yellow at the centre. *R. pomifera*, apple rose, resembles a small *R. canina* but with resin-scented leaves and conspicuous hips like small apples covered in bristles; *duplex* (alias 'Wolley Dod's Rose') is a garden hybrid with larger double pink flowers, central Europe. *R. primula* makes a wide shrub of 6 feet or more with neat, burnet-like leaves with an aromatic scent and small pale yellow blooms in May, Turkestan to northern China. *R. × pruhoniciana (R. moyesii × R. multibracteata)* is intermediate between the parents and has crimson flowers 2 inches across. *R. × pteragonis* covers garden hybrids between *R. hugonis* and *R. sericea*, of which var. *cantabrigiensis* is the best known; it makes a good display shrub with

4

1 'Rugosa' rootstock widely used for standards; var. *kamtschatica* is a less robust wild variety; var. *alba* has single white flowers and var. *albo-plena* ('Blanc Double de Coubert') double white; var. *rosea* ('Frau Dagmar Hastrup') has single pale pink blooms and var. *rubra* very large single magenta purple; var. *plena* ('Roseraie de l'Hay') has large double purplish flowers, eastern Asia. *R. sericea* resembles *R. hugonis* in general habit but the flowers mostly have only four petals and sepals. Very variable: var. *pteracantha* has long, thin, mahogany-red prickles, especially on young growth, and encouraged by hard pruning; var. *omeiensis* has the hip yellow below and tapered into the pedicel; var. *polyphylla* has numerous leaflets (up to 17), Himalaya, western China. *R. setigera*, prairie rose, makes a sprawling shrub with large trifoliate leaves and deep pink flowers $2–2\frac{1}{2}$ inches across in July, North America. *R. setipoda* is similar to *R. macrophylla* but has resin-scented glands on the flower stalks and fruits, western China. *R. sinowilsonii* resembles a stouter plant of *R. longicuspis* and has the largest leaves of any rose. It is definitely tender and is native of western China. *R.*

1 The scented single magenta-purple flowers of Rosa rugosa rubra. The branches are thick and prickly.
2 Rosa rugosa albo-plena 'Blanc Double de Coubert' has double pure white flowers.
3 The Scotch or Burnet Rose, Rosa spinosissima, has cream or yellow flowers.

profuse pale yellow flowers in May. *R. roxburghii*, chestnut rose, is a curious, distinctive shrub with smooth grey-brown branches from which the bark peels with age and robinia-like leaves. The flowers are up to 3 inches in diameter, flat, double, pink, followed by large prickly hips that resemble horse chestnuts when unripe; var. *normalis* is the wild single-flowered species, China and Japan. *R. rubiginosa*, sweetbriar, eglantine, resembles *R. canina* but has glandular foliage which gives off a deliciously sweet scent, especially noticeable after rain. Parent of the Penzance briars, and like them makes a good impenetrable hedge, Europe. *R. rubrifolia* is related to *R. canina* but is distinguished from all other species by the silvery purple of the foliage and stems. Flowers deep pink, $1\frac{1}{2}$ inches across, central and southern Europe. *R. rugosa* forms a stout shrub with thick, very prickly, downy branches, large, solitary, heavily scented flowers and large red hips like tomatoes. The type has purplish pink flowers, which appear in June and intermittently later in the season. Parent of the hybrid rugosas, useful as hedges, at the backs of borders and in the wild garden; 'Hollandica', a hybrid of uncertain origin, is the

*soulieana* throws vigorous arching stems 10–12 feet long with decorative foliage of small grey-green leaves and large sprays of 1½-inch white flowers followed by small orange-red hips, western China. *R. spinosissima*, Scotch rose, burnet rose, makes a low thicket of very bristly freely suckering stems up to 3 feet high in nature but twice this in cultivation, with burnet-like foliage, small-creamy white flowers and conspicuous purplish-black fruits up to ¾-inch wide. The flower colour varies from almost white through pale yellow to pink. Parent of the Scotch roses, of which those with bright yellow flowers are probably hybrids with *R. foetida;* those with crimson are probably descended from *R. pendulina;* var. *altaica* is taller than the type, with larger blooms; var. *andrewsii* has semi-double cup-shaped pink blooms; var. *bicolor* 'Grahamstown' and 'Staffa' are semi-double pink turning white-flushed; var. *hispida* has large single pale yellow blooms; var. *lutea* is single yellow and *lutea plena* double yellow; var. *luteola* has a 2-inch pale yellow bloom; var. *rosea* has single pale pink flowers, and var. *nana* small fairly double whitish blooms, Europe and western Asia. *R. stellata*, gooseberry rose, forms a small shrublet up to 2 feet tall with pale bristly shoots and trifoliate leaves. Flowers large (2½ inches), delicate rose purple; fruits bristly. With the green unripe fruits the plant looks surprisingly like a gooseberry. The type is covered in a down of starry hairs; var. *mirifica* lacks these, New Mexico. *R. sweginzowii* resembles *R. moyesii* but has flattened

6 inches apart to allow for a few failures. *Rosa multiflora* and the polyantha ramblers, *R. rubiginosa* and the hybrid sweetbriars and some rugosas are suitable for this treatment. Commercially obtained plants are all budded on *R. multiflora, rugosa* and *canina* or its allies. If planted with the bud-union below ground level, naturally suckering types will soon form large thickets. But this might prove to be an embarrassment in small gardens, where it is best to plant with the bud-union clear of the soil. However they are planted a careful watch should be kept for unwanted suckers from the stock. Seeds can be raised but a mixture of usually inferior hybrids is to be anticipated as roses grown side by side in gardens inter-cross readily. The few pests and diseases which attack these plants such as black spot, mildew and aphids can be dealt with in the ways described in the article Roses and their cultivation (Diseases; Pests).

1 Rosa virginiana forms a thicket-like shrub, with rose-pink flowers, followed by long-lasting red hips.
2 Rosa xanthina hybrid 'Canary Bird' has bright yellow, wide open flowers.
3 Rosa gallica, known as Rosa mundi.

prickles and glandular bristles on the fruits, north-western China. *R. virginiana* is a thicket-like shrub, notable for its glossy, colourful foliage, deep pink 2-inch flowers in midsummer and long-persistent red hips, eastern United States. *R. webbiana* forms a graceful, very prickly shrub with small leaflets and dainty blush pink flowers 1½ to 2 inches in diameter, Himalaya. *R. wichuraiana*—see under *R. luciae*. *R. willmottiae* forms a large arching shrub with small, dainty leaves and 1–1½-inch purplish-pink blooms in clusters, western China. *R. xanthina* resembles *R. hugonis*, but the brownish stems bear triangular prickles and the young leaves are felted, the flowers more or less double; the true single wild species is var. *spontanea*. 'Canary Bird' is a hybrid, probably with *R. hugonis*, northern China and Korea.

**Cultivation** Most rose species are hardy and readily accommodate themselves to a wide variety of soils and situations, but like the garden roses they are intolerant of overhead shade and do best in a sunny, not too exposed site. Pruning consists mainly in keeping the plants in shape and removing senile or dead branches. Propagation is by division of clumps, by suckers, layers or cuttings. Soft-wood cuttings may be taken in midsummer or hard-wood cuttings in early winter, after leaf fall. The latter should be about 1 foot long and deeply buried (for about three quarters of their length) and well firmed, especially after frost which tends to loosen the soil. Effective hedges can be made this way by planting the cuttings in position about

# S

## Santolina (san-to-lee-na)

From the Latin *sanctum*, holy, and *linum*, flax, an ancient name for *S. virens (Compositae)*. A genus of 10 species of hardy dwarf evergreen shrubs grown mainly for their finely divided and aromatic foliage. In summer ball-like flowerheads on slender stalks surmount the low mounds of foliage. The santolinas are natives of the Mediterranean lands and should be given a sunny position in any well-drained soil. They are particularly useful for the front of shrub borders, for covering banks and for the tops of retaining walls.

**Species cultivated** *S. chamaecyparissus* (syn. *S. incana*), 2 feet, forms a dense mound of grey-white, woolly, finely-divided leaves, flowers yellow, in heads about ½ inch across, freely produced in July, southern France; var. *corsica (nana)*, 1 foot, a more compact form from Corsica and Sardinia, suitable for the rock garden. *S. neapolitana*, 2–2½ feet. often now considered a variety of *S. chamaecyparissus*, differing from the latter in its longer, more feathery foliage, flowers bright lemon-yellow, Italy; var. *sulphurea*, a form with grey-green leaves and pale yellow flowers. *S. virens* (syn. *S. viridis*), 2 feet, forms mounds of emerald-green thread-like foliage, flowers golden-yellow; the cultivar 'Primrose Gem', has pale yellow flowerheads.

**Cultivation** Santolinas are easily grown in sunny situations in any light, well-drained soil. Annual pruning and removal of flower stalks immediately after flowering is very necessary to maintain a healthy compact plant. Old 'leggy' specimens may be cut back hard in the spring to encourage basal growth. Propagation is easily effected by cuttings of semi-ripe side shoots taken with a heel in late summer and inserted in sandy soil in a cold frame.

## Skimmia (skim-ee-a)

Adapted from the Japanese word *skimmi*, used for the species *S. japonica* (Ruta-

ceae). A genus of seven or eight species of handsome evergreen shrubs, with bright, single red berries in clusters which last through the winter, and leaves which are fragrant when crushed. The flowers are inconspicuous, but they make good specimen shrubs or informal hedges. If berried species are required, male and female forms should be obtained, as only one is hermaphrodite, the hybrid *S. × foremanii*.

**Species cultivated** *S. × foremanii* (syns.

*S. japonica foremanii, S. j. fisheri*), 3 feet, flowers white, spring, hermaphrodite, has large, scarlet, long-persisting fruit. *S. japonica*, 3–4 feet, flowers white, spring, Japan; vars. *fragrans*, very sweet-scented male form; *rogersii*, dwarf, compact variety, leaves curved, berries large. *S. laureola*, 2–3 feet, foliage aromatic, flowers yellow, spring, fruits red, Himalaya, needs protection and is rarely seen in cultivation, though it does well on alkaline soils. *S. reeve-*

1 Santolina chamaecyparissus (syn. S. incana) has finely divided grey-white leaves and forms a dense small shrub. It has yellow flowers in July.
2 The white flowers of Skimmia japonica are followed by bright red berries. Often the shrub is in flower and berry at the same time.

*siana,* 2 feet, flowers white, April, persistent berries crimson, China; does not like alkaline soils. *S. rubella* (syn. *S. reevesiana rubella),* 2 feet, flowers pink, male, late winter and spring, will tolerate some lime in the soil.

**Cultivation** The soil preferred is a well-drained, open loam or peaty soil, except where noted above, moist rather than dry. Most situations suit these shrubs. Planting can be carried out in autumn or spring and propagation is by seeds sown as soon as they are ripe in a sandy mixture in a cold frame; by cuttings of ripened wood taken in spring or summer and put in a frame at a temperature of 55–65°F (13–18°C), or by layering shoots in the autumn.

## Spiraea (spi-ree-a)

Probably from the Greek *speira,* a wreath or coil, referring to the twisted fruits *(Rosaceae).* A genus of 100 species of deciduous flowering shrubs widely spread over the northern hemisphere, which can be grown easily in most places, although they flourish in a loamy soil in a sunny position. They bear masses of small flowers. There are two main groups: one consists of those that are early-flowering; the other of varieties that flower in the summer.

**Species cultivated** All have white flowers if not otherwise stated. *S. albiflora* (syn. *S. japonica alba),* 2–3 feet, flowering in June to July, Japan. *S.* × *arguta,* foam of May, 6–8 feet, April to May, hybrid. *S.* × *billardii,* 6–7 feet, flowers bright rose, summer, hybrid. *S.* × *brachybotrys,* to 8 feet, flowers bright pink, June, hybrid. *S. bullata,* 12–15 inches, flowers rosy-crimson, July and August, Japan. *S.* × *bumalda,* 2–3 feet, flowers deep pink in flat heads, June, hybrid; vars. 'Anthony Waterer', flowers brilliant carmine, leaves variegated cream and pink in some forms; *froebelii,* flowers bright crimson. *S. calcicola,* 3–4 feet, sometimes more, flowers white, tinted pink outside, June, China. *S. canescens,* to 12 feet, shoots arching in habit, flowering June and July, China. *S. cantoniensis,* 5–6 feet, flowering in June, China, Japan; var. *lanceolata,* flowers double. *S. chamaedrifolia,* 6–8 feet, flowers tiny, fluffy, in large heads, May and June; var. *ulmifolia,* flowers larger. *S. douglasii,* to 6 feet, flowers rosy-red, in spikes, June and July, western North America, a rampant, suckering shrub. *S. gemmata,* to 9 feet, flowering in May, China. *S. henryi,* to 10 feet, flowers cream, June, China. *S. hypericifolia,* to 6 feet, flowering in May, Siberia. *S. japonica,* 3–5 feet, flowers pink in flat heads, June and July, Japan; vars. *atrosanguinea,* flowers deep rosy-red; *fortunei,* leaves deeply toothed, flowers bright red; *macrophylla,* leaves to 6 inches long, blistered in appearance (bullate), colouring well in autumn; *ruberrima,* rounded in habit, flowers rose-red. *S. latifolia,* to 6 feet, flowers pale pink, June to August,

1 The yellow flowers of Skimmia laureola come in spring in globular panicles. The foliage is aromatic.
2 Skimmia rubella, a useful shrub for winter effect on a chalky soil.

North America, rampant in habit. *S.* × *margaritae,* to 5 feet, flowers bright rose-pink, July, hybrid. *S. media,* to 6 feet, compact in habit, flowers in rounded heads, April and May, Europe, Asia. *S. menziesii,* to 5 feet, flowers deep rose, in erect panicles to 8 inches long, July and August, suckering in habit, western North America; var. *triumphans,* flowers bright purplish-rose. *S. mollifolia,* 3–6 feet, leaves silvery, flowers cream, June and July, China. *S. nipponica,* to 4 feet, flowering in June, Japan; vars. *rotundifolia,* to 7 feet, leaves and flowers larger; *tosaensis,* leaves narrow, flowers smaller. *S. prunifolia plena,* to 6 feet, flowers double, April and May, leaves orange in autumn, Japan. *S. salicifolia,* to 6 feet, flowers pink, June and July, Europe, Asia, vigorous, suckering species. *S. × sanssouciana,* 5–6 feet, flowers bright rosy-pink, in broad panicles, July, hybrid. *S. sargentiana,* to 6 feet, flowers creamy, June, China. *S. splendens,* 2½–3 feet, flowers rosy-pink, June, North America. *S. × syringaeflora,* to 3 feet, flowers pink in pyramidal panicles, summer, hybrid. *S. thunbergii,* to 5 feet, flowers in clusters all along the arching stems, March and April, China, Japan. *S. trichocarpa,* to 6 feet, flowers in sprays to 1 foot long, June, Korea. *S. × vanhouttei,* to 8 feet, flowers in clusters to 2 inches across, along the graceful stems, May and June, hybrid. *S. veitchii,* to 10 feet, flowers cream, June and July, China. *S. × watsoniana,* to 6 feet, flowers cream, June and July, hybrid. *S. wilsonii,* to 9 feet, flowering in June, China. *S. yunnanensis,* to 6 feet, flowers creamy-white, spring, China.

**Cultivation** These easily grown shrubs are happy in most soils except thin chalky ones which are shallow; on this type of soil *S. douglasii, S. menziesii triumphans* and *S. thunbergii,* are apt to get rather poor. Give the plants a sunny position and plant in autumn or winter. Mulching each spring with well rotted garden compost will ensure strong, floriferous growth. Prune the early-flowering varieties hard after flowering, so as to encourage the production of new wood; *S. douglasii* and *S. salicifolia* need little pruning; the remaining late-flowering kinds should have the old wood thinned out in the spring, and the younger growth shortened. Propagation is by suckers, but where these are not available cuttings of young shoots may be rooted in sandy soil under cloches, or in a frame, in shade during summer. The larger varieties may also be increased by root cuttings in winter.

---

### Stephanandra (steff-an-and-ra)

From the Greek *stephanos,* a wreath, and *andros,* a male, a reference to the arrangement of the stamens (Rosaceae). A genus of 3 or 4 species of deciduous shrubs from eastern Asia, which are grown for their graceful and elegant foliage, which colours well in a good autumn in some species, rather than for their uninteresting flowers. Their cinnamon-brown stems are most attractive during the winter months.

**Species cultivated** *S. incisa,* to 6 feet, flowers white or greenish-white, June; var. *crispa,* dwarf form, spreading in habit, leaves crinkled. *S. tanakae,* to

6 feet, flowers yellowish-white, June and July.

**Cultivation** These are easy shrubs to grow in almost any moist soil but they are best when placed in full sun to encourage good autumn colour. Pruning should be carried out annually in early spring just before growth starts. Cut out thin, damaged or diseased shoots, then remove about half the shoots, giving those remaining as much space as possible. This will encourage plenty of young growth from the base which carries the graceful leaves more abundantly and produces a good supply of young and colourful stems for winter display. Propagation is easy; young shoots taken in early summer and

1 Spiraea × bumalda 'Anthony Waterer' in July.
2 Spiraea salicifolia has willow-like leaves.
3 Spiraea nipponica rotundifolia.

---

inserted into sand in a greenhouse, root easily. Quite good results can be obtained from cuttings of bare stems, about 9 inches in length, taken during the winter and inserted in the open ground with a little sand at the base of each. Insert them to two thirds of their length into the soil and ensure that they are quite firm. Old plants can be divided and *S. incisa* can be increased by root cuttings.

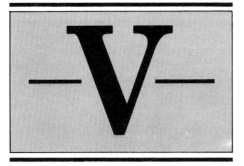

# Vaccinium (vak-sin-ee-um)

An ancient Latin name, possibly a corruption of *baccinum,* a little ˙berry *(Ericaceae).* A genus of between 300 and 400 species, both deciduous and ever-green, mostly shrubs but including a few trees, the fruit being a berry. They are mostly natives of the northern hemisphere, from the arctic region to high mountains in the tropics.

**Species cultivated** *V. angustifolium* (syn. *V. pennsylvanicum angustifolium*) (D), low bush, blueberry, low shrub, flowers white, tinged red, berries sweet, black, North America. *V. arctostaphylos* (D), Caucasian whortleberry, to 10 feet, flowers greenish-white, June, sometimes again in autumn, berries small, purple, Caucasus. *V. ashei,* rabbit-eye blueberry (D or SE), shrub to 18 feet, flowers pink, red or white, fruits black, North America. *V. corymbosum* (D), swamp blueberry, 6–12 feet, flowers white or pale pink, May, berries black, edible, leaves colour well in autumn, North America. *V. crassifolium,* thick-leaved whortleberry (E), trailing flowers red or white, fruits black, North America, slightly tender. *V. cylindraceum* (D), tall shrub, flowers yellow tinged red. *V. delavayi* (E), to 3 feet, flowers creamy-white, Yunnan. *V. erythrocarpum* (D), southern mountain cranberry (D), to 6 feet, flowers pink, fruits purplish-red, acid, North America. *V. floribundum* (E), mortina, 1–4 feet, flowers pink, berries red, tender, Ecuador. *V. glaucoalbum* (E), 2 feet, leaves blue-white beneath, flowers pinkish with persistent blue-white bracts, fruits black with a blue-white bloom, Himalaya. *V. hirsutum* (D), hairy huckleberry, 2 feet, flowers white, tinged pink, fruits purplish-black, edible, North America. *V. macrocarpon* (syn. *Oxycoccus macrocarpus*) (E), American cranberry, prostrate, creeping shrub, flowers pink, summer, berries scarlet; cultivars grown for the fruit, North America, northern Asia. *V. melanocarpum* (D), Georgia blueberry, to 4½ feet, flowers white or greenish, fruits purple, North America. *V. membranaceum* (D), greenish or pinkish-white flowers, fruits black, North America. *V. moupinense* (E), to 2 feet, flowers pink, fruits purple-black, western China. *V. myrsinites* (E), evergreen blueberry, low bush, flowers white, berries blue-black, North America. *V. myrtilloides* (D), sour top, to 1½ feet, flowers greenish or reddish,

**1 The Cowberry, Vaccinium vitis-idaea, an evergreen creeping shrub.**
**2 Vaccinium macrocarpon, the American Cranberry.**
**3 The Thin-leaved Bilberry, Vaccinium membranaceum, from America resembles the British native Bilberry.**

fruits blue-black, sweet, North America. *V. myrtillus* (D), creeping bilberry, whortleberry, whinberry, to 1 foot, flowers pink, fruits blue-black, Europe (including Britain), northern Asia. *V. nummularia* (E), to 18 inches, flowers pink, fruits black, edible; hardy in mild districts, ideal for unheated greenhouse, northern India. *V. ovalifolium* (D), oval-leaved blueberry, to 12 feet, flowers pink, fruits dark blue, North America. *V. ovatum* (E), to 10 feet, flowers white, fruit black, western North America. *V. oxycoccus* (E), small cranberry, straggling, flowers pink, fruits red, Europe, Asia, North America. *V. padifolium* (D), Madeiran whortleberry, shrub, 6–9 feet, flowers yellowish tinged purple, berries dark blue, Madeira, slightly tender. *V. pallidum* (D), dry-land blueberry, to 3 feet, flowers white, or white tinged red, fruits blue, North America. *V. parvifolium* (D), to 6 feet,

flowers pinkish-white, fruits red, North America. *V. retusum* (E), to 1 foot, flowers white and red, May, Himalaya. *V. simulatum* (D), 3–4 feet, flowers white, berries blue, North America. *V. urceolatum* (E), to 6 feet, flowers pink, fruits black, western China, tender. *V. virgatum* (D), southern black blueberry, to 3 feet, flowers white or pink, fruits black, North America. *V. vitis-idaea* (E), cowberry, mountain cranberry, dwarf, creeping shrub, flowers white or pink, June onwards, fruits red, acid, edible, an attractive and useful shrub for carpeting, particularly in heath or woodland gardens, Europe (including Britain), northern Asia, eastern North America.

**Cultivation** Vacciniums thrive in acid, heathy soils, usually in moist conditions, and combine well with rhododendrons and similar ericaceous plants. The smaller, choicer species do well in rock gardens or, when tender, in unheated alpine houses. Planting can be carried out from October to March–April. Propagation is from seed placed in sandy peat in spring, with a temperature of 55–65°F (13–18°C), or in many species by division, or from layers in autumn, or by cuttings of half-ripe shoots taken in summer, and placed in a shady frame.

## Viburnum (vi-bur-num)

The ancient Latin name for the British native wayfaring tree *(V. lantana)* *(Caprifoliaceae).* Shrubs and a few trees widespread over the northern temperate zone, mostly deciduous but some evergreen, with opposite leaves. The numerous flowers, generally white and sweetly scented, are closely packed into heads. The fruits are berries, which in some species are very decorative. Unless otherwise stated, the following named species normally reach between 5 and 7 feet. There are about 200 species from Europe, North and Central America, North Africa and northern Asia.

**Species cultivated** *V. acerifolium* (D), dockmackie, leaves maple-like, colouring well in autumn, flowers and red fruit undistinguished, North America. *V. alnifolium* (D), hobble bush (from the frequent habit of the lower branches taking root), acid soil and woodland conditions, large inflorescences, leaves turning red in autumn, North America. *V. betulifolium* (D), shrub to 12 feet, huge clusters of red berries hanging on far into the winter, China. *V. bitchiuense* (D), shrub to 10 feet, flowers white, sweetly-scented, April and May, berries black, Japan. *V. x bodnantense (V. fragrans* x *V. grandiflorum)* (D), valuable winter-flowering shrub with white flowers pink-flushed, fragrant, hybrid, the cultivar 'Dawn' is the best form. *V. buddleifolium* (SE), leaves unusually long and narrow, berries red to black, China. *V. x burkwoodii (V. carlesii* x *V. utile)* (E), valuable shrub, flowers sweetly-scented, white, pink in bud, early spring, of great adaptability and hardiness, without the leaf-curl often affecting *V. carlesii;* 'Park Farm Hybrid' has larger flowers in late spring. *V. calvum* (E) leaves small, leathery, flowers

white, fruits lustrous blue-black, China. *V. x carlcephalum (V. carlesii* x *V. macrocephalum)* (D), vigorous, erect shrub, flowers scented, in large heads, May, hybrid. *V. carlesii* (D), a rounded shrub, flowers, sweetly scented, pink in bud, opening to white, in rounded heads, April and May, Korea, subject to leaf-curl. *V. cassinoides* (D), withe-rod, leaves colour well in autumn, flowers, yellowish-white, June, berries blue-black, North America; var. *nanum,* smaller; neither will grow on chalk. *V. cinnamomifolium* (E), shrub or small tree, to 18 feet, berries blue-black, China. *V. davidii* (E), to 5 feet, leaves dark green, wrinkled, grown also for its turquoise-blue berries on the female plants, produced only when a male is present, China. *V. dentatum* (D), arrow-wood, shrub to 15 feet, with straight shoots rising from the base, fruits small, blue-black, unsuitable for chalk, North America. *V. dilatatum* (D), shrub to 18 feet, flowers white, profusely borne June,

fruits scarlet, numerous only if two or more bushes are grown, Japan. *V. erubescens* (D), tender shrub or small tree, flowers pinkish, June or July, berries red changing to black, China, Nepal; var. *gracilipes,* hardy, inflorescences larger. *V. foetidum* (SE), shrub to 10 feet, berries scarlet, the wood, when bruised, smells unpleasant, China, India. *V. fragrans* (D), 10–15 feet, flowers pinkish, sweetly-scented, autumn to spring before the leaves, China; vars. *candidissimum,* flowers white; *compactum,* a smaller form, not usually satisfactory. *V. furcatum* (D), to 12 feet, fine autumn leaf colour, grows well in lime-free woodland soils, Japan. *V. grandiflorum,* similar to *V. fragrans,* but with larger, deeper-coloured flowers. *V. harryanum* (E), to 10 feet, fruits shining black, China. *V. x hillieri (V. erubescens* x *V. henryi)* (SE), flowers cream, fruits red, becoming black; the unfolding leaves copper-tinted becoming suffused with bronze-red in winter, hybrid;

98

6

7

1 The evergreen Viburnum × burkwoodii has sweetly scented flowers.
2 The deciduous Viburnum dilatatum has a profusion of creamy-white flowers followed by scarlet berries where male and female forms are grown.
3 Viburnum betulifolium has shining dark red berries.
4 Viburnum opulus xanthocarpum, the yellow-fruited form of the Snowball Tree, carries its yellow berries throughout the winter.
5 Viburnum tomentosum 'Lanarth Variety'.
6 Viburnum × bodnantense 'Dawn' has white pink-flushed flowers.
7 Viburnum opulus sterile, the Snowball Tree, has solid ball-like clusters of flowers.

'Winton' is the best cultivar. *V. hupehense* (D), flowers white, early summer, fruits orange, finally scarlet in heavy trusses, leaves colour early in the autumn, China. *V. ichangense* (D), 5 feet or more, berries red, China. *V. japonicum* (syn. *V. macrophyllum*) (E), slow-growing, stout bush, flowers white, sweetly scented, June, berries red, Japan. *V. × juddii (V. carlesii × V. bitchiuense)* (D), open shrub, leaves shining green, flowers sweet-scented, in large heads, pink, becoming white, April and May, hybrid. *V. lantana* (D), wayfaring tree, large bush, or tree to 15 feet, flowers white, May and June, fruits small red, turning black, usually found on calcareous soils, Europe, including Britain. *V. lentago* (D), sheepberry, shrub or small tree, 20–30 feet, flowers creamy-white, fragrant, May and June, fruits blue-black, covered with bloom, leaves colour well in autumn, North America. *V. lobophyllum* (D), flowers white, June and July, fruits

bright red, China. *V. macrocephalum* (SE, D), Chinese snow-ball tree, to 12 feet, flowers white in large, globular trusses to 9 inches in diameter, needs good soil and shelter. *V. mongolicum* (D), spreading shrub, flowers white, May, fruits black, Siberia. *V. nudum* (D), 10–15 feet, leaves shiny, colouring well in autumn, flowers yellowish-white, freely borne, early June, berries blue-black unsuitable for chalk, North America. *V. odoratissimum* (E), leaves large, flowers pure white, scented, August, berries red, thrives in mild conditions only, when it may reach 20 feet, China, India. *V. opulus* (D), guelder rose, 10–12 feet, flowers white ('Whitsun bosses'), berries red, translucent, hanging on after the leaves, which colour brilliantly in autumn—particularly on lime and chalk, Europe, North Africa; vars. *compactum,* much smaller than the type; *nanum,* curious dwarf, tufted form which does not normally flower, 'Notcutt's Variety', large flowers and fruits;

*sterile,* has only the large sterile flowers justifying the name snowball-tree, but not producing berries; *xanthocarpum,* fruits yellow, persistent. *V. phlebotrichum* (D), flowers in nodding spikes, May, berries bright red, Japan. *V. propinquum* (E), leaves glossy, flowers greenish-white, June, berries blue-black, China; var. *lanceolatum,* leaves narrower. *V. × rhytidophylloides (V. rhytidophyllum × V. lantana),* very vigorous shrub somewhat like the next species, one of its parents, hybrid. *V. rhytidophyllum* (E), large, spreading, striking shrub to 20 feet, leaves distinctively wrinkled on the upper surface; flowerheads are formed in autumn, flowers yellowish or pinkish-white, opening in spring, berries red, turning black, freely produced only when two plants are present, China. *V. sargentii* resembles *V. opulus;* var. *flavum,* fruits yellow. *V. setigerum* (syn. *V. theiferum*) (D), flowers white, May and June, berries yellow, becoming brilliant red, the leaves continually change colour, China. *V. suspensum* (E), tender, flowers fragrant, white, rose-tinted, March, Japan. *V. tinus* (E), laurustinus (not a British native), grown in Britain for 400 years on account of its autumn to early spring flowering, 10–15 feet, flowers white, berries (not often produced) blue turning black, south-eastern Europe; vars. and cultivars include 'Eve Price', buds and flowers pink; 'French White', flowers particularly white; *hirtum,* stouter leaves (rather tender); *lucidum,* broader leaves and larger flowers (rather tender); *purpureum,* leaves darker than the type; *variegatum* (tender), leaves variegated with gold. *V. tomentosum* (D), to 10 feet, shrub of distinctive form on account of its horizontal branches which carry many snowball-like flowers on their upper surfaces, late May and early June, leaves colour in autumn, China, Japan, vars. and cultivars include 'Lanarth', most vigorous in growth; *mariesii*, extremely floriferous; *sterile (plicatum)* flowerheads lasting longer than in the type; *sterile grandiflorum*, a larger form. *V. trilobum* (syn. *V. opulus americanum*) (D), American cranberry bush, resembles *V. opulus* though the fruit turns scarlet in July and hangs through the winter. *V. utile* (E), slender-branched shrub, flowers white, May, berries blue-black, China. *V. wrightii* (D), tall shrub, flowers white, May, fruits red, Japan; var. *hessei*, dwarf form with large red berries.

**Cultivation** The viburnums are generally hardy shrubs thriving in any reasonably good moist soil. Little pruning is needed or desirable. In some species, as noted, the sexes are on different bushes and both must be grown to produce berries. On others, far more berries are produced if a second plant is present to provide cross-fertilisation. Propagation of the species can be from seed, but all kinds can be grown from cuttings, using any of the accepted methods, or by layering.

# W

## Weigela (wy-gee-la)

Commemorating the German Professor C. E. von Weigel (1748–1831) *(Caprifoliaceae)*. Deciduous shrubs with opposite leaves, the showy flowers for which they are cultivated resembling a foxglove in shape. All flower in May and June. They were formerly included in the genus *Diervilla*. There are about 12 species distributed in eastern Asia, and upwards of 40 hybrids and cultivars are recorded.

**Species cultivated** *W. coraeensis,* to 10 feet, flowers at first pale pink or whitish becoming carmine. *W. florida,* to 7 feet, flowers rosy-pink outside, paler within; vars. *foliis purpureis,* smaller with purple foliage and pink flowers; *variegata,* leaves margined with creamy white and pink flowers; *venusta,* smaller leaves and rosy-pink flowers. *W. hortensis,* 5–6 feet, flowers carmine; var. *nivea,* large pure white flowers. *W. japonica,* 6–7 feet, flowers whitish at first, changing to carmine; var. *sinica,* taller. *W. middendorfiana,* 2–4 feet, compact shrub, flowers striking yellow marked orange. Hybrids include 'Abel Carrière' flowers large soft rose; 'Bristol Ruby', ruby-red,

free flowering; 'Buisson Fleur', early and scented, rose with yellow stripe; 'Candida' white; 'Conquête', large pink flowers; 'Descartes', very dark crimson; 'Esperance', pale pink tinged pale yellow; 'Eva Rathke', deep crimson, late flowering and of slow growth. 'Fairy', clear soft rose with deeper markings; 'Fleur de Mai', early flowering, carmine fading to pink; 'Gustave Mallet', rose coloured; 'Heroine', pale pink; 'Ideal', early pale pink; 'La Perle', creamy white, flushed pink; 'Le Printemps', large, flowers,

---

The weigelas are handsome shrubs.
1 Weigela florida.
2 'Newport Red', a fine cultivar.
3 Weigela florida variegata.

---

peach pink; 'Lavallei', crimson with prominent white stigma; 'Looymansii Aurea', light golden foliage, flowers pink, needing some shade; 'Majestueux', pink within, deeper pink without; 'Mont Blanc', white, scented; 'Newport Red', bright red, 'Othello', clear pink; 'Stelnzneri', bright pink, 'Styriaca', rose-crimson; 'Vanhouttei', two shades of clear pink.

**Cultivation** Weigelas will thrive in any reasonably good soil in an open situation, though doing even better on fertile, moist soils. *D. middendorfiana,* however, needs some shelter and shade. As flowering takes place on last year's growth, pruning should consist of removing this after flowering. Propagation is from cuttings in late summer.

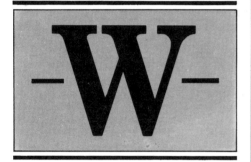

# EVERGREENS

Evergreens have an important role to play in our gardens, particularly during the winter, when their value is so much enhanced by the way in which they brighten otherwise dreary surroundings.

It is not, however, at this season alone that they add their lustre to the garden scene. In spring and summer, as well, their foliage, in many instances a rich dark green in colour and glossy in texture, provides interesting contrasts to the more delicate green of deciduous shrubs and trees. It acts also as an interesting foil to the brilliant colours of the floral displays of spring and high summer, while in autumn, its sombre hues make the leaf colours and bright berries shine more intensely by contrast

Although some herbaceous plants might be called evergreen, in the sense that their summer foliage does not die down in winter, and there are a few trees, such as the holly and the holm oak, that retain their leaves all the year round, in general, when we talk about evergreens, we are thinking of shrubs.

**Many evergreens have additional value in fragrant flowers or showy fruits.**
**1 The brilliant red young foliage of Pieris forrestii turns pale green as the season advances.**
**2 The shrub Phillyrea decora grows up to 10 feet. The smooth leaves droop to display spikes of flower.**
**3 Griselinia littoralis variegata, from New Zealand, grows up to 20 feet, and has leathery variegated leaves.**
**4 Rhododendron 'Temple Belle' has large single, bell-like flowers. The foliage is soft in both colour and texture.**
**5 Aucuba japonica crotonoides has shining leaves spotted with creamy-white. The white flowers are in early spring.**
**6 Santolina neopolitana, the Lavender Cotton, a sub-shrub, with yellow button flowers in July. The foliage is silver grey.**
**7 Berberis darwinii, a thorny plant, has small decorative orange flowers in early summer, followed by purplish fruits.**

## A selection of genera containing evergreen shrubs

| | | | | |
|---|---|---|---|---|
| Adenocarpus | Danae | Halimiocistus | Mahonia | Rhamnus |
| Andromeda | Daphne | Halimium | Myrtus | Rhododendron |
| Atriplex | Desfontainea | Hebe | Nandina | Rosmarinus |
| Aucuba | Elaeagnus | Hedera | Olearia | Ruscus |
| Azara | Embothrium | Helianthemum | Osmanthus | Santolina |
| Berberis | Erica | Hypericum | Osmarea | Sarcococca |
| Buxus | Eriobotrya | Ilex | Pachysandra | Senecio |
| Calluna | Escallonia | Itea | Pernettya | Skimmia |
| Camellia | Eucryphia | Kalmia | Philesia | Stranvaesia |
| Carpenteria | Euonymus | Laurus | Phillyrea | Sycopsis |
| Cassinia | Fabiana | Lavandula | Pieris | Tricuspidaria |
| Ceanothus | Fatsia | Leucothoe | Piptanthus | Vaccinium |
| Cistus | Garrya | Ligustrum | Pittosporum | Viburnum |
| Cotoneaster | Gaultheria | Lonicera | Prunus | Yucca |
| Daboecia | Griselinia | Magnolia | Pyracantha | |

1

2

3

4

5

6

7

# PICTORIAL GUIDE TO
# CLIMBING PLANTS

## Climbing Plants

House walls, garden walls, fences, archways, pergolas, trellises, poles, either single or erected tripod fashion and other vertical or near-vertical features, provide the gardener with another dimension in which to grow plants. There are attractive plants available for this purpose, many of which benefit from the extra shelter provided by a wall or fence.

**Types of plant** Suitable plants include those which are true climbers, clinging to some form of support, either by tendrils (e.g. clematis), by twining stems (e.g. honeysuckles) and those known as self-clinging climbers, which adhere to their supports by aerial roots (e.g. the ivies) or by sucker-pads (e.g. the Viriginian creeper and some of its relations). In addition to these true climbers, there are many woody or semi-woody plants which are not in fact, climbers but can be trained to grow against walls or fences with the aid of wire or a trellis. Examples of these are the well-known chaenomeles ('japonica'), climbing roses, ceanothus and certain cotoneasters.

**Types of support** Self-clinging climbers need little in the way of extra support except in their early stages. Once started they cling to walls, fences and the like and need little more attention. Some gardeners are a little wary of the more vigorous self-clinging climbers

*The garden brought into contact with the house by means of wall plants such as Wisteria and Clematis, flowering in May*

such as ivies, but, provided they are not allowed to interfere with drain-pipes, guttering, roof tiles or slates, etc., they are unlikely to harm the wall itself. It can be argued that they help to keep the wall dry and the house warm, by providing a leafy covering which keeps off even the heaviest rain.

Tendril climbers and twining climbers obviously need something to which to cling. In the open, garden poles, driven vertically into the ground or set tripod fashion, pergola posts and archways will provide support for twiners, but not for tendril climbers. These will need further support such as wire-netting placed loosely round the poles to which the tendrils can cling. The growths of non-climbers will need tying in to the support as they develop.

Against walls and fences there are various ways of providing support for plants. Trellis-work is a well-tried method and panels may be bought in various sizes. Before they are fixed to the wall they should be treated with a copper naphthenate wood preservative to prolong their lives. Suitable trellis may also be made at home, using lathing, which is obtainable cheaply from builder's merchants or timber merchants.

It may be made to a square-mesh pattern or to the traditional diamond mesh. So that the growths of the climbing plants can attach themselves properly the trellis should be fixed an inch or so away from the wall, using wooden distance pieces or spacers. Old cotton-reels are useful because they have a hole through which the fixing screw may pass. All fixing should be done firmly as eventually the mature plant may be quite heavy. Wall fixings such as Rawlplugs are admirable; an electric drill with a masonry bit is useful but not essential as the necessary fixing holes for the plugs can be made with a hammer and jumping bit. Where walls are painted or otherwise treated it is handy to arrange the trellis in such a manner that it can be easily taken down to enable the wall behind it to be painted. One way of doing this is to hinge the bottom of the trellis to a wooden bar of suitable dimensions fixed to the wall. The top of the trellis is fixed to a similar bar in such a way that it can be undone and the trellis and its plants gently lowered, thus minimising the risk of damage to the plants.

Panels of plastic-covered, heavy gauge wire-netting (Gro-Mesh) are obtainable in various sizes, and these provide excellent support for plants. They may be fixed to the wall in much the same way as wooden trellis.

1 Many climbing Honeysuckles are well known for their delightful fragrance. They are not difficult to grow in any ordinary soil if trained over arches or bushes as in the wild state. 2 Lonicera periclymenum, can reach 10 to 20 feet

Wires, preferably covered, stretched across the face of a wall or fence, about an inch away from it, will also provide adequate support for many plants. However, unless the wire is properly strained it may sag in course of time. Vine eyes (drive-in pattern for walls, driven into the perpendicular jointing, screw-in type for wooden posts) are useful devices for fixing wires for climbing plants. Straining bolts, which can be tightened when necessary to take up any slack, are also obtainable. Lead-headed wall nails, nails with flexible lead tags, are used for individual ties, when it becomes necessary to tie in long, woody growths such as those of climbing or rambler roses.

An unusual way of growing certain climbers such as clematis, honeysuckles, is to let them clamber over dead trees or even up the trunks and into the branches of living trees. It is better to avoid for living trees the very vigorous climbers such as *Polygonum baldschuanicum*, the Russian vine, although this is perfectly suitable for a dead tree, which it will quickly smother with its long, twining growths.

Some climbers may easily be grown in well-drained tubs or other large containers and this method is useful where there is no soil bed near the wall, or in courtyards, patios or on town balconies. John Innes potting compost is suitable but vigorous plants may need regular feeding when in full growth.

**Preparing the site** Most climbers and other wall plants will grow in ordinary garden soil, but of course, they will grow better and begin to cover their allotted space more quickly if they are given a richer diet. The soil should be deeply and widely dug, adequately drained, and the opportunity should be taken to dig in a good supply of garden compost, well-rotted manure, leafmould, spent hops, and other bulky manures, plus about 4 oz per square yard of bonemeal, well worked into the top 6 inches or so of soil. Sites by walls present certain problems which are not always appreciated by gardeners. The soil in such places is often poor, full of builders' rubble and other rubbish buried when the house was built. It is often dry, protected from rain by overhanging eaves. To ensure that the plants do well it is necessary to carry out considerable soil improvement. In some instances it may pay to remove the existing poor soil and rubble to a depth of a foot or so and replace it with good soil from elsewhere in the garden, adding quantities of rotted manure, compost, leafmould etc., all of which will not only provide plant

1 Humulus lupulus aureus, the golden hop, a hardy perennial climber that makes an effective screen in summer. 2 Morning Glory or Ipomoea (a synonym for Pharbitis tricolor), an annual twiner

foods but will also help the soil to retain moisture. Even so, in periods of drought, it may be necessary to water copiously, soaking the site from time to time.

If the soil is replaced it should be allowed to settle for some weeks before planting is done. During this time the wall supports can be fixed in position.

**Planting** The footings of walls usually project several inches beyond the line of the wall itself and to avoid these and the drier soil at the base of the wall, the plant should not be closer to the foot of the wall than 6 inches. Where there is enough room, a planting hole about 2 feet wide and 1½–2 feet deep should be taken out, to allow sufficient room for the roots to be spread out properly. If the soil is heavy clay it is better not to replace it but to use instead some specially made up planting soil. The basis of this might be old potting soil or good loam to which should be added generous quantities of garden compost and leafmould plus a couple of handfuls of bonemeal per barrow-load of the mixture to provide slow-acting food.

The roots of the plants should be well spread out round the hole, not cramped up or doubled over. Many climbers arrive in pots and to avoid damaging the roots it may be necessary to break the pot and gently tease out the drainage crocks and spread out the roots. Some plants arrive with their roots 'balled-up' in sacking. With these the root ball should be preserved; it is necessary only to cut the ties, after the plant has been placed in position in a planting hole of suitable size, and pull away the sacking. If this is difficult it may be left in place as it will rot away gradually and the roots will, in any case, grow through it into the soil beyond.

Planting should be done firmly, returning a little soil round the roots first and working this in among them and firming it with the hands. More soil is then added and firmed with the boot, provided the roots are adequately covered, until the hole is filled. The soil-mark on the stem gives a guide to the correct depth to plant, although it is usually best to plant clematis a little deeper than is indicated by the soil-mark (see Clematis).

Some temporary support should be provided for the plants until their growths reach the wire, trellis or other support and can begin to cling or twine. Even though this is temporary it should be firmly fixed to prevent the growths blowing about and being damaged. Short canes, twiggy sticks, strings or wires fixed to pegs driven into the ground, are all suitable.

**Training and pruning** Left to their own devices many climbers quickly become a tangled mass of growths, new shoots clinging to or twining round older ones, instead of neatly covering the supports provided and filling their allotted spaces. Some initial training may be needed to overcome this tendency. Such training consists in starting the new shoots off in the right direction and occasionally during the season ensuring that they are carrying on in the way they are desired to go. This is particularly necessary where it is required to train the shoots horizontally or nearly horizontally, since the natural growth of the plant is upward.

Shrubs trained flat against walls and fences usually need to have their breast-wood removed from time to time. Very young growths developing from forward-pointing buds can often be rubbed out to prevent their development; otherwise the secateurs will have to be used judiciously (see Breastwood).

Pruning is often needed to keep plants under control or to ensure the production of new flowering growths. Pruning methods for particular plants are discussed under the appropriate article (e.g. Clematis) elsewhere in the Encyclopedia (see also Pruning).

**Mulching** An annual mulch round the bases of the plants, but not actually touching the stems, will help to prevent the soil from drying out in hot weather, particularly near walls and fences, will keep down weeds and will supply plant foods and improve the soil texture as the mulch is gradually absorbed into the soil by the action of worms and weather. Such a mulch might consist of garden compost, leafmould, partially rotted leaves, or moist peat. Late spring is a suitable time to apply the mulch which should be several inches deep. The covering may be renewed from time to time during the summer.

**Providing protection** Some slightly tender plants may be grown successfully against walls in many parts of the country although in severe weather some protection may be necessary. Bracken fronds may be sandwiched between two layers of wire-netting to make an excellent protection which can be placed round the plant when necessary. Wire-reinforced plastic material can be used to make a roll, stapled together along the edges. This roll can be used to surround the plant but should be fixed firmly to a stake to prevent wind movement. Hessian sacking may be draped over the plants in bad weather but should not be too close to them. In fact, no form of protection should surround the plant too closely and it should be removed as soon as possible to allow light and air to get at the plants again.

**Supports** Supports will need some attention from time to time as the plants grow and, for vigorous specimens, it may be necessary to provide further supports in course of time. Many plants in full leaf present a good deal of wind resistance and inadequate supports or those which have been weakened through age, may easily be brought down, possibly doing irreparable damage to the plants or at least undoing the work of some years. Any suspect supports should be replaced as quickly as possible.

**Feeding** In time the plants will exhaust the plant food available in the soil, but before that time arrives some extra feeding will be necessary. Annual mulches will provide a good deal of food

1 Lonicera sempervirens, the trumpet honeysuckle, a tender, semi-evergreen climbing shrub, which produces scentless flowers in July. 2 Jasminum officinale, the sweet jessamine, also semi-evergreen which grows to 30 feet if trained

1 Passiflora caerulea, a beautiful climber for warm walls. 2 Polygonum baldschuanicum, a quick growing, climbing shrub. 3 Thunbergia alata, black-eyed Susan, an annual

in time but spring and summer feeds with sulphate of ammonia, nitrate of soda, Nitro-chalk, all at about 1–2 oz per square yard, or proprietary fertilisers at rates recommended by the manufacturers, are quick stimulants. Over-feeding must be avoided; small doses given at regular intervals are much more effective than large doses given infrequently. Feeding should cease by the end of August to avoid the production of soft, frost-tender growth. Bonemeal stirred into the top few inches of soil at up to ¼ lb per square yard in the autumn or winter will release plant foods slowly during the following growing season and possibly for longer.

**Annual climbers** There are a fair number of annual climbers which may be used to form quick screens if grown against appropriate supports. It almost goes without saying that the quickest results are obtained by growing the plants in rich soils and by feeding them with dilute liquid feeds at regular intervals once they are growing well. The exceptions are the climbing nasturtiums

## Climbers for Particular Purposes

### Annual

| | | |
|---|---|---|
| Cobaea (P as A) | Maurandiya | Rhodochiton |
| Cucurbita | (P as A) | (P as A) |
| Humulus (P as A) | Mina | Thunbergia |
| Ipomoea | Pharbitis | Tropaeolum |
| Lathyrus | | |

### Greenhouse

| | | |
|---|---|---|
| Allamanda | Dolichos | Pentapterygium |
| Antigonon | Eccremocarpus | Petraea |
| Araujia | Ficus | Philodendron |
| Aristolochia | Gloriosa | Piper |
| Asparagus | Hedera | Plumbago |
| Bomarea | Hibbertia | Rhodochiton |
| Bauhinia | Hoya | Rhoicissus |
| Beaumontia | Ipomoea | Smilax |
| Bougainvillea | Jasminum | Solanum |
| Cassia | Lapageria | Sollya |
| Cestrum | Metrosideros | Stephanotis |
| Cissus | Mikania | Streptosolen |
| Clerodendrum | Mitraria | Syngonium |
| Clianthus | Monstera | Thunbergia |
| Cobaea | Myrsiphyllum | Tibouchina |
| Colquhounia | Oxypetalum | Trachelosper- |
| Convolvulus | Parthenocissus | mum |
| Dipladenia | Passiflora | Tropaeolum |

### Tendril

| | | |
|---|---|---|
| Ampelopsis (D) | Lathyrus (D) | Passiflora (E) |
| Clematis (D & E) | Mutisia (E) | Smilax (D & E) |
| Eccremocarpus | Parthenocissus | Vitis (D) |
| (D) | (D) | |

### Twining

| | | |
|---|---|---|
| Actinidia (D) | Jasminum | Pueraria (D) |
| Akebia (SE) | (D & E) | Schizandra (D) |
| Araujia (E) | Kadsura (E) | Senecio (D) · |
| Aristolochia (D) | Lardizabala (E) | Solanum (D) |
| Berberidopsis (E) | Lonicera (D & E) | Sollya (E) |
| Billardiera (E) | Mandevilla (D) | Stauntonia (E) |
| Calystegia (D) | Muehlenbeckia | Trachelospermum |
| Celastrus (D) | (D) | (E) |
| Holboellia (E) | Periploca (D) | Wistaria (D) |
| Humulus (D) | Polygonum (D) | |

### Walls north and east

| | | |
|---|---|---|
| Berberidopsis | Hydrangea | |
| (E) | (D & E) | Vitis (D) |
| Ficus (E) | Lonicera (D & E) | |
| Hedera (E) | Pileostegia (E) | |

### Shrubs, Wall plants (not true climbers)

| | | |
|---|---|---|
| Abelia (D & E) | Cotoneaster | Indigofera (D) |
| Abutilon (D) | (D & E) | Itea (D & E) |
| Adenocarpus | Diplacus (D) | Jasminum (D & E) |
| (D or SE) | Escallonia | Kerria (D) |
| Buddleia (D & E) | (D & E) | Magnolia (D & E) |
| Camellia (E) | Feijoa (E) | Phygelius (E) |
| Ceanothus (D & E) | Forsythia (D) | Piptanthus (E) |
| Ceratostigma (D) | Fremontia (D) | Pyracantha (E) |
| Chaenomeles (D) | Garrya (E) | Ribes (D) |
| Colletia (D) | Hebe (E) | Rosa (D & E) |
| Corokia (E) | Hypericum | Rubus (D) |
| Crinodendron (E) | (D & E) | Schizandra (D) |

KEY:
D        Deciduous
E        Evergreen
P as A   Perennial grown as annual
SE       Semi-evergreen

1 The climbing form of the rose 'Caroline Testout' is ideal for a pergola. Flowering is almost continuous from June to November.
2 The Bougainvillea 'Miss Manila Hybrid', one of the loveliest greenhouse climbers.

which tend to make foliage at the expense of flowers if grown in too rich a soil. However, even these do better if the soil is not too poor and dry. Dead-heading will do much to keep the plants flowering instead of spending their energies on ripening seed. Some of these climbers may be grown from seed sown out of doors in spring where they are to flower, others give the best results if they are grown from seed sown in heat in the greenhouse. The methods of propagation recommended are described under the individual articles on the various genera.

**Greenhouse climbers** Many of the most beautiful climbers are too tender to be grown out of doors (although some succeed in the milder counties) but are fine plants for greenhouse or conservatories. They may be grown in large pots or other containers, or planted direct in the greenhouse border. In lean-to greenhouses the plants may be grown against the back wall and trained up and over the rafters. In span-roof greenhouses they are either grown at the end of the house opposite to the door or in the border below the staging and trained up between the staging and the wall and thence up the rafters. Less vigorous climbers may be grown in pots on the stanging and provided with some form of support in the way of canes, etc. Several of these greenhouse climbers make good house plants.

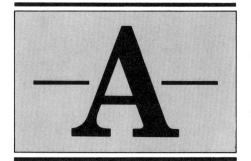

### Actinidia (ak-tin-id-e-a)

From the Greek *aktin*, a ray, in reference to the rayed stigmas of the female flowers. (*Actinidiaceae*). Decorative deciduous, hardy climbing plants of twining habit from eastern Asia. Some species are very vigorous and will climb to the top of a tall tree, while others are more suitable for planting against a house or a wall.

**Species cultivated** *A. arguta*, most vigorous, reaching the tops of tall trees. Leaves large, shining green, white flowers tinged green in June and July. *A. chinensis*, not so vigorous and more decorative in the garden, with large, heart-shaped leaves. Flowers creamy-white aging to buff. The egg-shaped fruits are covered with reddish hairs. Flavour insipid. Where fruits are required it is advisable to plant both sexes in close proximity. *A. kolomikta*, 6–10 feet, slender growths bearing attractive leaves, metallic green in the spring, later becoming variegated with pink and white markings. Fragrant white flowers in June. *A. melanandra*, tall, with numerous unisexual pale lemon-yellow flowers and pleasing dark grey anthers. The leaf stalk is bright red.

**Cultivation** Actinidias thrive in sun or shade and prefer a loamy soil but are not fastidious in this respect. Propagation is by seed sown in April in pots in a cold frame; by cuttings of half-ripened shoots in sandy compost in a cold frame, or by layering in November.

### Akebia (ak-ee-be-a)

This is the Japanese name (*Lardizabalaceae*). Climbing shrubs, suitable for training over old trees, porches or on trellises in the sun lounge. Natives of China and Japan, the akebias are genuine climbers supporting themselves by their twining stems.

**Species cultivated** *A. quinata* and *A. trifoliata* (syn. *A. lobata*) D or SE in some sheltered conditions. Both make growth up to 30 feet. The main difference is in the leaflets, *trifoliata*, with leaves in three parts, and *quinata* with five parts. The flowers are not exciting, male and female flowers being on the same raceme, the latter twice the size of the male flowers. They are dull purple in colour and faintly fragrant, blooming in April, and when they escape being caught by frost, unusual sausage-shaped fleshy fruits

**1** The pink and white variegated leaves of Actinidia kolomikta.
**2** Akebia quinata an evergreen climbing shrub with fragrant flowers.

form, violet in colour. These open when ripe, curling back to reveal the black seeds embedded in a white flesh.

**Cultivation** Light soil suits these climbers best and the growth benefits from considerable cutting back every three or four years. Propagate by layers made in autumn and severed the following spring. Cuttings made in July or August will strike under cloches or in a cold frame, or seed may be sown, once it is ripe, at the end of the summer and wintered in a cold frame.

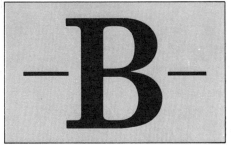

## Bougainvillea (bou-gain-vil-le-a)

Commemorating Louis Antoine de Bougainville (1729–1811), a French navigator *(Nyctaginaceae)*. Vigorous deciduous climbing plants from tropical and sub-tropical South America, remarkable for their brilliantly coloured floral bracts; showy plants for training on a wall in a large greenhouse. The flowers are insignificant, but the bracts persist for a long time.

**Species cultivated** *B. glabra*, 5–8 feet, rosy bracts, summer; *sanderiana* is an exceptionally free-flowering, rich rose variety. Both are decorative pot plants trained on wires. *B. spectabilis*, 15 feet, vigorous climber, lilac-rose bracts, March to June, dark green leaves. 'Mrs. Butt' has large, bright rose bracts. These should be planted in a border.

**Cultivation** Pot or plant out in February in a mixture consisting of 2 parts of turfy loam to 1 part of leaf-mould and sharp sand. Prune shoots of previous year's growth to within 1 inch of base each February. Plants require abundant water from March to September, should then be watered moderately until November, and given no water from then until March when growth starts. Winter temperature, 50°F (10°C). Cuttings, 3 inches long, should be taken in the spring with a small portion of old wood attached. Insert in pots of sandy soil in a frame with bottom heat. Hybrids may be raised from seed sown in brisk heat.

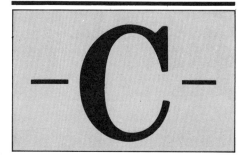

## Celastrus (se-las-trus)

From the Greek *kelastros,* an evergreen tree, probably referring to the fact that the fruits are retained through most of the winter *(Celastraceae)*. A group of vine-like climbing plants, the beauty of which lies in the brilliant fruits of gold and red which remain for a long period through winter; the flowers are small and inconspicuous. They thrive on most

## 2 Allamanda (al-la-man-da)

Named after an eighteenth-century professor of natural history, Dr Fr. Allamand *(Apocynaceae)*. Evergreen climbing plants from tropical America which need warm greenhouse conditions. Their large trumpet flowers make them among the most attractive of climbers.

**Species cultivated** *A. cathartica*, to 10 feet, has yellow flowers in June; vars. *grandiflora*, pale yellow flowers, 4½ inches across, *hendersonii*, yellow flowers, white-spotted in the throat, flushed brown outside, *nobilis*, bright yellow flowers with magnolia fragrance, *schotti*, large yellow flowers striped brown in the throat, *williamsii*, yellow flowers with reddish-brown throat, can be grown in bush form. *A. neriifolia*, erect-growing to 3 feet, with deep golden flowers streaked orange, June. *A. violacea*, 6–8 feet, large rosy-purple flowers in October. Does not do well unless grafted on to stock of *A. cathartica hendersonii*.

**Cultivation** Allamandas can be grown in containers or in the greenhouse border. Plants need copious water when growing, but little after August through autumn and winter. Shoots should be pruned back to within one joint of the main branches in January or February. Train new growth close to the roof. Minimum winter temperature is 55°F (13°C). Cuttings 3 inches long can be made from the ripened growth of the previous season and rooted in a temperature of 70–80°F (21–27°C).

1 One of the most attractive of climbing evergreen plants for the greenhouse is Allamanda cathartica from tropical regions of America.
2 The bougainvilleas are handsome, vigorous climbers for the wall of a cool greenhouse or conservatory.

soils but need plenty of room to twine round trellis and over outhouses as some species will grow 30 feet or more. The deciduous species described below are the ones most usually grown.

**Species cultivated** *C. angulata*, leaves up to 8 inches long, 6 inches wide, fruits orange and red, China. *C. hypoleuca*, large leaves, bluish-white on the undersides, fruits yellow and red in long clusters, China. *C. orbiculata* (syn. *C. articulatus)*, orange and red fruits, leaves turn yellow in autumn, N.E. Asia. *C. rosthorniana*, fruits orange and scarlet, China. *C. scandens*, unisexual, so both male and female plants needed, must be planted to obtain the orange and red fruits.

**Cultivation** Any ordinary garden soil is suitable. Plant in the dormant season from November to March. No pruning is required. Propagation is by root cuttings taken in December; 1 inch sections of root are laid horizontally in pots in sandy compost. Shoots may be layered in August or by seeds which may be sown in spring.

---

**Clematis** (klem-a-tis or klem-ay-tis) Clematis comprise the most useful and diverse group of shrubby climbing plants. The name is derived from the Greek *klema*, a vine branch, referring to their

1 Clematis 'Comtesse de Bouchaud' given an Award of Merit in 1936.
2 C. rehderiana, a Chinese species with cowslip-scented flowers.
3 C. jackmanii superba.

climbing habit. The large-flowered cultivars are showy and glamorous, and the smaller flowered species and hybrids are singularly adaptable and vigorous, and carry quantities of blossom. A wide selection of clematis may be had in flower from April until October.

All of them need some sort of support, unless they are being used as ground coverers. On a wall, they will cling to lattice, wires or to other wall shrubs such as wisteria, pyracantha or roses. Most clematis will flower as freely on a north aspect as elsewhere. Perhaps they look their best when growing in the open over other shrubs, such as lilacs, viburnums and shrub roses. Or they can be trained, with the help of some wirenetting, over tree stumps or used among heather to extend the heath garden's season of interest. They also make an effective vertical feature on a pole, arising from among lower shrubs or herbaceous plants.

**Clematis in cultivation** Most clematis are deciduous and very hardy. The few worthwhile evergreen species need a sheltered wall for protection.

**Species and small-flowered cultivars** This group is especially vigorous and disease-free. Their main season starts in April with *C. macropetala* and *C. alpina*, whose blue, lantern-like flowers are of somewhat double formation, particularly in the former. 'Markham's Pink' is a variant of *C. macropetala*, while cultivars of *C. alpina* include 'Columbine', pale blue; 'Pamela Jackman', deep blue and White Moth'. The evergreen *C. armandii*, with massed clusters of scented white flowers, blooms at the same time.

These are closely followed, in May, by *C. montana*, the most rampant of all clematis, quickly covering any garage or other eyesore, as well as small trees up to 30 feet high. Its white flowers, 2–3 inches across, are usually vanilla-scented. *C. montana rubens* is the pinky-mauve variety, particularly striking in 'Picton's Variety', paler but strongly scented is 'Elizabeth'. *C.* × *vedrariensis* and *C. chrysocoma*, both pink

---

1 **Clematis montana rubens given an Award of Merit in 1905. 2 Clematis florida sieboldii, a synonym for Clematis bicolor, a striking and rare form, given an Award of Merit in 1914. The central boss is composed of purple, petal-like stamens. 3 Clematis 'Nellie Moser', deservedly very popular, flowers profusely in early summer**

and very handsome, but odourless, are closely allied.

The purple *C. viticella* flowers from late June onwards and has a rich wine-red variety, *rubra*. Other variations on this theme are, 'Abundance', pinky-red; *alba luxurians*, white with green tips and 'Little Nell', mauve and white. Somewhat larger flowered, about 4 inches across, are *C. venosa violacea*, white with purple veins and margins; 'Etoile Violette', purple with a creamy eye; 'Mme Jules Correvon', wine-red with twisted sepals; 'Margot Koster', bright pink, and 'Huldine', translucent white, with mauve reverse.

Two buttercup-yellow clematis, with masses of 1½ inch long bell-flowers, from July to October, are *C. tangutica*, with charming fluffy seed heads as well, and *C. orientalis*. The pale, straw-yellow bells of *C. rehderiana* are strongly cowslip-scented.

**Large flowered cultivars** (a) The largest of these, with blooms from 7–10 inches across, have their main season in May and June, though sometimes with later flushes of smaller blooms. The best mid-blues are 'Lasurstern' and 'Lady Northcliffe', with 'Lord Nevill' a good runner up, its rather deeper colouring being

especially valuable in a very sunny position where much bleaching can be expected. For a light satiny blue, the dark-eyed 'Mrs Hope' and the somewhat similar 'Mrs Bush' are striking, while 'Mrs Cholmondeley' is particularly free-flowering, though with gappy blossoms. 'President' is the best-known purple and carries a generous second crop. 'Marie Boisselot' (syn 'Mme Le Coultre') is the most eye-catching large white but 'Miss Bateman' has the advantage of purple-tipped stamens, forming a conspicuous eye. *C. × henryi* is another fine white variety with dark stamens. The red clematis are really crimson and are not quite as large-flowered as the paler coloured cultivars. 'Ville de Lyon' is the best-known and most dependable, in flower from May till late August; 'Duchess of Sutherland' is the largest but not always strong growing. 'Barbara Dibley' is magenta all through but with its eight spiky sepals clearly belongs to a group that is typified by the popular 'Nelly Moser', mauve with a carmine central bar. 'Marcel Moser' is larger flowered but not so vigorous. In the same class are 'Barbara Jackman', bluish-mauve with a vivid crimson bar, and 'Lincoln Star', raspberry pink with reddish anthers. As the 'Nelly Moser' group bleaches to pale parchment, they are best sited where the sun does not strike them too much.

A very exciting and unusual looking group among these early summer-flowering cultivars, carries large double flowers. Usually, when flowering again later on, the second crop comes single. A selection here should include 'Beauty of Worcester', deep blue; 'Countess of Lovelace', pale blue; 'Vyvyan Pennell', lilac and blue; 'Daniel Deronda', purple; 'Proteus', rosy-lilac; 'Mrs Spencer Castle', slightly pinker than the last; 'Belle of Woking', silvery-grey and 'Duchess of Edinburgh', white.

(b) From the end of June onwards, the main display is given by clematis flowering on long young shoots made in the current season, with one extended six to eight week crop. Their blooms are 5–6 inches across. The purple *C. × jackmanii*, of which *superba* is an improved form, is typical. *C. × ascotiensis* is deep blue; 'Perle d'Azur', light blue; 'Mme Grange' and 'Mme Edouard Andre', deep crimson-red, best on a light background. 'Gypsy Queen' is purple with more sepals than *jackmanii*; 'Comtesse de Bouchaud', bright mauve-pink; 'Hagley Hybrid', dusky pink with a dark eye. 'Ernest Markham' is vivid magenta; it needs full sun to flower well, as does 'Lady Betty Balfour', bluish-purple with a creamy eye and a usefully late season centred on September. The rosy-lilac 'Mme Baron-Veillard' flowers even more generously from early August till October, and is happy on a north wall.

**Herbaceous Clematis** In addition to the

1 Clematis orientalis, flowering in late summer, received an Award of Merit in 1950. 2 Clematis 'Ville de Lyon' rambling over a pergola. An Award of Merit was given in 1901. 3 C. macropetala a Chinese species that obtained the Award of Merit in 1923 and Award of Garden Merit in 1934

climbers there are a few species which are suitable for the herbaceous border as they do not grow more than about 4 feet tall, making scrambling stems, sometimes rather weak, which need twiggy support. They are good plants for growing behind other plants which go out of flower in the early summer as their growths can be drawn forward to hide the gap thus created. In cultivation are *C. heracleifolia*, 3–4 feet, with tubular blue flowers; the tips of the sepals curving back like those of a hyacinth, August onwards; vars. 'Cote d'Azur', deep blue flowers; *davidiana*,

3

pale blue. *C. integrifolia,* 4 feet, violet, bell-shaped flowers, late summer. *C. recta,* 4 feet, fragrant white flowers freely borne in summer; var. *purpurea* is a striking form with purple leaves.

The herbaceous clematis should be planted in autumn or spring, in ordinary enriched garden soil and will flourish in sun or partial shade. Their stems die back in the autumn and should be cut down with the stems of the other herbaceous plants. Propagation is by division in autumn or by cuttings of young shoots rooted in a frame in summer.

**Pruning** Methods of pruning of climbing clematis vary according to the season of flowering. They can be considered under three headings. (1) Early spring flowering. These include the small-flowered species *C. alpina, C. macropetala, C. armandii, C. montana, C. chrysocoma, C. spooneri* and all their varieties and

cultivars. They need no regular pruning but if they become leggy or out of hand or are required to occupy only a small space, they can have all their flowering trails removed *immediately after flowering.*
(2) Early summer flowering, large-flowered cultivars, both single and double, that have already been considered as a group. It is perfectly natural for a good deal of flowering wood, in these, to die at the end of the growing season. All dead shoots should be removed in February or March when new growth is sufficiently advanced for live and dead to be easily distinguished. Thus, pruning consists in thinning out.
(3) The species and large-flowered cultivars with a flowering season from late June onwards should be cut hard back, annually, to within a foot or two of ground level. The safest time is March, but the plants look so unsightly in winter that many gardeners take a chance on pruning them in November, which is usually safe enough in our British climate.
**Cultivation** Clematis are gross feeders and amply repay generous manurial treatment with copious water supplies in the growing season. A wall site, where they are so often planted, is the driest in the garden, since the wall itself absorbs so much moisture. Plant them 15 inches or so forward from the wall, when possible, in autumn or spring. On sandy

or chalky soils that dry out easily, work in a large quantity of water-retentive peat, before planting and add annual surface mulches of peat as well as garden compost or other bulky organic materials, while the soil is still moist. Feed the plants generously with slow acting organic manures, preferably bulky, such as spent hops, farmyard or deep-litter chicken manure, but hoof and horn and bonemeal are also good. The addition of lime to the soil is scarcely ever either necessary or desirable

Clematis should always be kept cool at their roots. In sunny positions, either cover them at the base with stone slabs, tiles or with a thick mulch; or else grow shade-casting plants around them.

There is one serious clematis trouble, known as wilt disease, the cause for which has yet to be discovered. Young plants of the large-flowered cultivars are the usual victims. A young shoot or shoots will suddenly collapse and die, having been affected by a rot at ground level. There is no known preventive or cure but, although apparently dead, a plant will more often than not throw a new shoot from the base, some weeks or months later. To encourage this, rather deep initial planting is a good plan, with an inch or two of stem below the soil surface. A plant that wilts repeatedly on the same site, should be given the opportunity to grow healthily by moving it to another position.

Earwigs can be troublesome in late summer, eating out great gashes from the flowers and reducing foliage to a skeleton. They should be controlled with a BHC, derris or pyrethrum spray.

**Propagation** A few species such as *C. montana*, *C. tangutica* and *C. flammula* can be raised from seed, but the best general method of propagation is from cuttings. Each cutting consists of a leaf (the opposite leaf being removed at the base of the petiole), a node (joint) and 1½ inches of stem below this. Select young shoots on which the leaf is fully expanded, in May and June. Keep in a close case (propagating frame) and spray at weekly intervals with Captan to prevent grey mould fungus from gaining entry.

---

## Cobaea (ko-be-a)

Commemorating Father Barnadez Cobo, a Spanish Jesuit and naturalist, who lived in Mexico, the home of these plants (*Polemoniaceae*). A small genus of tender perennial plants, climbing by means of tendrils, usually grown as annuals. One species only is likely to be found in cultivation. This is *C. scandens*, the cup and saucer vine, so named because of the shape of the beautiful long-stemmed flowers, which resemble those of a Canterbury bell. They open cream and gradually turn deep purple. They appear continuously from May to October, or even throughout the winter. A quick-growing evergreen climber to 20 feet, this is particularly useful for large conservatories where two or three plants can soon cover a wall. There is a white-flowered form, *flore albo*, and a variegated form, *variegata*.

**Cultivation** Seed should be sown (edgeways in the pots) in a temperature of 50–55°F (10–13°C) in late February, or in a frame in April and young plants potted up singly when they have made two or three leaves. They can then either be planted out of doors in June in sheltered gardens or planted in a cold greenhouse or conservatory border. Alternatively, they can be potted in large pots or tubs in a compost of equal parts of leafmould and loam with a scattering of sand, and the laterals pinched back to two or three buds to prevent straggly growth. Water regularly and feed weekly with a liquid feed during the early summer.

Plants occasionally survive the winter outdoors in warm areas but are usually so slow to make new growth that much quicker results are obtained by raising new plants from seed. They may be

---

1 **Clematis 'Nelly Moser' is one of a number of climbers used to grow over archways**

2 **Cobaea scandens, a half hardy climbing plant from South America**

grown in a light warm living room, but need ample space and adequate support for their tendrils. A sticky nectar is liable to drop from the open flowers, so the position indoors should be chosen with some care.

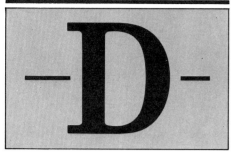

# D

**Dipladenia** (dip-la-dee-ne-a)
From the Greek *diploos,* double, *aden,* gland, referring to a pair of glands on the ovary *(Apocynaceae).* Hot house, evergreen twining plants, first grown here in the mid nineteenth century, natives of tropical America, bearing racemes of beautiful periwinkle-like flowers opening in long succession. They are slender plants suitable for training up stakes or wires fixed to the structure of the greenhouse, when they flower very freely. When flowering is over, remove the dead blooms and prune as necessary to retain a good overall shape and bushiness.

**Species cultivated** *D. atropurpurea,* 10 feet, maroon-purple flowers, in summer. *D. boliviensis,* 8–10 feet, white and creamy-yellow flowers, summer. *D. sanderi,* 10 feet, rose-red flowers, summer. *D. splendens,* 8–12 feet, white, mauve and rose flowers, summer; vars. *amabilis,* rose pink; *brearleyana,* pink turning to crimson; *profusa,* large carmine flowers, up to 5 inches across.

**Cultivation** Pot in a compost of rough fibrous peat with a quarter of its bulk of silver sand added. Young plants are repotted in February and brisk drainage is essential, especially if plants are put into a greenhouse border. Plants in large pots or in borders need a top-dressing of fresh compost annually. Summer care against attack from red spider mite is necessary and daily syringeing is required. Water frequently and give liquid feeds throughout the summer, then give only very little water during the winter. Propagation is by cuttings taken in March inserted in sand in a propagating case in a temperature of 70–80°F (21–27°C). These cuttings are best taken from the new shoots formed after pruning, when growth is cut back to within two or three buds of the previous year's growth in February.

**Dipladenia sanderi, one of the finest of climbing plants for the warm greenhouse. It came from Brazil in 1896.**

**Eccremocarpus** (ek-re-mo-kar-pus)
From the Greek *ekkremes*, pendant, and *karpos*, fruit, describing the pendulous seed vessels *(Bignoniaceae)*. An attractive evergreen half-hardy annual climbing plant. There are very few species and of these one only is in cultivation. This is *E. scaber*, the Chilean glory flower. It grows up to 15–20 feet, clinging to suitable supports by means of tendrils at the ends of the leaves. The flowers, borne in clusters from late spring to autumn, are tubular in shape, scarlet or orange-red and yellow in colour. There is a golden-flowered variety, *aureus*, and an orange-red variety, *ruber*.
**Cultivation** *E. scaber* is very easily raised from seed sown in pots of sandy soil in March or April. Plant out in June in a light, rich soil against south or southwest facing walls, with trellis, wires, etc., for support. Roots are hardy, but in exposed gardens should be covered with old ashes or matting in severe weather.

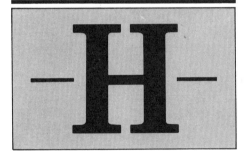

**Hedera** (hed-er-a)
The ancient Latin name *(Araliaceae)*. Ivy. A small genus of evergreen climbing or trailing plants which attach themselves to supports by means of aerial roots. They are grown for their leathery, often decorative, variegated leaves. They were planted extensively in Victorian gardens, and there has been a renewed interest in them in recent years. Several species and hybrids are now used as house plants. When plants reach the top of their support they cease to produce aerial roots, growth becomes bushy, the leaves lack lobes and the plants produce flowers and fruits (usually black). Cuttings taken from mature growth will not revert to the climbing plant habit, but will remain bushy.
**Species cultivated** *H. canariensis*,

Eccremocarpus scaber, the Chilean Glory Flower, is a climbing plant which will grow outside, given the protection of a warm wall.

Canary Island ivy, vigorous climber, 3–5 lobed leaves up to 8 inches across, leathery; vars. *azorica*, leaves with 5–7 lobes, tender; *variegata*, leaves green and silvery-grey, margined with white. *H. chrysocarpa*, Italian ivy, leaves 4 inches wide, fruits yellow. *H. colchica*, Persian ivy, strong growing, leaves up to 8 inches long, 4 inches wide, dark green; var. *dentata*, leaves toothed, *dentata variegata*, variegated yellow. *H. helix*, common ivy, a native plant which may grow 80–100 feet up trees, leaves variable in size and number of lobes; vars. *aureo-variegata*, leaves flushed yellow; 'Buttercup' (also known as 'Golden Cloud' and 'Russell's Gold'), small leaves, flushed yellow; *caenwoodiana*, small, narrowly lobed leaves; 'Chicago', large leaves, 3-lobes; 'Chicago' *variegata*, variegated cream; *conglo-merata*, slow growing, growth dense, leaves small, wavy, suitable for rock garden; *congesta*, slow growing, growth dense, leaves more or less triangular, grey-green; *deltoidea*, leaves 3-lobed, the two basal ones overlapping; *digitata*, leaves broad, 5-lobed; *discolor*, small leaves, flushed red, mottled with cream; 'Eva', leaves small, margined cream, variegation very variable; 'Glacier', leaves grey, margined cream; *gracilis*, graceful, slender growth; 'Jubilee' (or 'Golden Leaf'), small leaves, central vein red, yellow mark at base; 'Little Diamond', central lobe long pointed, variegated cream and pale green; *lutzii*, dense growth, lime green and cream, darker green flecks; *palmata*, slow growing, palmately lobed leaves; 'Pittsburgh' mid-green, cream veins; *purpurea*, leaves bronze-purple in winter; 'Shamrock', very dark green leaves, basal lobes overlapping; *tortuosa*, curled and twisted leaves; *tricolor*, leaves grey-green, edged white, rosy in winter. Other varieties and cultivars may be offered in trade lists from time to time.

*H. hibernica*, Irish ivy, strong growing, large leaves up to 6 inches wide, bright green in colour, usually 5-lobed, useful for ground cover under trees and in other shady places.

**Cultivation** Ivies will grow in any aspect out doors and in any kind of soil. Plant in autumn or early spring. When used as ground cover peg the shoots to the soil to encourage growth. Prune in April and feed as required for rapid growth. When grown in pots indoors John Innes potting compost No. 1 is suitable; provide good drainage. Plants may be allowed to trail, may be trained up sticks or bark-covered branches or trained to a fan or frame of any form. Water moderately in winter; freely in summer, when established plants should be fed occasionally. It should be noted that the varieties are more often grown as house plants and as such are liable to damage by frost, but if put out of doors in late May and gradually accustomed to lower temperatures, will then tolerate frost. Propagation is by cuttings rooted out of doors in autumn or in winter in the home or greenhouse.

Ivy will not damage healthy trees or sound buildings, although the growths should not be allowed to clog gutters or to grow between gutters or down-pipes and the brickwork.

1 Variegated Ivy covers a balustrade.
2 Hedera helix 'Chicago', a cream variegated form grown as a pot plant.
3 Hedera 'Glacier' has grey and cream leaves, giving a frosty effect.
4 A golden-leaved form, Hedera 'Buttercup' covers an old low wall.
5 Hedera 'Jubilee', a distinctive Ivy with elegantly pointed variegated leaves.
6 The black fruit of the Ivy.

## Hibbertia (hib-ber-te-a)

In honour of George Hibbert, an early nineteenth-century patron of botany *(Dilleniaceae)*. Evergreen plants of shrubby or climbing habit normally requiring cool greenhouse cultivation. Several succeed out of doors in the milder climates of some districts. They are chiefly natives of Australia.

**Species cultivated** *H. bracteata*, low shrub, of branching habit, yellow flowers ¾-inch wide, May and June, produced on the ends of the side growths. *H. dentata*, of trailing or twining habit, large bright yellow flowers, 1–1½ inches across, early summer. *H. montana*, 18 inches, of upright habit, ¾-inch wide, yellow flowers, early summer. *H. pedunculata*, 2 feet, spreading branches, yellow flowers, 1 inch wide, June. *H. perfoliata*, trailing growth, bright yellow flowers, 1½ inches wide, early summer. *H. volubilis*, 4 feet, of trailing or strong climbing habit, flowers yellow, 2 inches across, summer, scented, but not pleasantly so.

**Cultivation** The climbing species are trained on a greenhouse framework. All require copious watering during active growth but not so much in winter. Temperature from March to October, 55–75°F (13–24°C) with a winter minimum of 45°F (7°C). They are propagated by 3-inch long shoot cuttings, made from nearly ripe growth, rooted in a compost of equal parts of coarse sand and peat, with a temperature of 55-65°F (13-18°C) in a propagating case. Several species are hardy out of doors in the Isles of Scilly.

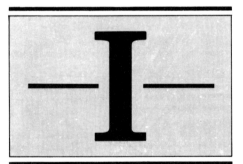

## Ipomoea (i-po-mee-ya)

From the Greek *ips*, bindweed, and *homoios*, like, in reference to the twining habit of growth *(Convolvulaceae)*. A genus of 300 species of evergreen and deciduous climbing and twining herbs, including the sweet potato, and a few trees and shrubs, mostly from the tropics, Asia, Africa and Australia. First introduced in the late sixteenth century. Some of the greenhouse species, which like plenty of root room, are amongst the prettiest of climbing plants. They do best if planted in borders.

**1 Hibbertia, a greenhouse climber.**
**2 The blue flowers of Ipomoea.**

**Species cultivated** *I. batatas*, sweet potato, 2–4 feet, tubers edible, greenhouse. *I. tricolor* (syn. *I. rubro-caerulea*), red, summer, greenhouse. *I. hederacea*, Morning Glory, blue, summer, half-hardy. *I. purpurea*, purple, summer, half-hardy. *I. pandurata*, white and purple, perennial, summer.

**Cultivation** The seeds of annual species, whether greenhouse or half-hardy, should be sown (notch seed slightly with file) 2–3 in a 3-inch pot in a warm house in early spring using a compost of fibrous loam, decayed manure and lumpy leafmould, otherwise the plants are prone to a chlorotic condition. Transfer the plants to a larger pot as required, without disturbing the roots. Train up a tripod of canes until ready for planting. The half-hardy species may be planted out at the beginning of June in a sheltered border on a south wall. Evergreen ipomoeas may be propagated by cuttings or layers.

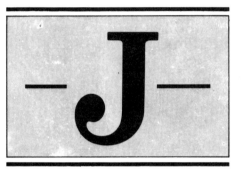

# J

## Jasminum (jas-min-um)

A Latinised version of the Arabic name, *ysmyn (Oleaceae)*. Jasmine. A large genus of climbing, trailing, and erect shrubby flowering plants native of tropical and sub-tropical regions, introduced in the mid-sixteenth century. There are both evergreen and deciduous species, some of which have very fragrant flowers.

**Species cultivated** Stove: *J. gracillimum*, 4 feet, white, fragrant, winter, Borneo. *J. sambac*, 6 feet, evergreen, white, fragrant, autumn, tropical Asia. Coolhouse: *J. grandiflorum*, 30 feet, white, most beautifully fragrant, flowers early summer (hardy in sheltered parts in warm climate). *J. mesnyi* (syn. *J. primulinum*), 6–10 feet, yellow, winter. Hardy: *J. nudiflorum*, winter jasmine, 15 feet, deciduous, yellow, November–March. *J. officinale*, common jasmine, 30–40 feet, white, June–September, very fragrant. *J. stephanense*, 15–20 feet, pale pink, very sweetly scented, flowers June–August.

**Cultivation** Stove and coolhouse species should be potted or planted in February or March, in a compost of equal parts by volume of loam, peat and leafmould with a little sand. Prune them to shape in February and train the shoots to walls, pillars, or trellis. Watering should be moderate during the winter, but copious

1 The white flowers of Common or Summer Jasmine, J. officinale, are very sweetly fragrant especially in the evening during the late summer months.
2 Jasminum mesnyi, with yellow flowers in winter is an evergreen climber for a cool greenhouse or for a sheltered wall in a mild locality.

between March and October. Keep the stove species in a temperature of 55–65°F (13–18°C), and the coolhouse species 45–55°F (7–13°C) from September to March. Syringe daily March–April and give adequate ventilation when weather permits. Coolhouse species benefit from standing outdoors in a sunny place from June–September. The hardy species should be treated as slightly tender in cold districts and the north. Plant them in ordinary soil, rich but well-drained, preferably at the base of south or south-west walls October–November or February–March. After flowering, remove only those shoots which have flowered. Propagate greenhouse species by cuttings of firm shoots in March–September placed in sandy peat in a temperature of 65–75°F (18–

24°C) or hardy species by cuttings 3–6 inches long placed in sandy soil in a cold frame September–December, or by layering in spring or summer.

## Lonicera (lon-is-er-a)

From the name of a German botanist, Adam Lonicer, 1528–86 *(Caprifoliaceae)*. Honeysuckle. This genus of nearly 200 species, is of great garden importance, and has shrubby and climbing deciduous and evergreen species. Many of them have extremely sweetly scented flowers. Most species and hybrids are hardy, and two are among the finest of our native hedgerow plants, filling the summer evening air with their fragrance. The species are widely spread over the Northern Hemisphere.

**Species cultivated** Climbing: *L. alseusmoides* (E), leaves narrow, flowers yellow and purple, July to October, fruits blue-black, China. *L.* x *americana* (D), 25–30 feet, flowers fragrant white, ageing to yellow, flushed purple outside, June and July, hybrid. *L.* x *brownii* (SE), scarlet trumpet honeysuckle, 10–15 feet, flowers orange-scarlet, May to August, hybrid; vars. *fuchsioides,* similar, *plantierensis,* flowers coral-red and orange. *L. caprifolium* (D), 15 feet, yellowish, fragrant, June and July, Europe; var. *pauciflora,* flowers flushed purple on the outside. *L. ciliosa* (D), flowers yellow, tinged purple, Western North America. *L. dioica* (D), yellow and pink, June and July, North America. *L. etrusca* (D), 20–30 feet, creamy-yellow and purple, fragrant, July to August, Mediterranean region. *L. flava* (D), 10 feet, yellow, fragrant, June, south-east USA. *L. giraldii* (E), vigorous, purple-red flowers, whole plant rather hairy, summerflowering, China. *L. glaucescens* (D), yellow, summer, North America. *L.* x *heckrottii* (D), rather a shrubby climber, deep yellow and pink, fragrant, summer, hybrid. *L. henryi* (E), 20–30 feet, glossy dark green leaves, flowers small, red and yellow, June and July, fruits black, China. *L. hildebrandiana* (D), giant honeysuckle, 60–80 feet, flowers fragrant, creamy-yellow, ageing to orange, 4 inches or more long, June to August, Burma, China, Siam, hardy only in the milder counties, otherwise needs cool greenhouse treatment. *L. implexa* (SE), 8–10 feet, yellow flushed pink, June to August, Mediterranean, not fully hardy. *L. japonica* (E), 8 feet, red and white, very fragrant, June and July, Japan, Korea, China; vars. *aureo-reticulata,* veins at leaves bright yellow, seldom flowers; *halliana,* white and yellow, very fragrant, all summer; *flexuosa (repens),*

leaf veins purplish, red and white flowers. *L. periclymenum* (D), woodbine, 10–20 feet, yellow-white to purple, fragrant, June to August, Europe, North Africa, Asia Minor; vars. *belgica,* early Dutch honeysuckle, deep purplered to yellow, May and June; *serotina,* late Dutch honeysuckle, red-purple, July to October. *L. sempervirens* (E), trumpet honeysuckle, 15 feet, yellow and scarlet flowers, June to August, hardy only in the south-west of Britain, USA. *L. similis delavayi* (E or SE), white, ageing to yellow, August, China. *L. splendida* (E), 15–20 feet, leaves bluish-green, flowers cream, reddish outside, June to August, Spain. *L.* x *tellmanniana* (D), 15–20 feet, leaves large, flowers copperyyellow, June and July, hybrid, prefers shade. *L. tragophylla* (D), 15 feet, showy orange-yellow flowers, June, China, prefers shade.

Shrubby: *L. alpigena* (D), 6 feet,

1 One of the deciduous Honeysuckles, Lonicera hildebrandiana grows up to 80 feet and has large fragrant flowers, creamy yellow, fading to orange.
2 Lonicera x tellmanniana a vigorous hybrid Honeysuckle, likes the shade.

1 Lonicera periclymenum, the Common
Honeysuckle or Woodbine, grows wild in
Britain and has strongly fragrant flowers.
2 Lonicera scrambles naturally and is
used here to cover a pillar.

yellow and red, April and May, Central
Europe. *L. angustifolia* (D), 9–10 feet,
pink and white, fragrant, April,
Himalaya. *L. chaetocarpa* (D), 6 feet,
primrose-yellow, May, China. *L. chrys-
antha* (D), 12 feet, pale yellow, May and
June, north-east Asia. *L. ciliosa* (D), 6
feet, orange-yellow, June, western North
America. *L. coerulea* (D), 3–5 feet,
yellow-white flowers, blue fruit, April
and May, Northern Hemisphere. *L.
fragrantissima* (SE), 6–8 feet, creamy-
white, very fragrant, December to
March, China. *L. hispida* (D), 3–5 feet,
yellowish-white, May and June,
Turkistan. *L. involucrata* (D), 4 feet,
flowers yellow with red bracts, June,
North America. *L. korolkowii* (D), 8–12
feet, leaves greyish-blue, flowers rosy-
pink, June, fruits red, Turkistan; var.
*zabelii*, flowers deeper in colour. *L.
ledebourii* (D), 9 feet, orange, June,
California. *L. maackii* (D), 10–15 feet,
white to yellow, fragrant, May and June,
fruits red, Manchuria, Korea; var.

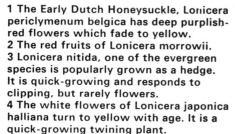

1 The Early Dutch Honeysuckle, Lonicera periclymenum belgica has deep purplish-red flowers which fade to yellow.
2 The red fruits of Lonicera morrowii.
3 Lonicera nitida, one of the evergreen species is popularly grown as a hedge. It is quick-growing and responds to clipping, but rarely flowers.
4 The white flowers of Lonicera japonica halliana turn to yellow with age. It is a quick-growing twining plant.

podocarpa, a better form, branches more horizontal, freely-fruiting, China. *L. morrowii* (D), 8 feet, creamy-white to yellow, June, Japan. *L. myrtillus* (D), 3 feet, creamy-white, fragrant, May, fruits orange-red, Himalaya. *L. nitida* (E), 6–10 feet, densely leafed with very small leaves, much used for hedging, rarely flowers, China. *L. pileata* (E), 3–5 feet, small, yellowish-white fragrant flowers, May, fruits violet-purplish, China, sometimes used for planting under trees or on banks, but does not flower reliably. *L. x purpusii* (D), 6–8 feet, cream, fragrant, winter, hybrid. *L. pyrenaica* (D), 3 feet, slow-growing, cream and pink, May and June, Pyrenees, Balearic Isles. *L. quinquelocularis* (D), 8–10 feet, flowers white, ageing to yellow, June, fruits translucent white, Himalaya. *L. rupicola* (D), 3–4 feet, flowers fragrant, pink, May and June, Himalaya. *L. spinosa albertii* (syn. *L. albertii*) (D), prostrate, flowers fragrant, pinkish-lilac, May, Turkistan. *L. standishii* (SE), 6–8 feet, creamy-white, very fragrant, November to March, China. *L. syringantha* (D), 6–8 feet, rosy-lilac, very fragrant, May and June, China. *L. tartarica* (D), Tartarian honey-suckle, 8–10 feet, flowers pink, May and June, fruits red, Russia, Turkistan; vars. *alba,* white; *sibirica,* flowers rosy-red. *L. thibetica* (D), 4–6 feet, leaves white below, flowers fragrant, lilac-pink, May and June, fruits red, Tibet, western China. *L. trichosantha* (D), 5–6 feet, flowers pale to deep yellow, June, fruits red, China. *L.* × *vilmorinii* (D), 6–9 feet, flowers yellow, summer, fruits pink, hybrid. *L. xylosteum* (D), fly honeysuckle, 10 feet, yellowish white, May–June, Europe.

**Cultivation** Generous treatment of these climbers and shrubs produces good results. On the whole they are not very fastidious about soil, although they do better in one which is on the moist side. The shrubby species do best in full sun, the climbing kinds like shade at the

1 Lonicera periclymenum has formed a quick-growing screen supported by a light trellis by this door.
2 The ripening fruits of Lonicera periclymenum in late summer.
3 Lonicera × americana, a strong-growing hybrid with long yellow and pink flowers in June and July.
4 Lonicera sempervirens, the Trumpet Honeysuckle is an evergreen, or semi-deciduous species for mild districts.

roots, but should be so planted that the top can reach full light. Plant in October or March; any pruning which is required to restrict size should be done in early spring. Support in the form of fences, arbours or walls is needed by the climbers, and since they climb by twining, the wall or fence should have some wire or trellis to which they can cling. The species used for hedges *L. nitida,* is an attractive, small-leaved evergreen of dense habit; which grows quickly and responds well to clipping. It should be planted out when not more than 18 inches high at 18 inches apart, in October or April. Cut back to 9 inches high after planting to make sure that the base is well furnished with shoots. Thereafter trim as required in the growing season until the height wanted is obtained (see also Hedges, Screens and Shelterbelts). A particularly popular variety is 'Baggesen's Gold', which lives up to its name with a sun-burst of golden-yellow leaves in the summer months and turns yellow-green in the autumn. However, the most com-mon form for hedging is 'Ernest Wilson'. Propagate loniceras from cut-tings of firm young shoots in July or August placed in sandy soil in a shaded frame, or by layering, August to November. Seed, when available, can be sown in well-drained soil in a temperature of 55–60°F (13–16°C) in February–March.

## Lygodium (ly-go-dee-um)

From the Greek *lygodes,* twining, referring to the habit of the plants (*Schizaeaceae*). A genus of about 40 species of climbing ferns, found in sub-tropical, tropical and temperate parts of the world. They climb clock-wise by means of their fronds and in nature scramble over shrubs and small trees.

**Species cultivated** *L. japonicum* (syn. *Ophioglossum japonicum*), 8–10 feet, pinnules to 8 inches long, Japan to Australia, cool greenhouse. *L. palmatum,* 4 feet, Hartford fern, handsome fronds, somewhat maple-like in appearance, eastern United States, cool greenhouse.

**Cultivation** The most useful species for pot cultivation is *L. palmatum.* It requires a very porous soil consisting of equal parts of leafmould and chopped sphagnum moss. Copious watering is necessary from March to September, a little less at other times. Most species are much more vigorous and make a large amount of fibrous roots so they need to be planted into a bed of soil, or a pocket made with rocks and grown on the greenhouse staging.

The ferns can be shown off to the best advantage by using thin wires fixed from the roof to the soil, and each frond can climb on its own wire. These fronds can can be trained in different ways, whichever is the most suitable for the house or area to cover. They may also be trained on sticks, trellis-work or pillars.

These plants are semi-deciduous but it is advisable to cut the old fronds off when the young ones start to appear otherwise they will be difficult to separate.

Lygodiums can remain in the same position for three or four years, but a liquid nitrogen feed must be given once a week during their growing season. They should be given a shady position in the greenhouse; the winter temperature should not fall below 45°F (7°C).

New plants can be raised from spores which can be found on the upper part of the fronds. These are sown on the surface of a mixture of fine sand and peat in a propagating case, in a temperature of 75–85°F (24–29°C) at any time. Otherwise plants may be divided at potting time, from February to April.

1 A climbing fern for the cool greenhouse, Lygodium japonicum grows up to 10 feet. It is native of an area stretching from Japan to Australia.
2 Maurandia scandens, a climbing plant which uses its sensitive leaf-stalks to cling to its support.

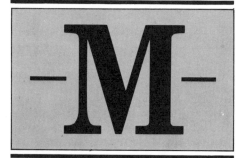

## Maurandia (maw-ran-de-a)

Commemorating Mme Catharina Maurandy, student of botany, Cartha-gena, c.1797 (*Scrophulariaceae*). This small genus, mainly of half-hardy climbing perennials has a few Mexican species worthy of cultivation in the greenhouse. The climbing kinds climb by the aid of their sensitive leaf-stalks, in the manner of a clematis, and are quite suitable for cultivation in a suspended wire basket. The funnel-shaped flowers are large and showy.

**Species cultivated** *M. barclaiana,* to 6 feet, violet-purple, rose or white, summer. *M. erubescens,* to 6 feet, rose and white, summer. *M. lophospermum,* to 6 feet, rosy-purple, summer. *M. scandens,* to purple and violet, summer.

**Cultivation** A mixture of equal parts of loam and leafmould or peat and a little sand suits them. Pots or wire baskets are suitable and these climbers need some sort of support upon which to fix their leaf-stalks, such as trellis work or twiggy sticks. In the growing season when plants are flowering, water with a weak liquid fertiliser, but in winter keep the plants nearly dry, with a minimum temperature of 45–55°F (7–13°C). Though perennial, the maurandias are sometimes treated as half-hardy annuals. Plants may also be grown out of doors from June onwards in sunny, protected places, such as against south-facing walls. They should be lifted and taken into the protection of the greenhouse in September. Propagation is by seed, sown in John Innes seed compost in March in a temperature of 60–70°F (16–21°C), potting the seedlings into individual small pots when they are 1 inch high. Cuttings will root in spring or summer in a closed propagating frame with bottom heat.

# P

## Parthenocissus (par-then-o-sis-us)

From the Greek *parthenos*, virgin, and *kissos*, ivy, an adaptation of the English common name Virginia creeper *(Vitaceae)*. This genus has 15 species of deciduous, tendril-climbing plants, natives of temperate Asia and America. The best known of these is the Virginia or Virginian creeper, *P. quinquefolia*, the leaves of which in autumn, colour strongly in shades of red. This plant in various forms is very widespread in North America, where it is also known as woodbine (not to be confused with our native woodbine, *Lonicera periclymenum*). It is synonymous with *Ampelopsis quinquefolia* and *Vitis quinquefolia*.

*Parthenocissus henryana* is a Chinese plant of much beauty of leaf. On the upper surface of dark green the main venation is in white, while the underside of each leaf is of a pinkish tint. The full colour is most strongly developed when the plant is growing on a north wall. In most species in this genus the tendrils end in flattened suckers by means of which the plants can cling even to the

**1 Parthenocissus henryana, one of the finest of foliage plants for a north wall. It is a self-clinging climber.**
**2 Parthenocissus quinquefolia, the true Virginia Creeper or American Ivy.**

surface of a pane of glass. In the remaining species the tendrils are split at the ends and twine round objects to support the plant. These tendrils with sucker tips, the divided or lobed leaves and certain characteristics of the flowers distinguish *Parthenocissus* from the related genera *Vitis* and *Ampelopsis*. The flowers of all parthenocissus species are green and relatively inconspicuous, nor are the fruits particularly decorative, unlike those of the vitis, which include the grape vines.

**Species cultivated** *P. henryana*, a tall climber needing the protection of a wall, see above. *P. himalayana*, tender dark green leaves, very good red in autumn, Himalaya. *P. inserta*, similar to *P. quinquefolia*, but not self-clinging and less vigorous, fine autumn colour, North America. *P. quinquefolia*, large, dull green leaves to 4 inches long, eastern North America, see above. *P. thomsonii*, leaves purple when young, red-purple in autumn, Himalaya. *P. tricuspidata*, leaves 3-parted, very good red and crimson autumn colouring, Japan and China; var. *veitchii*, particularly brilliant autumn colouring. All the above may be found listed or referred to under various synonyms in the genera *Ampelopsis* or *Vitis*.

**Cultivation** Ordinary garden soil suits these climbers which, though they will

easily ascend into trees, are seen to much greater advantage clinging to a wall, or a pergola, in which situations also the autumn leaf colouring is generally very rich. Most of them can be rooted from cuttings in September or October, placed in a frame, or the long shoots can generally easily be layered.

## Passiflora (pas-se-flor-a)

From the Latin *passus*, suffering, and *flos*, a flower, hence Passion-flower, the Spanish Roman Catholic priests arriving in newly colonised South America found in the plants features which they regarded as symbols of the Crucifixion *(Passifloraceae)*. This genus of 500 species of tender tendril climbers, mostly from tropical America, has many species with arrestingly beautiful blossoms, and some with edible fruit. The only species which may be grown upon an outside wall in the south and west of Britain is *P. caerulea*. There is some disagreement among experts about the colour of the five petals and five sepals. W. J. Bean, the British shrub expert, says they are blue and the American horticulturist, L. H. Bailey, says they are pink, though to the man or woman with normal sight they are apparently greenish-white. About the remarkable circle of thread-like radiating filaments called the corona there is no disagreement; it is purple, inclining to blue. This plant was used by the Spanish priests to give the native 'Indians' a lesson on the Crucifixion as prophetically figured by the leaves, tendrils, petals and sepals, the stamens and stigmas.

**Species cultivated** *P. alata*, tall climber, flowers fragrant, to 5 inches wide, sepals and petals crimson, outer filaments banded with red, white and blue, spring to summer, Brazil, stovehouse. *P.* x *allardii*, vigorous climber, flowers large, sepals and petals white, shaded with pink, corona deep blue, hybrid, cool greenhouse. *P. antioquiensis* (syn. *Tacsonia van-volxemii*), vigorous climber, flowers 5 inches or more across, bright red, summer, Colombia, greenhouse, but hardy in the extreme south-west, particularly on the Isles of Scilly. *P.* x *belottii*, strong climber, flowers to 5 inches across, sepals pink flushed green, petals rose, filaments blue, hybrid, warm greenhouse. *P. caerulea*, vigorous climber, described above, June to September, sometimes into November in mild autumns, fruits egg-shaped, orange, inedible, hardy in the south and west against warm walls, Brazil; the parent of many hybrids; var. 'Constance Elliott', flowers ivory-white. *P. edulis*, purple granadilla, woody climber, flowers to 3 inches across, sepals green outside, white inside, petals white, filaments white with purple bands, summer, fruit egg-shaped, yellow ripening to deep purple, pulp edible, Brazil, warm greenhouse. *P. incarnata*, maypop, may apple, vigorous climber, flowers to 3 inches across, sepals lavender, petals white or lavender, filaments purplish-blue, summer, fruits yellow, egg-shaped, edible, south-eastern United States, cool greenhouse. *P. mixta*, climber, flowers 3 inches or more across, sepals and petals orange-red, corona lavender or purple, summer, tropical South America, greenhouse or out of doors in the mildest places; var. *quitensis*, differing in minor botanical details. *P. quadrangularis*, giant granadilla, vigorous climber, flowers up to 4½ inches across, sepals greenish outside, pink or white inside, petals pale pink, corona banded with blue and reddish-purple, summer, fruits egg-shaped, purple, 8 inches to 1 foot long, pulp edible, tropical South America. *P. racemosa*, vigorous climber, flowers 4–5 inches or more across, sepals and petals crimson, corona purple, white and red, stove greenhouse, Brazil. *P. umbellicata*, vigorous climber, flowers small, purplish-brown, hardy in the milder counties against protected walls, South America.

**Cultivation** The soil mixture for the stove species should consist of equal parts of loam and peat and ¼ part of coarse potting sand. Pot cultivation is quite suitable if a large pot is used, for under-potting encourages the plant to flower rather than produce too much extension of growth. The plants should be pruned in February, removing weak growth completely and shortening the strong shoots by one third. These climbers may be trained up to the greenhouse roof and will stand full sun. The temperature from March to October should be 65–75°F (18–24°C), and from October to March 55–65°F (13–18°C). Water them generously April to September, but sparingly at other times. The greenhouse plants should have a temperature from March to October of 55–65°F (13–18°C) and October to March of 45–50°F (7–10°C).

*Passiflora caerulea* may be planted in ordinary garden soil, preferably at the foot of a warm wall, though even here a severe winter may destroy all the top growth; however, some new shoots generally appear later from the unharmed roots. All species may be propagated from seed, or very easily from 6-inch cuttings, rooted under glass in a propagating frame with bottom heat, from April to September. They may also be propagated by layering in summer.

1 A tendril of Passiflora caerulea, by which it clings to a support.
2 The egg-shaped fruits of Passiflora caerulea are often produced, more particularly after hot summers. They are fleshy but inedible.
3 The strangely beautiful flowers of Passiflora caerulea are typical of the genus. The plant is hardy in the south.

## Pharbitis (far-by-tis)

From the Greek *pharbe*, colour, in reference to the brilliantly coloured flowers *(Convolvulaceae)*. This widespread genus of 60 tropical and subtropical, tall, twining, annual and evergreen plants differs only in botanical details from *Ipomoea* and *Convolvulus,* and the species are often placed in the former genus. Those grown in this country are cultivated for the sake of their colourful funnel-shaped or bell-shaped flowers, usually borne in great profusion. It is a remarkable experience to see, in a large greenhouse, the vigorous growths of *P. learii* mounting to the roof and bearing huge clusters of its large, funnel-shaped bright blue flowers, which later turn to pinkish-mauve.

**Stovehouse species cultivated** *P. cathartica* (E), to 16 feet, purple, August to September, West Indies. *P. hirsutula,* annual, violet to white, Mexico. *P. learii* (E), blue dawn flower, 20 feet, blue to pinkish-mauve, tropical America. *P. mutabilis* (E), blue to purple with a white throat in clusters, South America.

**Coolhouse species cultivated** *P. lindheimeri,* perennial, light blue, Texas. *P. triloba,* annual, pink or purple, tropical America. *P. tyrianthina* (D), shrubby, twiner to 10 feet, dark purple, August to November, Mexico.

**Cultivation** Stovehouse species grow well in John Innes potting compost No 2, and should be potted between February and April. A temperature of 65–75°F (18–24°C) is required in summer, and between 55–65°F (13–18°C) in winter. Water generously in the growing season, but moderately at other times and prune into shape if necessary in February. Coolhouse species are treated in a similar manner, but do not require so high a temperature in summer and the winter minimum can be 45°F (7°C) though 50°F (10°C) is better. Propagate from seed, sowing the annual species three to a pot in a temperature of 65°F (18°C) in March, or, where the perennials are concerned, by cuttings taken between March and August, and placed in sandy peat in a close frame in a temperature of 75–85°F (24–30°C), or by layering the long shoots. *P. learii* can be grown from its own runners which it drops to the soil at the end of the season.

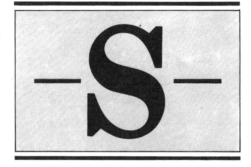

## Stephanotis (steff-an-o-tis)

From the Greek *stephanos,* a crown or wreath, and *otos,* an ear, a reference to the arrangement and shape of the stamens *(Asclepiadaceae)*. A genus of five species of evergreen twining climbers whose stems exude a milky latex if damaged. All are natives of Madagascar. The only species now cultivated is *S. floribunda,* the clustered wax flower, Madagascar chaplet flower or Madagascar jasmine, which produces its highly fragrant white flowers sporadically throughout the year. These flowers are much used in floristry, especially in wedding bouquets. It is a plant for a tropical house where the minimum winter temperature is 60°F (16°C). Plant it in a greenhouse border in an ordinary, well-drained soil against a wall where support is provided either in the form of wires or a trellis. When first planted it may be slow to grow away but once established it will grow rampantly. Train the shoots as they develop. Once growth really begins it develops so rapidly, twining as it grows that if training is neglected such a tangle develops that it becomes difficult to control. Reduce unwanted and thin shoots whenever they develop, and before growth begins again in the spring, cut back all side shoots to within an inch of the main stems and maintain only enough of these to form a reasonable framework. All surplus shoots should be removed. Top dress annually with well-rotted compost or a dressing of a complete fertiliser. Plants may be grown in pots but they need more attention than do plants in a greenhouse border. After the cuttings have rooted, put three plants to a pot and pot on as each pot fills with roots, finishing, usually, in an 8-inch pot. As the young plants establish themselves in each pot, the developing shoots should be shortened. When the final pot is reached, make a framework either with canes or wire and train the shoots over this. Pinch back all shoots that develop to about two leaves and the sublaterals which form, back to one leaf. Each year cut out some of the older stems and tie in their place some younger ones. Feeding is necessary at regular intervals every year but use nitrogenous fertilisers cautiously and always balance these with potash so as to prevent vigorous growth at the expense of flowering. Mealy bug and scale can become serious pests if control is neglected. Spray with malathion when the pests are first noticed and continue until control is achieved. Propagation is by cuttings which can be taken at almost any time of the year. It is probable that cuttings of young shoots taken in spring as growth is beginning to give best results. Detach them with a heel and dip them into a rooting hormone powder to stop bleeding. Insert them in sand, with a bottom heat at a temperature of 75°F (24°C), either in a closed propagating case or under mist.

**Stephanotis floribunda has very fragrant, waxy, white flowers.**

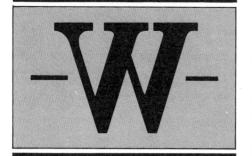

## Wisteria (wist-ear-ee-a)

Named after Caspar Wistar (1761–1818), an American professor of anatomy *(Leguminosae)*. A genus of ten species of deciduous shrubs from North America and eastern Asia, with pinnate leaves and pea-like flowers in long 'chains', climbing by means of the stems which twine round any nearby supports. These shrubs climb vigorously to a great height and as they age the twining stems take on a woody, twisted look that adds even more to their attractiveness and appeal.

**Species cultivated** *W. floribunda*, Japanese wisteria, flowers violet or violet blue, the 'chains' short; June or July and sometimes later; vars. *alba*, flowers white in 'chains' 18 inches or more long; *macrobotrys*, 'chains' longer, flowers lilac, tinged purplish; *rosea*, flowers pale pink, marked with purple; *violaceo-plena*, flowers double, violet. *W. × formosa (W. floribunda × W. sinensis)*, flowers pale violet-pink, which open more or less at the same time on the same 'chain' of about 10 inches long. *W. sinensis*, Chinese wisteria, flowers blue-violet, sweetly scented, opening more or less simultaneously and densely packed on the same 'chain' up to 1 foot long, May and June, one of the most reliable; vars. *alba*, flowers white; *plena*, the best double kind. *W. venusta*, flowers large white, scented, May and June; var. *violacea*, flowers violet.

**Cultivation** Wisterias will grow in any ordinary well-drained soil. A sunny, sheltered position is essential. Provide adequate support for displaying the hanging 'chains' to best advantage. Unnecessary vigorous shoots should be cut hard back in winter. Flowering takes place on short spur growths which should be encouraged. It is possible to train plants as standards on their individual stems by selection at an early stage, pruning away all unnecessary, long growth shoots. Propagation from seed is not altogether satisfactory as poor forms may result. Layering is the best method.

1 Wisteria sinensis, a favourite climbing plant, flowers in May.
2 One of several forms of Wisteria floribunda, with long racemes of purple and white flowers.

# PRUNING

## SHRUBS AND CLIMBING PLANTS

## Pruning ornamentals

Ornamental shrubs and trees by no means all require pruning; certainly not regularly. A number profit from it, however, even though they may survive without it. Pruning ornamentals is simply a matter of assisting them to appear at their best.

Whether to prune or not to prune depends to a great extent on the nature, performance and growth characteristics of individual species and specimens. The subject is not difficult to understand.

**Pruning before flowering** Many shrubs flower during the second half of summer and after. These should be pruned early to allow time enough for the production of the maximum amount of new growth which should bear flowers of the best quality. However, not all shrubs which flower late need pruning—hibiscus, for example.

Among those shrubs that flower in late summer are *Buddleia davidii*, hypericums, deciduous ceanothus, *Spiraea × bumalda*, perovskias, *Ceratostigma willmottianum*, *Leycesteria formosa*, *Hydrangea paniculata grandiflora*, hardy

1 Perovskia atriplicifolia is one of the shrubby plants that benefit from being cut hard back before flowering.
2 Perovskia atriplicifolia 'Blue Spire' having been pruned will throw up good flowering shoots in the summer.
3 Fuchsia magellanica, a hardy species, looks dead in the spring following the complete dying away of growth during the winter.
4 Fuchsia magellanica should be cut hard back in the spring to encourage the production of flowering shoots.
5 Fuchsia magellanica after pruning.

fuchsias, and *Potentilla fruticosa* in its many varieties.

The buddleia, perovskia and ceratostigma should be cut hard back in spring, to encourage as much new growth as possible (in any case, buddleias will become large and ungainly if left alone, even though they will survive). Treat deciduous ceanothus and the taller hypericums in this way, too, if necessary though they do not demand it. Leycesteria may be required to grow very tall; if it is cut back in spring, it will do so. *Hydrangea paniculata grandiflora* will grow particularly vigorously and flower profusely if cut hard back in spring.

*Spiraea* x *bumalda* will soon make a probably undesirable thicket if it is not relieved of some of its older wood and its young growths shortened in March. And, while *Potentilla fruticosa* rarely requires much attention, March is also the time for any pruning that may be needed. Hardy fuchsias—*F. magellanica riccartonii*, for example—when cut back in spring, thrust up strong new growth to bear fine flowers in late summer. The old stems, tied together at their tops, as the year wanes, will give some protection to the crowns against winter weather. Left unpruned, fuchsias flower a little sooner, but in time can attain somewhat unmanageable proportions.

**Pruning after flowering** Early-flowering shrubs on the whole require to be pruned after they have flowered. This allows new flowering wood a chance to arise and mature in readiness for another year's display. It also allows existing unflowered wood scope for full development, so that it may also flower, probably the following year. The point is that many shrubs flower on one-year-old and older wood. Sufficient of this must be promoted and encouraged to ensure regular and worth-while crops of flowers.

The growths to cut away are, conveniently enough, those that have just flowered. This, basically, makes much of the pruning of this kind of shrub self-explanatory.

Forsythia is a good example of an early-flowering shrub calling for pruning after it has bloomed. If the job is done before the leaves have fully developed, flowered wood is more easily seen and removed and the risk of severing the growths that will flower the following

1 Forsythia is an example of an early-flowering shrub that is pruned after it has flowered in early spring.
2 The stems that have flowered of Forsythia suspensa are cut hard back.
3 The branches of the shrub after the pruning has been completed.
4 Ribes sanguineum, the Flowering Currant, is pruned after flowering.
5 Old flowered wood is cut hard back.
6 The shrub, when pruning has been completed, looks like this.

133

1 The gracefully arching Berberis x stenophylla needs no pruning.
2 The deciduous Daphne x burkwoodii also does not need pruning.
3 Some plants do not require pruning at all, notably evergreens. With shrubs such as Rhododendrons the old flowerheads need to be removed.
4 The old flowerheads of Ericas are cut back with shears.

year is reduced. Forsythia is a shrub which is better for minimal pruning, otherwise it may well throw up much non-flowering, leafy growth. Removal of spent growth, only, therefore suits it very well as a general rule.

*Kerria japonica* flowers on the early side and the flowered growth is best cut away when the blooms have faded. *Spiraea arguta* and *S. thunbergii* repay similar attention. Philadelphus, or mock orange, flowers in early summer, so does weigela or diervilla. These shrubs also need pruning after they have finished flowering. They soon make unproductive thickets if the older growths are not cut away. Kept clear of spent wood, they will remain in good form, producing ample new growth which will flower when it ripens.

Syringas (lilacs) require the removal of spent flowerheads when at last the petals have all browned and shrivelled. The buds below the flowerheads should not be damaged; new flowering growth will be produced from these. Thin, twiggy growth, can be cut away at the same time. Brooms (cytisus), too, respond by producing new growth if they have their old shoots with developing seed-pods removed. This pruning helps to ensure that there need be little or no cutting back into old wood as the plants mature, because brooms respond poorly to this.

It should also be remembered that there are plenty of shrubs which do not require any pruning at all, even though they flower in the spring and summer period. The viburnums, which flower in spring and summer are examples. The winter-flowering species and hybrids also need little attention.

A number of evergreens flower during the first half of the year. *Berberis stenophylla* is one, well-known for its sprays of golden-orange flowers and as an excellent hedging shrub. *Berberis darwinii*, with miniature holly-like leaves, produces its orange flowers in April and May. This, too, makes a good specimen shrub and hedging plant. Both these evergreens may be pruned after they have flowered, though when they are grown as individual specimens, such attention is not essential. Indeed, left unpruned, full pleasure can be taken from their annual crop of handsome dark fruits. When they are used for hedging purposes, however, the need for control does arise.

**No pruning needed** *Mahonia aquifolium* and *Mahonia japonica* are two very showy, early-flowering evergreens which need no pruning at all. Nor does the evergreen *Garrya elliptica,* whose silver catkins are so handsome during February, although it is better for removal of its dead catkins. If necessary, light trimming is permissible in May. However, those familiar with garrya's excellence for indoor decoration may have trimmed away some of the growth while its catkins were at their best.

Deciduous, winter-flowering shrubs such as daphne, chimonanthus and hamamelis, call for no pruning, though chimonanthus when grown against a wall will. Laterals will require to be shortened after flowering is over.

Evergreen escallonias, flowering in summer, need no regular pruning; any which may become necessary should be done when flowering is over. Evergreen ceanothus, with the exception of those that flower late, come in the same category, particularly when they are grown on walls.

Magnolias, in general, evergreen or

deciduous, need no pruning. As far as *Hydrangea macrophylla* varieties (the mophead hydrangeas) are concerned, congested old wood and spindly shoots should be cut away in spring, though regular pruning is unnecessary. Faded flowerheads should be allowed to remain on the plants during the winter in order to afford some protection to the young growth buds. Cut the dead heads away in spring.

The general run of relatively non-flowering evergreens, including conifers, grow away very satisfactorily without the need for pruning, but should it become necessary to reduce their height, this should be done in early May. Where such evergreens are used as hedges, light clipping from early to late summer may be done; conifers, however, should be trimmed in early May or August. Rhododendrons need not be pruned unless in time they become straggly. The fairly hard cutting back likely to be necessary under such circumstances should be done in April or May. This will result in the loss of blossom for a season or two, but recovery will follow. If it is practicable the seed pods of rhododendrons should be removed after the flowers have fallen, breaking them away carefully in order not to damage the buds behind them.

**Trimming and pinching** Lavender, santolina and the evergreen greyish-leaved senecios, do not require pruning so much as being kept in good shape. To this end

1 Wisteria is a climber which must be spurred back to encourage the production of flowering shoots.
2 After pruning, shrubs grown against a wall are tied in to supports.

lavender and santolina should have spent flower-stems removed after the flowers have faded and then receive a mere trim over in spring in order to keep them compact. If this is not done, lavenders in particular will straggle, making it difficult to restore the bushes to good condition. Avoid cutting back into old wood.

The removal of awkwardly placed branches in spring, will assist *Senecio laxifolius,* for example, to maintain a good shape. Mere pinching of soft growth tips during summer is an easy means of eliminating wayward shoots and encouraging bushiness. Hebes respond well to April pruning, should they need to be brought back under control. Pruning at this time is often necessary, in any case, to remove frost-damaged shoots. Summer trimming keeps these shrubs compact.

Heathers (ericas and callunas) will thrive very well, left quite naturally, unpruned. On the other hand, those that flower in summer can be trimmed over in spring; the winter and spring-flowering kinds may be attended to after the flowers have faded. It must be emphasised that such pruning is not essential, even though it tends to

improve appearances and may be convenient in individual cases.

**Pruning for bark effects** A number of shrubs and trees bear particularly brilliant bark if they are encouraged to throw up plenty of new wood. Examples are certain dogwoods such as *Cornus alba sibirica*—vividly red—and willows such as *Salix vitellina britzensis*—glowing orange. Hard spring pruning is necessary to induce these to produce the maximum amount of young wood with the brightest bark. *Rubus giraldianus* is one of the showiest of the brambles with 'whitewashed' stems. The strongest and most spectacular canes arise from healthy plants which have been cut back annually after flowering.

**Wall shrubs and climbers** Many shrubs lend themselves to being trained against walls, as well as making good free-standing specimens. Examples include *Cotoneaster lactea* and pyracanthas, both evergreen, grown for their colourful autumn and winter fruits. Prune these lightly during summer, in order to encourage them to grow as required.

Chaenomeles (cydonia, japonica or flowering quince) is a deciduous shrub which responds well to wall culture. It needs to be spurred back when grown in this way. Cut away laterals after flowering, and then pinch out the tips of resultant young growths during summer. Alternatively, leave the plant unpruned until early autumn, then shorten the lateral shoots well back. Keep forward-

pointing growths (breastwood) cut back or pinched back as they develop.

Wisteria is a climber which requires to be spurred back, not only to encourage flowering, but to curtail the long whippy growths which are characteristic and freely produced at the expense of flowering growth. The end of July is the time when, if practicable, all side growths made during the current year should be reduced to about 6 inches in length. A further shortening to an inch or two may take place in November.

*Hydrangea petiolaris,* an excellent climber for north walls, conveniently requires no pruning at all. The hederas, or ivies, also self-clinging, can strictly speaking, be left alone too. But clipping them over in spring will keep them tidy and encourage the production of fresh young growth. The summer-flowering fragrant white *Jasminum officinale,* needs no pruning either, though it may be thinned in spring, if necessary. Old, neglected plants may need more drastic treatment. Thin the growths of winter jasmine after flowering, if necessary. Honeysuckle can be left alone, but thin in spring, if necessary, too.

Clematis pruning is straightforward enough if given a little thought and if basic facts about the genus are noted.

The small-flowered species can be left alone, though if the late flowering kinds among them grow too vigorously, hard pruning in February will correct matters. After flowering is the time to attend to the early flowering kinds, should they become a little out of hand.

Splitting the large-flowered varieties into their groups: varieties belonging to the *jackmanii* and *viticella* groups require hard cutting back to the lowest pair of healthy buds on each stem, every February, just as the buds begin to show green. Flowers are prolific on their new growth of the current year. Clematis in the *florida, lanuginosa* and *patens* groups need no pruning at all to all intents and purposes, after the initial cutting back in February after planting. They may, however, need a little pruning in February, where growth definitely appears dead. And should growth ever become beyond control, then they should be cut back hard in February.

**General winter pruning** This pruning, in general, should aim at keeping shrubs and trees in reasonable shape, keeping branch systems simple and open, and where appropriate, aiming at producing an adequate supply of young healthy wood. During the dormant period, however, most deciduous specimens may need major overhaul, particularly if they have been neglected. Some shrubs are

1 One of the main aims of pruning is to control the shape of the branches. An ornamental Vine spurred back for training over an archway.
2 Golden Elder, Sambucus nigra aurea, is cut hard back to ensure good leaves.

best pruned in winter, when pruning becomes necessary, deciduous berberis, for example. Deciduous cotoneasters can also be brought back under control, where such action is called for, in wintertime, preferably in February.

**Pruning principles** Cuts should be clean and made back to a joint or growing point, or flush to a main stem, so as to leave no snags and stumps. Failure to do this will almost certainly lead to dead snags. With no developing bud to draw up sap, the wood dries and dies. Shrubs to be cut down should be cut right down.

Before making cuts, particularly those that are a little awkward, it pays to decide sensibly the best direction for saw or secateurs, for example. Snags and stumps are very much more likely to arise where there has been crude and hasty cutting. Neither is necessary. Undercut large branches before making main cuts. They will fall cleanly, without stripping the bark.

Pruning must always be purposeful, directed towards maintaining uncluttered and healthy specimens; bearing in mind, of course, that some specimens are twiggy by nature. Pruning should not be mere snipping. It should be borne in mind that many shrubs and trees (as indicated above) thrive well enough if they are left entirely alone. Pruning just for the sake of it is very unsound.

You should never attempt to reduce a specimen to a convenient shape, unless it is a hedging plant. Proper balance and natural appearance are paramount. And, while by skilful pruning larger-growing specimens may be kept within bounds in confined spaces, it is nearly always better to have chosen, in the first place, shrubs or trees of suitable proportions.

All pruning is a matter of doing what is obviously best for individual shrubs and trees, according to their natural habit.

**Tools for the job** Light to medium pruning may be done easily enough with secateurs. There are many different makes. It may be wise to have two pairs, one for lighter work and the other for heavier tasks. It is important to choose a pair which you can use comfortably.

Cuts should always be made in the same plane as the secateur blades. Twisting will result in mangling cuts and straining the tool. Making sloping cuts for the purpose of shedding rain is wise, but cuts must still be made in the same plane as the secateur blades. Cuts should not, of course, be so sloping as to slice wood away from behind a bud or growing point, allowing it to dry out.

Secateurs as opposed to shears, should be used for pruning or shaping certain hedges, where practicable. Examples include the larger-foliaged chamaecyparis varieties and the thujas. Cherry laurels and other large-leaved evergreens should be pruned rather than clipped, otherwise the cut leaves will turn brown and die, and look unsightly.

There are several powered trimmers, driven from the electric mains, portable generators, petrol engines, batteries, by flexible drive, and by power take-off units from motor mowers or cultivators.

Loppers, both short-arm and long, are useful. Short-arm loppers or pruners enable tougher cuts to be made with efficiency and speed where it is impracticable to use secateurs. Both anvil-cut and scissor-action kinds are available. Blades are short and very strong. Long-arm loppers, their blades operated by long arms, a form of remote control, enable distant and more inaccessible cuts to be made.

There is a fair range of pruning saws,

1 Treat large pruning cuts with a lead-based paint or a proprietary compound.
2 Use sharp secateurs and cut just above the buds to avoid damage.
3 A thin-bladed pad saw is useful for thinning overcrowded basal shoots.
4 A hand saw cuts awkward shoots.

both single-sided and double-sided. Especially useful is the Grecian pruning saw, short-handled or long. It is curved and pointed and cuts on the backstroke, making awkward cuts very easy.

Pruning knives were once widely used, but have largely been superseded by secateurs for general pruning. Some craftsmen, however, still use them, particularly in nurseries. They are still useful to have on hand for general purposes, and are still the best instrument for the all-important job of paring smooth the edges of large pruning cuts, especially those made by the saw. They should be used carefully; cuts are best made away from the user.

For the sake of efficiency and safety all pruning tools should be kept in good order, sharp, clean and well-oiled.

White lead paint, bitumastic paint and proprietary tree-healing compounds should be used for sealing large cuts, to ensure that they heal rapidly and to prevent the entry of disease spores.

# INDEX

Only generic names have been included from the main alphabetical sequences of shrubs and climbers;
specific and varietal names have only been included where they occur in the introductions or are illustrated.
Page numbers in *italic* refer to illustrations.

## A

*Abelia*, 20, 109
  *A. grandiflorum*, *20*
*Abeliophyllum*, 20
  *A. distichum*, 20
*Abutilon*, 21, 109
  *A. 'Master Hugh'*, *21*
  *A. megapotamicum*, *21*
  *A. vitifolium album*, *21*
*Acer japonicum*, 13
  *A. palmatum dissectum*
  *atropurpureum*, 16
  *A.p. dissectum palmatifidum*, 16
*Actinidia*, 109, 110
  *A. kolomikta*, *110*
*Adenocarpus*, 109
*Aesculus parviflora*, 13
*Akebia*, 109, 110
  *A. quinata*, *110*
*Allamanda*, 109, 111
  *A. cathartica*, *111*
*Ampelopsis*, 109
  *A. veitchii*, 17
*Antigonon*, 109
*Araujia*, 109
*Arbutus unedo*, 13
*Aristolochia*, 109
*Aronia arbutifolia*, 13
*Artemisia abrotanum*, 13
*Arundinaria*, 13
*Asparagus*, 109
*Aucuba japonica*, 13, *14*
autumn colour, 16-18
azaleas *see Rhododendron*
*Azara lanceolata*, 13
  *A. microphylla*, 13

## B

*Bauhinia*, 109
*Beaumontia*, 109
*Berberidopsis*, 109
*Berberis*, 13, 22-3
  *B. 'Barbarossa'*, *22*
  *B. 'Bountiful'*, 18
  *B. 'Buccaneer'*, 18
  *B. 'Cherry Ripe'*, 18
  *B. darwinii*, 18, *22*, 134
  *B. gagnepainii*, 22
  *B. morrisonsiensis*, 18
  *B.* × *rubrostilla*, *23*
  *B.* × *stenophylla*, 134, *134*
  *B. thunbergii*, 16, 18
  *B.t. atropurpurea*, 16, *23*
  *B. verruculosa*, 16
*Billardiera*, 109
*Bomarea*, 109
*Bougainvillea*, 109, 111, *111*
broom, 12, 134
*Buddleia*, 13, 24-5, 109
  *B. davidii*, 12, *24*, 132
  *B. globosa*, 24
*Buxus sempervirens*, 13

## C

*Callicarpa*, 25
  *C. giraldiana*, *25*
  *C. rubella*, 25
*Calluna*, 26, 135
  *C. 'Multicolor'*, *26*
  *C. 'Ruth Sparkes'*, *26*
  *C. vulgaris*, 26
*Calystegia*, 109
*Camellia*, 10, *12*, 13, 26-7, 109
  *C. japonica 'Tricolor'*, *27*
  *C. 'Lady Clare'*, 27
  *C.* × *williamsii*, *12*
  *C.* × *williamsii 'Donation'*, 27
*Caryopteris* × *clandonensis*, 14, 16
*Cassia*, 109

*Ceanothus*, 28-9, 109, 132
  *C. dentatus*, 28
  *C. thyrsiflorus*, 28
  *C. 'Trewiothen'*, *28*
*Celastrus*, 109, 111-12
  *C. orbiculata*, 13
*Ceratostigma willmottianum*, 132
*Cestrum*, 109
*Chaenomeles*, 29, 109, 135
  *C. japonica*, 29
  *C. lagenaria*, 29
*Chimonanthus praecox*, 13
  *C.p. grandiflorus*, 13
*Choisya ternata*, *12*, 13, 30, *30*
*Cissus*, 109
*Cistus*, 13, 30
  *C.* × *cyprius*, *31*
  *C.* × *cyprius albiflorus*, *31*
*Clematis*, *104*, 109, 112-16, 136
  *C. 'Comtesse de Bouchaud'*, *112*
  *C. florida sieboldii*, *113*
  *C. macropetala*, *114*
  *C. montana rubens*, *113*
  *C. 'Nellis Moser'*, *113*
  *C. orientalis*, *114*
  *C. rehderiana*, *112*
  *C. 'Ville de Lyon'*, *114*
*Clerodendron*, 109
  *C. fargesii*, 15
  *C. trichtomum*, 13
*Clianthus*, 109
climbing plants, 104-30
  feeding, 107-8
  greenhouse, 109
  planting, 106-7
  protection, 107
  pruning, 107, 132-7
  site preparation, 105-6
  support, 104-5, 107, 138, *138*
  training, 107
*Cobaea*, 109, 116-7
  *C. scandens*, 116
*Colletia*, 109
*Colquhounia*, 109
*Columnea*, 30-1
  *C. gloriosa*, *31*
continuity of display, 15-16
*Convolvulus*, 109
*Cornus*, 19, 32-3
  *C. alba sibirica*, 13, 135
  *C.a. variegata*, 13
  *C. kousa*, 33
  *C. mas*, 33
  *C. sanguinea*, 32
  *C. sibirica*, 32
  *C. stolonifera*, 13, 19
*Corokia*, 33, 109
*Corylus avellana contorta*, 19
*Cotinus*, 13, 19, 34-5
  *C. americanus*, 17
  *C. coggygria*, 13, 17, *18*, *34*
*Cotoneaster*, 13, 34-6, 109
  *C. adpressus*, 18
  *C. conspicuus*, 35
  *C. cornubbia*, 18
  *C. dammeri*, 18
  *C. dielsianus*, 18
  *C. frigidus*, 18
  *C. horizontalis*, 17-18, *35*
  *C. lactea*, 135
  *C. salicifolius*, 18
  *C. simonsii*, 13, 18
*Crinodendron*, 109
*Cucurbita*, 109
*Cytisus*, 36-7, 134
  *C. battandieri*, 37
  *C.* × *burkwoodii*, *36*, 15
  *C.* × *kewensis*, 12, *36*
  *C.* × *praecox*, 12, *36*
  *C. scoparius*, 12, *37*

## D

*Daphne*, 38
  *D.* × *burkwoodii*, *134*
  *D. laureola*, 38
  *D. mezereum*, 13, *14*, 38
*Daphniphyllum*, 38-9
  *D. macropodum*, 39
density of planting, 12
*Desfontainea spinosa*, 39, *39*
*Desmodium*, 40
  *D. spicatum*, 40
*Deutzia*, 13, 15, 19, 40-1
  *D. gracilis*, 40
  *D. lemoinei*, 15
  *D. 'Magician'*, *41*
  *D. rosea eximia*, 15
*Dipladenia*, 109, 117
  *D. sanderi*, 117
*Diplascus*, 109
*Dolichos*, 109
dogwood, 19, 32-3
*Dolichos*, 109

## E

*Eccremocarpus*, 109, 117-18
  *E. scaber*, 118
*Eleagnus*, 41-2, *41*
  *E. pungens*, 42
  *E.p. aureovariegata*
  *E.p. variegata*, 13
*Embothrium coccineum*, *10*
*Enkianthus*, 42-3
  *E. campanulatus*, 16, *42*
*Erica*, 43-5, 135
  *E. carnea*, 13, 45
  *E.c. alba*, 44
  *E. cinerea coccinea*, *43*
  *E.c. 'Golden Hue'*, 45
  *E.* × *darleyensis*, 13
  *E. hyemalis*, 44
  *E. tetralix*, 43
*Eriobotrya*, 46
  *E. japonica*, 46
*Escallonia*, 13, 47, 109
  *E. 'Apple Blossom'*, *46*
  *E. 'Peach Blossom'*, *46*
*Eucryphia*, 47
  *E. 'Nymansay'*, 47
*Euonymus alata*, 13, 17
  *E. fortunei gracilis*, *14*
evergreen shrubs, 101

## F

*Fatsia*, 48
  *F. japonica*, 48
feeding, climbing plants, 107-8
*Feijoa*, 109
*Ficus*, 109
firethorn, *13*
Forrest, George, 10
*Forsythia*, 13, 48-9, 109, *133*, 134
  *F. 'Beatrix Farrand'*, *48*
  *F. spectabilis*, 49
Fortune, Robert, 10
*Fothergilla*, *11*, 49-50
  *F. major*, 49
*Fremontia*, 109
*Fuchsia*, 50-2, 133
  *F. 'Beauty of Bath*, 51
  *F. 'Burning Bush'*, 51
  *F. fulgens*, 51
  *F. magellanica*, 132
  *F.m. riccartonii*, *133*
  *F. 'Mrs Popple'*, 50
  *F. 'Tennessee Waltz'*, *52*

## G

*Gardenia*, 53
*Garrya*, 53, 109

  *G. elliptica*, 13, *13*, *53*, 134
  × *Gaulnettya*, 53-4
  × *Gaulnettya wisleyensis*, *54*
*Gaultheria*, 54
  *G. procumbens*, 13, 18
  *G. shallon*, 54
*Genista*, 13, 54-5
  *G. cinerea*, 55
  *G. sagittalis*, 55
  *G. villarsii*, 55
Ghent azaleas, 16-17
*Gloriosa*, 109
greenhouse climbing plants, 109

## H

*Hamamelis*, 55-6
  *H. japonica*, 13
  *H. mollis*, 12-13
  *H.m. brevipetala*, 13
  *H.m. pallida*, 13, *56*
*Hebe*, 13, 56, 109, 135
  *H. 'Midsummer Beauty'*, *57*
  *H. armstrongii*, 57
  *H. 'Autumn Blue'*, 57
  *H. 'Carl Teschner'*, 57
  *H. macrantha*, 57
  *H. pinguifolia 'Pagei'*, 57
*Hedera*, 13, 109, 118-19
  *H. 'Buttercup'*, 119
  *H. 'Glacier'*, 119
  *H. helix 'Chicago'*, *119*
  *H. 'Jubilee'*, 119
*Hibbertia*, 109, 120, *120*
*Hibiscus*, 16
  *H. syriacus*, 13, *14*, 16
*Hippophaë rhamnoides* 13
*Holboellia*, 109
honeysuckle, *105*, 122-5
*Hoya*, 109
*Humulus*, 109
  *H. lupulus*, *106*
*Hydrangea*, 15-16, 19, 58-60, 109
  *H. aspera*, 59
  *H. macrophylla*, 16, *58*, 59, 135
  *H.m. 'Hamburg'*, *58*
  *H.m. lilacina*, 59
  *H.m. mariesii*, *58*
  *H.m. rosea*, 59
  *H. paniculata*, 16, 59
  *H.p. grandiflora*, 132, *133*
  *H. petiolaris*, 136
  *H. quercifolia*, 16
  *H. serrata*, 16
  *H.s. rosa alba*, 59
  *H. villosa*, 16, 59
*Hypericum*, 13, 61-3, *63*, 109, 132
  *H. calycinum*, 16
  *H. elatum 'Elstead'*, 16, *61*
  *H. olympicum*, 61
  *H. patulum*, 13
  *H.p. forrestii*, 18
  *H.p. 'Gold Cup'*, 16
  *H.p. 'Hidcote'*, 16, *61*
  *H. polyphyllum*, 62
  *H. 'Rowallane'*, 16
  *H. 'Sun Goddess'*, 16
  *H. 'Sungold'*, 16

## I

*Ilex*, 13
*Indigofera*, 109
*Ipomoea*, *106*, 109, 120-1, *120*
*Itea*, 109
ivy, 118-19

## J

*Jacobinia*, 63
  *J. coccinea*, *63*

Japanese maples, 16
*Jasminum*, 109, 121
  *J. mesnyi*, 121
  *J. officinale*, *107, 121,* 136

## K

*Kadsura*, 109
*Kalmia*, 64
  *K. latifolia*, *64*
  *K.l.* 'Brilliant', *64*
*Kalmiopsis*, 64-5
*Kerria*, 109
  *K. japonica*, 13, *134*
*Kolkwitzia*, 65
  *K. amabilis*, *65*

## L

*Lapageria*, 109
*Lardizabala*, 109
*Lathyrus*, 109
*Laurus nobilis*, 13
*Lavandula*, 65-6
  *L.* 'Hidcote', *66*
  *L. spicata*, *66*
*Leycesteria formosa*, 132
*Ligustrum* 66-7
  *L. lucidum*, *66*
  *L. ovalifolium*, *67*
  *L. vulgare*, *67*
lilac, 14, 134
*Lonicera*, 109, 122-5
  *L.* × *americana*, *125*
  *L. hildebrandiana*, *122*
  *L. japonica halliana*, *124*
  *L. morrowii*, *124*
  *L. nitida*, 19, *124*
  *L. periclymenum*, *105, 123, 125*
  *L.p. belgica*, *124*
  *L. sempervirens*, *107, 125*
  *L.* × *tellmanniana*, *122*
*Lygodium*, 126
  *L. japonicum*, *126*

## M

*Magnolia*, 109
*Mahonia*, 68-9
  *M. aquifolium*, 13, 16, *68, 69, 134*
  *M. bealei*, 68
  *M. japonica*, *68*, 134
*Mandevilla*, 109
*Maurandia*, 109, 126
  *M. scandens*, *126*
*Melianthus*, 69
  *M. major*, *69*
*Melicope*, 70
  *M. ternata*, *69*
*Metrosideros*, 109
Mexican orange, *12*, 13, 30, *30*
*Mikania*, 109
*Mina*, 109
*Mitraria*, 109
mock orange, 14-15, 71-3
*Monstera*, 109
*Muehlenbeckia*, 109
*Mutisia*, 109
*Myrsiphyllum*, 109

## O

*Osmanthus*, 70
  *O. armatus*, *70*
*Oxypetalum*, 109

## P

*Pachysandra terminalis*, 13
*Parthenocissus*, 109, 127
  *P. henryana*, 17, *127*
  *P. quinquefolia*, 17, *127*
  *P. tricuspidata veitchii*, 17
*Passifolora*, 109, 127-9
  *P. caerulea*, *109*, *128*
*Pentapterygium*, 109
*Periploca*, 109
*Pernettya*, 13, 70-1
  *P.* 'Bell's Seedling', 18
  *P.* 'Donard Pink', 18
  *P.* 'Donard White', *18*
  *P. lilacina*, 18

*P. mucronata*, 18, *71*
*Perovskia*, 132
  *P. atriplicifolia*, *132*
*Petraea*, 109
*Pharbitis*, 109
  *P. tricolor*, *106*
*Philadelphus*, 13, 14-15, 19, 71-2, *73*
  *P.* 'Avalanche', *73*
  *P.* 'Beauclerk', *73*
  *P.* 'Bouquet Blanc', *73*
  *P. coronarius*, 12, 15
  *P.c.* 'Belle Etoile', 15
  *P.c.* 'Enchantment', 15
  *P.c.* 'Silver Showers', 15
  *P.* × *lemoinei*, *73*
  *P. microphyllus*, 15
*Philodendron*, 109
*Phlomis fruticosa*, 13
  *P. terminalis*, 13
*Phygelius*, 109
*Phyllostachys*, 13
*Pieris*, 73
  *P. japonica*, *74*
*Pileostegia*, 109
*Piper*, 109
*Piptanthus*, 109
planting:
  climbing plants, 106-7
  shrubs, 11-12
*Plumbago*, 109
*Polygonum*, 109
  *P. baldschaunicum*, *108*
*Potentilla fruticosa*, 133
privet, 19, 66-7
propagation, 19
pruning:
  climbing plants, 107, 132-7
  shrubs, 19, 132-7
*Pueraria*, 109
*Pyracantha*, 13, 73-4, 109
*Pyracantha atalantioides*, *74*
  *P. coccinea lalandii*, *75*
  *P. rogersiana*, 13, *75*

## R

*Rhodochiton*, 109
*Rhododendron*, 10, *11*, 75-83, *75*, 135
  *R.* 'Blue Diamond', *80*
  *R. campylocarpum*, *77*
  *R.* 'China', *77*
  *R. cinnabarimum*, *77*
  *R.* 'Daybreak', *81*
  *R.* 'Elizabeth', *77*
  *R.* 'Exbury hybrids', *80*
  *R.* 'Hinodegiri', *81*
  *R. keysii*, *77*
  *R.* 'Lord Swaythling', *82*
  *R. macabeanum*, *78*
  *R.* 'Mermaid', *81*
  *R. obtusum*, *78*
  *R. ponticum*, 17
  *R.* 'Queen Wilhelmina', *82*
  *R. quinquefolium*, *82*
  *R.* 'Red Carpet', *82*
  *R.* 'Seven Stars', *77*
  *R.* 'Silver Slipper', *81*
  *R. simsii*, *78*
  *R. superbum*, *78*
  *R.* 'Susan', *82*
  *R. wardii*, *77*
  *R. williamsianum*, *77*
  *R. xanthostephanum*, *82*
*Rhoicissus*, 109
*Rhus*, 13, 19, 34
  *R. cotinoides*, 17
  *R. cotinus*, 17
  *R. typhina*, 19
  *R.t. lancinata*, 17
*Ribes*, 109
  *R. americanum*, 13
  *R. sanguineum*, *133*
*Romneya coulteri*, 13
*Rosa*, 84-93, 109
  *R.* × *anemonoides*, *85*
  *R. banksiae lutea*, 84
  *R. californica*, *85*
  *R. canina*, *85*
  *R.* 'Caroline Testout', *109*
  *R. chinensis minima* 'Rouletti', *86*
  *R. damascena* 'Hebe's Lips', *86*
  *R. ecae*, *86*

*R. filipes*, *87*
  *R. gallica versicolor*, *87*
  *R.* × *harisonii*, *87*
  *R. hugonis*, *87*
  *R. moyesii*, *88*
  *R. pomifera*, *88*
  *R. primula*, 88
  *R. rugosa albo-plena* 'Blanc Double de Coubert', *88*
  *R.r. rubra*, *90*
  *R.r.* 'Sarah van Fleet', *88*
  *R. spinosissima*, *90*
  *R. virginiana*, *92*
  *R. xanthina* 'Canary Bird', *92*
Rose of Sharon, 16
*Rosmarinus officinalis*, 13
*Rubus*, 109
  *R. giraldianus*, *135*
*Ruscus aculeatus*, 13
*Ruta graveolens*, 13

## S

St John's wort, 16, 61-3
*Salix vitellina britzensis*, *135*
*Sambucus*, 13
  *S. nigra aurea*, 13, *136*
*Santolina*, 94
  *S. chamaecyparissus*, 13, *94*
*Schizandra*, 109
*Senecio*, 109
  *S. laxifolius*, *135*
  *S. maritima*, 13
shrubs:
  autumn colour, 16-18
  continuity of display, 15-16
  definition, 10
  planting, 11-12
  planting density, 12
  propagation, 19
  pruning, 19, 132-7
  site preparation, 10-11
  spring-flowering, 13-14
  ways of using, 10
  winter-flowering, 12-13
*Sibiraea laevigata*, 17
site preparation:
  climbing plants, 105-6
  shrubs, 10-11
*Skimmia*, 94-5
  *S. japonica*, 13, *19*, *94*
  *S. laureola*, 95
  *S. rubella*, 95
*Smilax*, 109
smoke bush, 17
snowball bush, 15
soil:
  climbing plants, 105-6
  shrubs, 10-11
*Solanum*, 109
*Sollya*, 109
*Sorbaria arborea*, 13
*Spiraea*, 13, 95-6
  *S. arguta*, 13, *134*
  *S.* × *bumalda*, *132*, 133
  *S.* × *bumalda* 'Anthony Waterer', *96*
  *S. nipponica rotundifolia*, *96*
  *S. salicifolia*, *96*
  *S. thunbergii*, *134*
spring-flowering shrubs, 13-14
stag's horn sumach, 17
staking, 11-12
*Stauntonia*, 109
*Stephandra*, 96
*Stephanotis*, 109, 129
  *S. florabunda*, *129*
*Streptosolen*, 109
support:
  climbing plants, 104-5, 107, *138, 138*
  shrubs, 11-12
*Symphoricarpos laevigatus*, 13
*Syngonium*, 109
*Syringa*, 13, 134
  *S. microphylla*, 14
  *S. persica alba*, 14
  *S. vulgaris*, 14, *15*
  *S.v.* 'Alphonse Lavellee', 14
  *S.v.* 'Esther Staley', 14
  *S.v.* 'Katherine Havemeyer', 14
  *S.v.* 'Madame Lemoine', 14
  *S.v.* 'Mont Blanc', 14
  *S.v.* 'Souvenir de Louis Spath', 14

## T

*Thunbergia*, 109
  *T. alata*, *108*
*Tibouchine*, 109
*Trachelospermum*, 109
training, climbing plants, 107
tree hollyhock, 14
*Tropaeolum*, 109

## V

*Vaccinium*, 97
  *V. corymbosum*, 18
  *V. macrocarpum*, 18
  *V. membranaceum*, 97
  *V. myrsinites*, 13, 18
  *V. vitis-idaea*, 97
*Viburnum*, 13, 98-100
  *V. betulifolium*, 99
  *V.* × *bodnantense* 'Dawn', *99*
  *V.* × *burkwoodii*, 14, *99*
  *V.* × *carlcephalum*, 14
  *V. carlesii*, 14
  *V. davidii*, 13
  *V. dilatatum*, 99
  *V. farreri*, 12
  *V.f. candidissima*, *12*
  *V. hupehense*, 19
  *V. macrocephalum*, 14
  *V. opulus sterile*, 13, 15, *99*
  *V. opulus xanthocarpum*, *99*
  *V. tinus*, 13
  *V. tomentosum grandiflorum*, 15
  *V.t.* 'Lanarth', *17, 99*
  *V.t. plicatum*, 15
*Vinca major*, 13
  *V. minor*, 13
Virginia creeper, 17
*Vitis*, 109
  *V. coignetiae*, 13, 17, *18*
  *V. inconstans*, 17

## W

*Weigela*, 13, 19, 100
  *W.* 'Bristol Snowflake', 15
  *W.* 'Eva Rathke', 15
  *W.* 'Feerie', 15
  *W. florida*, 15, *100*
  *W.f. variegata*, 15
  *W.* 'Newport Red', *100*
  *W. styriaca* 15
winter-flowering shrubs, 12-13
winter sweet, 13
*Wisteria*, *104*, 109, 130, *135*, 136
  *W. floribunda*, *130*
  *W. sinensis*, *130*
witch hazel, 12-13

## Picture credits

**H. Allen:** 128(tl)  **Amateur Gardening:** 22(b), 26(b), 37(l), 74(bl)  **D. Arminson:** 15(tr&b), 58(b), 62(r), 79(br), 96(b), 100(bl&br), 132(bl,bc&br)  **P. Ayres:** 14(b), 76(tl&tr), 77 (tl&tr), 79(bl), 80(c&b), 82(tl,tr&bl), 83(bl&br), 94(b), 95(t&b)  **J. Banks:** 15(tl)  **K.A. Beckett:** 48(b), 57(tr)  **M. Beeston:** 21(b)  **C. Bevilacqua:** 14(tr)  **T. Birks:** 70(t), 73(t)  **P. Booth:** 64(b), 75(b)  **H. Bruty:** 126(t)  **R.J. Corbin:** 51(tl), 52(t), 55(tr), 57(cr), 60(br), 66(r), 99(tl), 108(r), 124(br), 125(t), 132(tl&tr), 133, 134(tl,tc&b), 135(l), 138, 139  **J. Cowley:** 127(l), 135(r), 136(b), 137  **C. Dawson:** 108(l)  **J.E. Downward:** 20(b&t), 46(l), 56, 74(br), 87(t&bl), 98(br), 120(b)  **V. Finnis:** 19(bl), 20(t), 33(b), 36(bl), 46(r), 47, 55(tl), 57(cl), 61(bl&cl), 64(t), 69(tl), 72(tr), 85(br), 86(tl), 93, 105(b), 107(l), 112(tr), 113(tr), 114, 115, 119(bl), 125(br)  **P. Genereux:** 44(t), 49(t), 67(l), 98(tr)  **A. Hamilton:** 85(t), 121(b)  **M. Hatfield:** 136(t)  **P. Hunt:** 29(b), 31(bl), 33(tr), 34(l&r), 35(r), 36(t), 37(br), 41(b), 45(tr), 57(bl), 58(cl), 59(tl), 60(tr), 109(tl), 110(t), 114/5, 119(cl&cr), 127(r)  **A.J. Huxley:** 27, 49(t), 88(tl&tr), 91  **George Hyde:** 14(tl), 23(l&r), 29(t), 32(b), 43(l), 67(tr&br), 99(b), 113(br), 121(t), 125(c), 128(bl)  **A. Jermy:** 78(b)  **Leslie Johns:** 26(tr), 45(tl), 106(r), 107(r)  **D. Kesby:** 66(b), 73(b), 124(tl), 134(tr)  **E. Knowles:** 58(t), 86(tr), 94(t)  **J. Markham:** 96(tl&tr), 119(b)  **Elsa Megson:** 11(b), 18(t), 19(t), 72(l), 75(tl), 81(tl), 92(t), 128(r)  **Mon Jardin:** 111(b)  **F. Naylor:** 122(t)  **M. Newman:** 28(tr)  **M. Nimmo:** 123(r)  **S. Norris:** 120(tr)  **Picturepoint:** 111(t)  **M. Pratt:** 60(tl&bl)  **R. Procter:** 17(t)  **M. Slingsby:** 63(t)  **E. Satchell:** 69(b)  **A. Schilling:** 119(tl)  **Harry Smith Collection:** 10, 11(t), 13(tl&tr), 16/7, 22(t), 24(l&r), 25, 26(tl), 27(bl&br), 28(tl&b), 30, 31(t&br), 32(t), 33(tl), 35(l), 36(br), 37(tr), 38, 39, 40, 41(t), 42, 43(r), 48(tl), 50, 51(tr&b), 52(b), 53, 54, 55(b), 57(tl&br), 58(cr), 59(tr&b), 61(br), 62(l), 63(b), 66(l), 68(tr&b), 71(l), 72(cr&br), 74(t), 75(tr), 76(tc,bl&br), 77(b), 78(t&c), 79(t), 81(tr&b), 82(br), 83(t), 84, 85(bl), 86(b), 87(br), 88(b), 89, 90, 90/1, 92(b), 98(tl&bl), 99(tr), 100(t), 104, 105(t), 106(l), 108, 109(b), 112(tl&b), 113(l), 116(b), 117, 118, 119(tr), 120(tl), 122(b), 124(tr&bl), 125(bl), 126(b), 130(t&b)  **Tourist Photo Library:** 97, 123(l)  **C. Watmough:** 65  **D. Wildridge:** 12(t), 16, 129  **D. Woodland:** 12(b), 13(tc), 17(b), 18(b), 19(br), 71(r), 80(t)